CAR
WARS

CAR
WARS

How General Motors Europe Built
'The Car of the Future'

John Butman

GRAFTON BOOKS

A Division of the Collins Publishing Group

LONDON GLASGOW
TORONTO SYDNEY AUCKLAND

Grafton Books
A Division of the Collins Publishing Group
8 Grafton Street, London W1X 3LA

Published by Grafton Books 1991

British Library Cataloguing in Publication Data

Butman, John
    Car wars: how General Motors Europe built 'the car
    of the future'.
    1. Cars. Design & construction
    I. Title
    629.23

    ISBN 0-246-13541-7

Printed in Great Britain by
William Collins Sons & Co Ltd, Glasgow

CONTENTS

ACKNOWLEDGEMENTS

I never expected to write a book about cars. I am neither a car buff nor a collector. I don't pretend to have the knowledge of the inner workings of cars (particularly the mechanicals) or of the car industry that many motoring journalists have. My interest is with the *process* of creating a product of the complexity of today's car. I have been exposed to, and written about, many other complex endeavours (such as computer development and marketing) and the car development process seemed to me to be the most vast, complicated and significant in our everyday lives.

I first became fascinated with the auto industry during the eighteen months I worked as staff writer and creative director with Spectrum Communications Ltd, London, from November 1986 to April 1988, and then as an independent writer through November 1989. Spectrum Communications is a communications agency and production company specializing in corporate communications, including special events, videos and multi-image presentations.

During that period I helped to develop and write speeches and media scripts for the launch events for the new Vauxhall Senator and Cavalier. While conducting my research, I was exposed to the process of new car development and found that the key business issues of the day – from manufacturing automation to globalization – are manifested and played out perhaps more intensely in it than in any other business or industry.

In exploring the development of J'89 I have received generous assistance from Vauxhall Motors Ltd, Adam Opel AG and General Motors Europe, but have in no way been sponsored or commissioned by these companies. I was granted access to people and facilities in Luton, Rüsselsheim and other locations, and I believe that I was treated with openness and honesty by those with whom I spoke. However, the car industry is so competitive and security-minded that there were many issues which could not be discussed fully by insiders. And, although I spoke to many people outside General Motors Europe and read widely as well, there undoubtedly are parts of the car development process that play a greater or lesser role in this book than they actually do in 'real life'. I have attempted to provide a portrait of the process as I experienced it at one time during the late 1980s.

My thanks begin with the members of the Vauxhall Motors team with whom I worked on the launch of the new Cavalier, especially Peter Batchelor, Executive Director of Sales and Marketing, and his assistant Margaret John; John Butterfield, then Manager of Marketing Communications and his staff, particularly Celia Wing; and Peter Negus, in product planning.

Thanks also to Eric Fountain, Ken Moyes, Maureen Clarke, Brian Millen and Glyn Davis of the Vauxhall Motors Public Relations staff. In addition, I received help from or conducted interviews with George Ashby, David H. Blair, Peter Bonner, Ian Coomber, Neil M. Gardner, Robert Hendry, George I'Ons, Peter Johnson, Peter Lord, Kevin Moxey, Manoj Patel, Paul Tosch, Bruce Warman and Philip Watson, all of Vauxhall Motors Ltd.

In Rüsselsheim, West Germany, where Adam Opel AG is based, I owe much gratitude to Christopher J.D. Mattingley of the public relations staff, who was my interpreter, guide and companion on many interviews and visits throughout Opel. Wayne Cherry, Director of Design, and his staff, including Moni Butz, George Gallion, Fromund Kloppe, Erhard Schnell and John Taylor, were extremely helpful and accommodating, as was Peter Döring, responsible for J car co-ordination. I also received help from or conducted interviews with Roland Bansch, Manfred Duvenkamp, Hans-Joachim Emmelmann, Friedrich W. Lohr, Dr Jürgen Lowsky, K. Ludwig, Hans-Jürgen Pache, Dietmar Pfeiffer, Hans G. Riemann, Joseph Schulze and Christian Weiss at Opel.

I also conducted interviews with Gunther Zech, Manager of the Dudenhofen Proving Ground; Dieter Krocker at General Motors Europe in Zurich; Uwe Bahnsen, then Education Director at the Art Center College of Design (Europe) and former Director of Design for Ford of Europe and Virginia Pepper, also of the Art Center; Rodney Calvert and Brian D. Cheney of the Millbrook Proving Ground; David Dyster of the Society of Motor Manufacturers and Traders Ltd; Terry Edwards, Chris Hamley, Adam Salt and others at Lowe Howard-Spink, the advertising agency for Vauxhall; Dr Thomas Helming and his staff at FKFS, the organization that manages the aerodynamic facility at the University of Stuttgart; Ronald C. Hill and Angus Whyte of the Art Center College of Design in Pasadena, California; David Willsher of Swan National Rentals Ltd; Jack Newlands of Marlboro Motors and Tony Palmer of Shaw and Kilburn, both Vauxhall dealerships.

The photographs reproduced in the book were kindly supplied by General Motors US, General Motors Europe, Vauxhall Motors and Adam Opel AG, with the following exceptions: the photograph of the Sierra was provided by Ford, those of the Cray supercomputer by Electronic Data Systems, Millbrook proving ground by Millbrook, the still from the TV commercial by Lowe Howard-Spink, the launch at the Royal Lancaster by Spectrum Communications Ltd, and Paul Tosch by *Luton News*.

My thanks to the members of the Spectrum Communications staff who were my associates during that period, particularly Nicholas Matthews, who brought me to England in the first place, and his family; Peter Berners-Price and Tony Crawford, directors of Spectrum Communications Ltd; Jamie Neal, producer of the J'89 launch events; and Tim Elliot, Leigh Johnstone and Melanie MacDonald, as well as John Furneaux of the design firm, Furneaux-Stewart.

Finally, thanks to my literary agent, Jane Judd, for her help in developing the book; my editor at Grafton Books, Richard Johnson, for his guidance and expertise; my friend Joost Tjaden who was pressed into service as a reader; my son, Jeremy, and most especially my wife Nancy, for all her support and no-nonsense advice.

INTRODUCTION

'No one spends Saturday morning waxing the fridge.'

Motor industry proverb

There is an old adage about creating a poem that also describes the creation of a new automobile: no car model (no product, for that matter) is ever really completed, it's simply abandoned. When launch day looms, when the budget is exhausted, when the market is hot, when a competitor's manoeuvre demands an answer, when another project takes precedence – that is when the new model is pushed out the front door.

In the case of a car, great quantities of time and money have been consumed in the process of creation: five to seven years on average, and several hundreds of millions of pounds. But the abandonment is short-lived. Even as the new car basks in the showroom – surrounded by bright pennants and an urgency of placards known as 'car toppers' – the designers and engineers and marketeers are already back at work, fiddling and tinkering, fixing and improving.

The result is that, by the end of its life, the new model may be very different to what it was in its infancy. And beneath its skin (sheet metal, fabric, glass and plastic) may lurk the skeleton of a predecessor – chassis and structural members, mechanicals and engines which comprise a 'platform', and can live far longer than any one model that rests upon it. So it's really more accurate to say that no new car is ever really completed – or even begun; it is always in a state of evolution.

The final decades of the twentieth century have been called the information age – and computers, communications systems and electronic devices have stolen our attention away from the products of the past. But now the car industry is re-emerging as one of the key business and industrial activities: a proving ground for new processes and product technologies, a battlefield of global competition, a paradigm for how mature manufacturing organizations are forced into change.

And that is what this book is about: the restless, evolving process that results in one of mankind's favourite yet most troublesome objects, the car.

The process is a sprawling and complicated one, partly because a car itself is so complex – comprising some 10-15,000 structural, mechanical, electrical, electronic, cosmetic and 'soft' parts. Technology also contributes to the complexity. The product has gradually been transformed from a mechanical substitute for the horse and carriage into a semi-disposable, electro-mechanical appliance. Design and engineering functions used to work separately, sequentially and often at cross purposes, but are gradually moving toward a more co-operative, simultaneous, computer-aided process. And manufacturing has evolved from an engineering handicraft to a flexible, computer-integrated, volume assembly operation.

Car making is not only complex but mercurial, and the 1970s and '80s were the most tumultuous decades ever for the auto industry. First, the Arab oil shocks of 1974 and 1979 tipped the giant industry off balance. From 1975 and into the '80s, partly as a result of these disturbances, Japan mounted an unrelenting invasion of Western markets which led to its becoming the leading car-producing nation in the world.

In reaction, most car makers based in Europe (whatever their parentage) have been through a tortuous period of applying the brakes – consolidating, reorganizing and reducing production capacity. But, just as production capacity was adjusting itself to reduced demand, demand started to pick up again in 1984; and, although analysts predicted the boom would blow up at any moment, it didn't. In 1987 Western Europe surpassed the United States to become the largest car market in the world.

The special nature of the product itself is another complicating factor. A car is more than a car: it reflects the priorities of the era, the country, the people that shape it. It also contributes to defining those priorities. It is both chicken and egg, leader and follower. More than any other consumer product, the car is three-dimensional shorthand for who and what you are. Thus the rise of national automotive stereotypes: the soft, superficial American; the spartan, ultra-engineered German; the bland, practical Japanese; the safe Swede; the stylish Italian; the idiosyncratic Brit.

But these images are evolving too. From a product based on national obsessions, the car is beginning to reflect the changing requirements of a unifying world. The car must be more culturally neutral now, but also more narrowly focused by specific market segment – to appeal to the 'sporting' set, for example, or to executive buyers or the affluent young. Safety is taking precedence over speed as a positive attribute. Compatibility with the environment is a high priority.

Many people argue convincingly that the car-making process is so unwieldy not because of its complexity but primarily because it is badly managed, and because the mammoth manufacturing organizations are calcified and byzantine. The proof is to be found with the Japanese manufacturers: as a group, they have defined the 'world best practice', meaning that they are able to bring products of the highest available quality to market faster and more productively than car makers in any other part of the world.

Auto books tend to be about exceptional cars: the great marques and high performance cars. This one is about a seemingly ordinary car called J'89. The 'J' denotes an intermediate size, front-wheel-drive General Motors platform, and J'89 is the second J platform model. In Germany, J'89 is marketed as the Opel Vectra. In the United Kingdom, it is known as the Vauxhall Cavalier.

But J'89 is not so much ordinary as standard. The car was created by an international team, with an American chief of design, German engineers and British packagers. It was designed and built with extensive use of computer-aided design and engineering and computer-aided manufacturing. It is the result of a development process that seeks to integrate marketing, engineering, design and financial objectives. It is manufactured with components and subassemblies from suppliers around the world and assembled in the facility of greatest convenience. And it is packaged for the world market.

J'89 is also a weapon in an all-out business battle for a substantial share of the European auto market. General Motors still may be the world's largest car producer (not to mention the world's largest industrial company of any kind) but its share of the US market is inexorably slipping away (down to 34% in early 1990 from 60% in 1959) and it ranks only fifth in Europe.

However, since the glum times of the early '80s, GM's European subsidiaries – Vauxhall and Opel – have staged a remarkable turn-around. Now the faltering American giant is looking to them and to the buoyant European market to improve its position worldwide. Its hopes are centred on two major markets, Germany and the United Kingdom, and two best-selling cars. One is the T car, better known as the Kadett in Germany and the Astra in Britain. The other is J'89.

The new Cavalier 'is a coathanger car', wrote Richard Bremner in the *Independent*, 'for the chap who plies the nation's motorways, jacket dangling from the ceiling, Marlboro smouldering in the ashtray, appointments list uppermost in mind.'

That may be true – the Cavalier has found its greatest acceptance as a company fleet car – but J'89 is more than a 'repmobile'. It is complexity, weapon, symbol, tumult on wheels and one of today's most telling products. It is a car shaped by technology, by global competition, by the current trials of a giant car company in the midst of change, and by key events of the past.

This is the story of J'89.

1 · BIG NUMBERS

'We like to do things in a big way in the United States.'

Alfred P. Sloan, Jr, former GM Chairman

Considering the growth of the automotive market (almost steadily upwards since 1900), the size of the worldwide market today (thirty-four million cars produced in 1988) and the total number of cars in use (about 400 million), you might be tempted to assume – if you were a car manufacturer – that the demand for your product was virtually inexhaustible.

That *is* what car makers, particularly US car makers, seemed to assume up until the end of the 1970s. But the oil shocks, the rise of the Japanese manufacturers and the near-saturation of the North American market sent the world motor industry spinning.

Today, although the market continues to grow, it is no longer safe to assume that it's growing in predictable ways. So if you're planning to invest some £340 million or more in a single new model (as GM Europe did with J'89), you had better understand how it fits into the global marketplace. You had better understand the numbers and how they are changing.

In the United Kingdom, the Society of Motor Manufacturers and Traders (SMMT) is one of the principal sources of motor industry data. Its offices are in a three-storey stone and yellow brick mansion, Forbes House, situated rather grandly at the apex of a crescent driveway off Halkin Street not far from Buckingham Palace. The statistics department, however, is not grand at all. Located in the basement, it's a hodge-podge of cubicles and desks and computer screens and shelves haphazardly stuffed with publications containing information on the motor vehicle industry from near and distant parts of the world.

From a corner table encircled by these shelves Ken Barnes, a methodical statistician of middle age, is finishing compiling the figures for the next edition of an industry bible published by the SMMT: *The Motor Industry of Great Britain*, or the *MIGB* as it is commonly known.

David Dyster, the Statistical Service Manager, rules here – a busy man behind heavy glasses with a quick, distracted manner and a slight rasp in the voice. Although the SMMT collects data from around the world, he says, they do not supply the potentially illuminating figure I am seeking: the percentage of the gross world economy the motor industry represents.

Dyster patiently explains that the vagaries of definitions (at exactly what percentage of in-plant manufacture does car making cease to be production and become assembly?); exchange rates (in which country do you report a sale – where the car is produced, sold, or where the parent is headquartered?); reporting procedures (when is a vehicle considered to be produced – when it comes off the assembly line or when it reaches the showroom, or somewhere in between?); and a hundred other factors make it difficult enough to compile the figures they do supply, let alone to calculate the size of the entire industry.

Much of motor industry analysis and forecasting is based on two essential sets of figures – the same ones that are essential to any business or industry – supply and demand. Supply roughly equates to new car production, and is based on figures supplied by the manufacturers. Demand roughly equates to the number of new car registrations and is based on Department of Transport records. Figures for exports, imports and the balance of trade are based on tracing where production originated and where sales took place, or were intended to take place.

These figures (and many others) can be analysed and formatted in a thousand different ways: production by manufacturer, plant location, model, month, year, engine size, body type; sales by postal code, type of customer, dealer, engine size, month or year. Such analysis is just what the statisticians who toil in the basement of the T block building at Vauxhall headquarters in Luton, Bedfordshire (and their counterparts at General Motors Europe headquarters in Zurich) use to determine what their markets are and where they are headed.

According to most estimates, there are about 400 million cars, of all makes and model years, in use throughout the world. Although, according to the Worldwatch Institute's estimate, that's only half the number of bicycles and less than the 600 million telephones and 660 million televisions in use worldwide, it is still a lot of cars, especially given the relatively high price of a new automobile. The car is usually named as the second most expensive purchase, after a house, that most people make.

If the 'cars in use' figure is divided by the total world population (just over five billion people) you arrive at a worldwide 'persons per car' figure of about twelve (whether they can drive or not). But, of course, the concentration of cars varies tremendously from country to country. By looking at the persons per car figure for individual countries, you get a good idea of which markets have enough cars to go around (saturated markets) and which are likely to have continuing growth in demand.

For example, it would not be advisable to increase capacity in anticipation of increased exports to the US territory of Guam (one of the Mariana Islands in the Pacific Ocean) because it tops the persons per car list, with an estimated 1.1 persons per car in 1988. The United States is also rampant with cars, having about 121 million in use in 1988, or about 1.7 persons per car.

In most of the EC countries the figure hovers around three persons per car, with the United Kingdom at 2.7 – an indication that there is still room for growth, but only a limited amount, before demand levels off as it has in the US.

China, not surprisingly, has one of the lowest concentrations of automobiles with an estimated 1440 people per car in 1988. Although the number is misleading, because China produces many more trucks and buses than cars, it is obvious that China is a market of gigantic potential, and there are several joint ventures under way between Chinese concerns and European and American producers to tap it.

One of the most significant persons per car figures is for Japan, at four people per car. That means that car owners make up a much lower percentage of the population in Japan than in any of the northern European countries, and that the Japanese domestic market is probably far from saturated. In fact, although Japan exported a greater number of passenger cars than were sold in the domestic market in 1988, new registrations there are now starting to climb. If there were to be a real boom in demand in Japan, it could change the face of the industry – with, presumably, more Japanese-made cars being sold at home, and more being imported into Japan from the United States and Europe.

Worldwide, passenger cars are produced by about forty major manufacturers (those with an annual production of over 50,000 cars) in about twenty-five countries. Passenger car production has grown steadily since 1900, except for slumps in the early 1930s and early 1980s. Since World War II, the share of world production by country has shifted dramatically. The US share of world motor vehicle production (passenger cars and commercial vehicles) has dropped steadily from about 76% in 1950 to just over 23% in 1988, or about eleven million vehicles.

The Japanese percentage of world production, by contrast, has sky-rocketed. According to the Motor Vehicle Manufacturers Association of the United States (MVMA), Japan produced just 32,000 vehicles in 1950, or 0.3% of the world production. But in the watershed year of 1980, Japanese production surpassed that of the United States for the first time, and by 1988 the Japanese were producing about 26% of the world's total vehicle production, over 12.5 million vehicles. That represents an increase over less than forty years of nearly 4000%.

The percentage of world vehicle production of the EC countries has grown steadily since the war, from a 20% world share in 1950 to about 36% in 1988, or about thirteen million passenger cars. Of the European annual production total, West Germany produces the most, almost a third. France is next, with about a quarter, then Italy and Spain; the UK comes fifth with about 9%, or just over one million cars.

In terms of demand – registrations and sales of new cars – the world scene has also shifted dramatically. The two largest car markets by far are the United States and Western Europe, accounting for almost three-quarters of total world sales. But demand in the US peaked in 1985-6, and picked up in Europe (and Japan) in 1986-7. In 1987,

Europe surpassed the US in total new passenger car registrations, reaching just over eleven million sold in contrast to the ten million sold in the US. Within Europe, West Germany, with the highest population, is the largest market in terms of new car sales, with 22% of the European total. The UK, Italy and France – roughly equal in population – each account for about 17% of European sales.

The other important statistics – for exports and imports – are perhaps the most telling in terms of the world economy. Japan is the world's largest exporter of cars, shipping about 4.4 million of them around the world in 1988; it imported just over 150,000. West Germany, the world's second largest exporter, runs a distant second to Japan, with 2.4 million cars shipped in 1988. The United States is the largest *importer* of cars, bringing in about 4.5 million in 1988. They exported only 800,000 cars in 1988, but of course the US makers, particularly Ford and GM, are already well represented in Europe – cars made by US makers in European countries are not considered US exports. The United Kingdom has a poor ratio of exports to imports as well, exporting 261,146 cars in 1988, while importing 1,356,902.

So, in brief: the world auto market is still growing. One forecast, by the Data Resources Incorporated 1989 Automotive Forecast Report, is that demand for new cars will continue to rise (as it has for the past ninety years or so), reaching some thirty-eight million a year by 1995, and that the demand will be strongest in Europe and Japan, flat in the United States. The biggest car producer and exporter is Japan, but the Japanese domestic market is not yet saturated. The biggest importer is the United States, but the market there is oversupplied.

In other words, the statistics confirm the popular and cautionary tale: the fortunes of the US are down, the fortunes of Europe are partially up and partially down (down, because the number of European cars exported to the US is falling), and Japan is in the strongest position of all.

All that sounds big, but just how big *is* big? The United Nations *Industry and Development Global Report 1988/89* states simply that, 'The international auto industry is one of the most important in the world in terms of its size, economic significance and employment generation.'

Despite the much-discussed shift toward service-based industries in recent years, manufacturing still accounts for about 80% of world trade. Although the computer and electronics industries have been hot, vehicle manufacturing is a bigger industry than either, according to *Fortune* magazine: bigger than chemicals, building materials, aerospace, computers, food production – in fact, it is the largest industry except one: petroleum refining. 'The titans of twentieth-century industry, motor vehicles and oil' is how *Fortune* describes them. Together, the inseparable 'twin titans' dwarf the other industrial sectors.

Of the world's ten largest industrial companies – listed by *Fortune* and ranked by 1988 annual turnover – seven are directly involved in the motor industry.

1. *General Motors*
2. *Ford Motor*
3. *Exxon*
4. *Royal Dutch/Shell*
5. International Business Machines
6. *Toyota Motor*
7. General Electric
8. *Mobil*
9. *British Petroleum*
10. IRI *(Instituto per la Ricostruzione Industriale*, an Italian conglomerate)

Even the three which are not directly involved – IBM, GE and IRI – derive some significant portion of their business from it. Although the petroleum refiners produce non-automotive products such as heating oil, industry sources estimate that 30-40% of the refiners' world output is motor spirit.

Of the top hundred industrial companies, thirty-six are motor vehicle manufacturers or petroleum refiners. Another twenty produce metals or rubber or plastics or electronics, heavily used in the industry. Total revenue for the hundred largest industrial companies worldwide came to over $2.3 trillion US in 1988 and sales of the thirty-six motor vehicle manufacturers and petroleum refiners accounted for 46% of that astronomical total.

But the arms of the great motor industry encompass more than just the giant manufacturers and petroleum refiners. You could not remove cars and petrol from the economy without eliminating a lot of associated businesses and industries, services and activities. The principal ones include the suppliers of raw materials, including steel, glass, rubber, plastic, fabric and paint and the hundreds of companies that deliver everything from nuts and bolts, gaskets and key rings to body pressings and complex electronic sub-assemblies. The MVMA estimates that one in every six businesses in Europe, Japan and the United States is dependent on motor vehicles, that one fifth of all wholesale sales and a quarter of all retail sales come from motor vehicles.

In a 1989 SMMT report called *Economic Significance of the UK Motor Vehicle Manufacturing Industry*, it is estimated that every job in vehicle manufacturing supports 1.4 more jobs among suppliers and about 2.8 jobs in the British economy as a whole. That amounts to almost a half million jobs in 1987, or about 2% of the total work force of twenty-eight million. Although this sounds a lot, it is down by about 50% from a decade ago, and far less than other vehicle manufacturing countries; in the United States, for example, the MVMA estimates that nearly 15% of the work force is employed in the motor vehicle and related industries.

This is the so-called 'multiplier effect' – the trickling (and sometimes flooding) up, down and sideways of the activities of the motor industry. The multiplier effect takes into account the 7,500 car dealers, 21,000 petrol stations and 17,000 repair garages operating in the UK. But there are dozens of other businesses and disciplines that derive all or part of their livelihood from cars and motorways, not to mention traffic and accidents: the insurance industry and its motor vehicle cover; the financial services industry, with some £3 billion in loans to retail outlets engaged in the motor trade; the police, the courts, hospitals, detective and law firms, newspaper, magazine, marketing, advertising and entertainment people who cater to the motor industry. And beyond all that, there is an effect too great to calculate: the general increase in commerce and trade that results from the mobility of people and goods made possible by motor vehicles.

Although UK motor vehicle exports accounted for £6.8 billion in

1988 – more than any other manufactured product – motor vehicle imports were valued at nearly £13 billion, which caused the UK motor industry to suffer a trade deficit of £6.1 billion. Even so, the Government collects 11.5% of its *entire tax revenue* – approximately £16 billion in 1988-9 – from fuel duties, vehicle excise taxes, VAT on both fuel and vehicles and £1.5 billion from the special car tax which is unique to the UK.

With the creation of the single market in 1992 and the opening-up of the Eastern European countries, the European car market can only grow larger. The twelve EC countries have a combined population of 322 million people, larger than the United States (about 246 million), the USSR (about 286 million) and Japan (about 123 million).

In comparison to the US market, which is dominated by three major domestic manufacturers (GM, Ford and Chrysler), there are ten key European producers, not including Japanese transplants, and, among the top six of those, no one holds an unassailable lead – as can be seen in the 1988 share by sales and registrations.

1.	VAG (Volkswagen, Audi and Seat)	14.9%
2.	Fiat Group	14.8
3.	PSA (Peugeot and Citröen)	12.9
4.	Ford	11.3
5.	Japanese (imports and transplants)	11.3
6.	GM (Opel and Vauxhall)	10.4
7.	Renault	10.1
8.	Mercedes	3.4
9.	Rover	3.4
10.	BMW	2.7
11.	Volvo	2.1

(Source: *Financial Times* survey, 13 September 1989)

Competition among these companies is intense, and they are looking with some worry at the Japanese. Although all the Japanese companies combined (a total of seven major producers) had just over 11% of the European new car market in 1989, the *Economist* Intelligence Unit estimates that they could capture some 18% by 1995. That is why the setting of standard import quotas is a major issue in the creation of the single European market.

Japanese companies are doing in Europe what they have done in the United States, and what the US companies did long before them in Europe: establishing so-called 'transplant' companies. Transplants are companies manufacturing or assembling cars in a foreign country, but still owned and controlled by the parent in the home country.

The Japanese are moving into the UK so aggressively (having invested some $1.8 billion in the country to date) that Kevin Done of the *Financial Times* asserts, 'It now appears a racing certainty that, by the second half of the 1990s, Japanese car makers will account directly for around a third of UK car production of around two million units a year. Japanese car makers have already announced plans to develop a capacity for building more than 500,000 cars a year.' Nissan operates a plant in Sunderland, Toyota announced plans in 1989 to build a plant in the UK and Honda has a joint venture with Rover. Mazda is considering a relationship with Ford and other Japanese companies are studying the best way to attack the European market.

But the Japanese incursion is just the latest development in a long decline of the UK-based, UK-owned motor industry. After the war, the worldwide demand for cars increased rapidly, and British manufacturers exported vehicles to the US, Australia and elsewhere. Since about 1970, however, the story has been one of declining production and falling exports. In 1968, UK car makers produced over 2.2 million vehicles and exported nearly a million of them. In 1988, production stood at 1.5 million vehicles, with exports at about 300,000. Naturally, there was a concurrent drop in employment in the UK motor industry, with an estimated 180,000 people leaving the business during the early '80s. At Vauxhall alone, employment plummeted from around 33,000 people in 1978 to 11,132 in 1989.

The good news is that production is now rising in the UK – 1988 marked the highest production level since 1978 – and the sales market is also very strong. The bad news is that there is scarcely a car maker left in the UK that one could call British. As motoring correspondent Kevin Eason wrote in *The Times*, 'A new game has been devised for motoring enthusiasts: spot the British car company.'

The growth in production is coming from the new Japanese plants, the new Peugeot facility at Ryton, Coventry, and from the two Americans, Ford and Vauxhall. The Rover Group cannot be called truly British because of its ties with Honda. Jaguar is now owned by Ford, which also owns Aston Martin and AC cars. GM owns Group Lotus. Only Rolls-Royce truly qualifies as a British manufacturer.

But the lack of true-blue British manufacturers is only representative of the alliances, joint ventures and mergers that now characterize the motor industry in Europe and worldwide. General Motors has alliances with at least thirteen other companies, including Saab, Suzuki, Isuzu, Bertone, Toyota and Daewoo. In addition to Jaguar and Aston Martin, Ford has deals with Nissan, VW, Peugeot and Kia. Fiat has links with Lada and Seat and Zastava (a Yugoslavian producer). The most dramatic alliance, because of the great size of both partners, is that of Mitsubishi and Daimler-Benz. A chart showing what's called the 'interpenetration' of auto manufacturers is such a tangle of criss-crossing lines as to be almost indecipherable.

In the UK, there are still three major producers who *seem* British, at least, by virtue of the longevity of their operations in this country. Ford dominates the UK market, with a 26.5% share of new car sales in 1988. The Rover Group still produces more cars than any other UK maker, but is not the sales leader because it is also the largest exporter. In second place – partly on the strength of the new Cavalier – is Vauxhall Motors.

General Motors has a scale that is difficult to comprehend, but it is a presence that, in the retail market at least, remains in the background. Many people in the UK are unaware that Vauxhall Motors Ltd is part of General Motors, and has been since 1925. This is probably because GM does not have the market identity that can come when the product name and company name are the same, like Ford. Rather, GM cars are known by the names of their subsidiaries or divisions – Vauxhall, Opel, Holden, Chevrolet, Buick, Cadillac, Pontiac or Oldsmobile – rather than 'GM'. Only GM, of all the major producers, does not have its name on the bonnet.

Even those who do know that Vauxhall is the child of General Motors are often surprised to learn that GM is not only the world's largest vehicle manufacturer, but also the largest industrial company in the world, the largest industrial company that has ever existed on earth, measured by any number of standards.

General Motors operates some three hundred plants in countries around the world. Vauxhall Motors Ltd has two plants, one in Luton and one in Ellesmere Port, near Liverpool. Adam Opel AG in West Germany is a wholly owned subsidiary of GM, and operates three plants in Germany. GM Continental operates an assembly operation in Antwerp, Belgium and GM España operates one in Zaragoza, Spain.

GM is the world's largest employer, with about 775,000 people working for its divisions worldwide in 1989. McDonald's runs a distant second, with about 540,000 employees and IRI is the largest European employer, with about 420,000 people on the payroll.

GM sold just under eight million cars and trucks in 1989. In early 1990, despite steadily falling sales, it still enjoyed a 34% share of the US car market, and produced about 17% of the total world output of cars. In 1989, GM had worldwide sales of $126 billion. That puts it easily at the top of the list of biggest vehicle makers, which are (ranked by 1989 sales, in millions of dollars) as follows:

1.	General Motors	126,974
2.	Ford	96,932
3.	Toyota	52,655
4.	Daimler-Benz	45,176
5.	Fiat	41,931
6.	Chrysler	36,156

GM's vast annual turnover is not only larger than that of any other industrial company, it is also larger than the gross national product of many countries, including Argentina, Austria, Belgium, Iran, Norway, Sweden, Switzerland and South Africa, and is not much less than the GNP of the Netherlands and Saudi Arabia.

Although the GM name may not be highly visible in the Western European consumer marketplace, it enjoys (or suffers from) an extremely high profile as a business organization. For years, it was a company to be studied and emulated, a model of industrial organization and sales success. Since its founding in 1908 as the

General Motors Corporation, the company has made a profit in every year but two – 1921 and 1981. It was the first US company to earn a billion dollars in profit (in 1949) and by the end of the 1950s GM had a share of the US vehicle market greater than 60%.

But since the events of the mid-1970s, when the inexorable slide of GM's fortunes began, the company has become a popular paradigm for everything that is – and can go – wrong with a big manufacturing concern today. In America, the list of GM's troubles – as articulated by the press, industry analysts, shareholders, authors, business executives, car owners and just about everybody else – is a long one.

The complaints in the US concern the products: the cars have poor build quality. The styling is superficial. The interiors are plasticky. The ride is soft and the handling squishy. The engines are outdated and can't compete with new Japanese technologies. The car packaging is sometimes misguided, with features that nobody wants to buy.

The complaints concern the US organization, too: some of GM's plants are old and antiquated, with over-capacity and low productivity. Others are so highly automated and complex as to be almost impossible to keep running. Their labour union agreements are inflexible and out of date. Management is insulated from the real world, and some of the top managers are finance men who know 'nothing' about building or marketing cars. The managers are greedy and make too many decisions based upon their own financial interests – particularly how their salaries and benefits will be affected in the short term – rather than the long-term interests of the company. In the US, General Motors has been on top for so long that it has lost its competitive edge, critics say. It is a world unto itself, in which people do what is right for their careers, not for their customers. GM cares about money, not cars or customers.

In the '80s, Chairman Roger Smith was awarded a large slice of the blame for GM's problems. He is, by most reports, the quintessential corporation man who has served the company loyally in a variety of positions, many of them involving finance. He is not considered to be, in industry jargon, 'a car man' – someone trained in engineering or manufacturing or design who loves cars for themselves.

During his tenure, which began in 1981 and ended in 1990, Smith began a restructuring of the corporation that involved an investment of some $70 billion in new plants, equipment and corporate acquisitions. He diversified through acquisition, purchasing Hughes Aircraft, a leading US aerospace company, and Electronic Data Systems, a leader in data processing services.

Smith established a joint venture with Toyota called New United Motor Manufacturing Inc, or NUMMI, based in California, which builds a new line of cars called Geo, and he set out to create a whole new marque called Saturn, with a new approach to car manufacturing based in an all-new, super-automated plant in Tennessee. By most analyses, however, none of these manoeuvres has been as successful as hoped. Smith himself contends that the results are yet to be seen, that he has put in place the makings of a new General Motors for the 1990s.

Although GM's profits grew in the late 1980s (on paper anyway, and with strong contributions from Europe and non-auto operations), the company has come to be perceived as a faltering giant, a dinosaur that may eventually collapse on top of itself, a company so huge and layered as to be almost completely unwieldy.

But, of course, GM is not alone in its troubles. Most of the older car companies have had to struggle with change in order to meet the challenge of the Japanese. General Motors, particularly in the United States, is such a large, high-profile company that it makes an extremely easy target. But, by the middle of 1990, there were clear signs that GM was on the brink of an upswing. Both Chrysler and Ford were struggling, and GM had announced new models that were gaining both critical and popular acclaim. In addition, GM President Robert Stempel was named the new Chairman and Chief Executive, to succeed Roger Smith. Stempel appeared to be a popular choice internally. As the first engineer ever to head GM, he is considered a real 'car man' who will focus more on products than on finance; and, as former chief of European operations, he understands the all-important international marketplace.

For GM in Europe the outlook is much more positive – a story of fast-rising sales, healthy profits, a gain of three points of market share since 1981, factories stretched to the limit. Net sales from GM's European operations rose from $14,476,600,000 in 1987 to $17,850,300,000 in 1989. But the most startling and telling figure

is for profits. GME was the most profitable European auto manufacturer in 1989, with a profit of 9.3%. Also in 1989, the great
General Motors corporation had a higher net income from GM
Europe – $1,830,000,000 – than from its US operations, where
net income was $1,279,000,000. The European profit was made on
a sales volume of less than half the US total. GM sold 3,437,000
cars in the US in 1989 and 1,595,000 in Europe.

As *Fortune* magazine put it in an article called '*Why US Car makers Are Losing Ground*' (23 October 1989), 'While GM stumbles at
home, its smaller European operation has dazzled customers with a
succession of snappy German Opels and English Vauxhalls.'

And one of those snappy little numbers is J'89.

2 · LINEAGE

'I am a young executive. No cuffs than mine are cleaner;
I have a slimline brief-case and I use the firm's Cortina.'

from Executive *by John Betjeman*

According to its makers, J'89 began life as a clean sheet of paper.
It was to be a brand new car – completely re-styled, re-engineered
and re-packaged – not a superficial 'facelift', the industry term for
the freshening-up of an existing model. As sheets of paper go in
the auto industry, J'89's was pretty clean, but one couldn't say the
car was developed from scratch.

Most new models incorporate such mechanical and structural
elements as engines, suspension and seats from a preceding model
if there is one, or from siblings if there isn't, and J'89 would be
no different. Its chassis, front-wheel-drive layout, intermediate size
and basic configuration would be similar enough to its predecessor
to keep the 'J' designation.

So J'89 would be the second generation J car (the first J platform
having been launched in 1981) but, confusingly enough, it would be
the third generation Cavalier. The first Cavalier, launched in 1975,
was on a smaller platform, dubbed the U.

Such anthropomorphic talk of siblings and generations is typical
of the motor industry, which tends to view its products not as
mechanical devices but as people, or at least, as living creatures.
There are 'families' of cars and each family has a heritage, each
individual model has bloodlines.

The definition of what makes a worthy heritage for a motorcar,
however, is different than for a human being. People are expected

to marry, of course, and the better the quality of the marriage, the better the issue will be. Theoretically anyway, the good families keep on getting better over the generations.

But for a car manufacturer, the purest family tree seems to be one that is based completely on inbreeding, or perhaps virgin birth – each new model springing from a single parent or from two parents that bear the same family name. Rolls-Royce comes close to the ideal, having made just one marriage and that to a fine family, the Bentleys. Of course, there was an American offspring (Rolls-Royce of America Inc) which was not much talked about, and died in infancy (1920-31).

Most volume manufacturers, however, have gone through consolidations and mergers, nationalizations and de-nationalizations over the years, or have origins they'd prefer not to talk about. The family tree of the Rover Group, for example, is so convoluted that most of the individual branches – Morris, MG, Austin and Triumph – have grown together and their individual characteristics have been lost. Trace Volkswagen back far enough and you bump up against ancestor Ferdinand Porsche, which is fine, but also Adolf Hitler (who laid the cornerstone of the VW factory in Wolfsburg in 1938), which is problematical in terms of public relations. Peugeot has made marriages with Citröen, Chrysler and Talbot, and the Chrysler relationship ended in a messy divorce. Although both Ford and Vauxhall have clear bloodlines, they lead directly back to their American ancestors.

American volume car makers, no matter how pure their ancestry, have long yearned for a bit of royalty in their blood. Even the finest family members – the likes of Cadillac and Lincoln – are humble in comparison to the European luxury cars. Thus, the ardent wooing and winning of the few remaining almost-virgin European marques by the Americans: Jaguar by Ford, Saab by GM, Lamborghini by Chrysler.

Even with all this crossbreeding and intermarrying, the emphasis on automotive heritage persists. Whether the specific family is noble or not, *every* new car seems to be allowed into the great, encompassing ancestry of motorcars.

*

J'89's roots are relatively easy to trace. Although it would unquestionably be a European car – designed in Germany, assembled in Germany and the UK, sold only in European markets – it could not escape the influence of its American parent, General Motors.

General Motors is unusual in the motor industry not just for its size, but for its nature. Its name says it: this is a company born to be big, impersonal and institutional. GM was founded, not by an obsessive, auto-loving inventor or engineer – like Henry Royce or Karl Benz or Henry Ford – but by an obsessive, business-loving entrepreneur. Billy Durant, son of a successful lumber merchant, began his career as a cigar salesman in Flint, Michigan in the early 1880s. He quickly built his employer, the George T Warren Cigar company, into one of the biggest cigar companies in the state.

Durant appears to have left the company by 1884, and got involved in a variety of other endeavours in Flint, including real estate, construction, public utilities and the operation of a skating rink.

Around 1886, Durant joined a carriage-manufacturing concern. He eventually took that company over and built it into the largest carriage maker in the United States; he personally became known as the 'King of the Carriage Makers'. In 1904, although he didn't think much of automobiles at first, Durant accepted a request to help out with the ailing Buick Motor Company, also based in Flint.

Buick was the platform Durant needed to build a *really* big enterprise. He incorporated the General Motors Company in 1908, and then started buying. By 1920, he had bought or joined forces with more than thirty companies. They included car makers Olds, Oakland, Cadillac and Chevrolet; suppliers of components such as McLaughlin Motor Company; and supporting companies such as Champion Spark Plug, DELCO and Dayton Wright Airplane. Durant was restless and energetic and, in classic entrepreneurial style, loved to start businesses but had little interest in running them. According to his colleague, Walter Chrysler, 'Durant could charm a bird right down from a tree'. He even tried to buy Ford, but was turned down.

In November 1920, Durant's flamboyant style caught up with him. His personal finances were a mess and were found to be deeply, dangerously entangled with the finances of the corporation itself.

He was forced to resign. He left the company he had founded and went on to a variety of other activities, including two more tries at automobile manufacturing. According to Lawrence R. Gustin in his book *Billy Durant, Creator of General Motors*, Durant was still cooking up big schemes in his old age. In 1940, at the age of seventy-eight, he was planning to build a great network of bowling centres across the United States. He died in 1947.

Unlike Ford, Chrysler, Benz and Rolls, Durant is seldom mentioned as a member of the pantheon of automotive pioneers. He wasn't a genuine 'car man', he left the company in disgrace, he didn't see the company through to its days of greatest glory. But General Motors is the way it is – huge and conglomerate – primarily because of the way Durant conceived and assembled the company. Durant was also responsible for bringing Alfred P. Sloan Jr into the company, the man who became the closest thing GM has to a patriarch and spiritual leader.

Sloan was president of one of the many companies Durant bought, the Hyatt Roller Bearing Company, purchased in 1916. He served General Motors from that year until his retirement in 1956, spending nearly twenty years as Chairman. Sloan is the man most credited with the development of the GM operating policies and management structures that became world famous, much studied, long-lasting and are now much maligned.

Sloan was also responsible for moving GM into the European marketplace. In his memoir *My Years with General Motors* (published in 1963 and recently re-issued with a new introduction by Peter Drucker, the eminent management expert) Sloan recounts his thinking behind the expansion: 'In building up our Overseas Operations Division, we were obliged, almost at the outset, to confront some large, basic questions: we had to decide whether, and to what extent, there was a market abroad for the American car – and if so, which American car offered the best growth prospects. We had to determine whether we wanted to be exporters or overseas producers. When it became clear that we had to engage in some production abroad, the next question was whether to build up our own companies or to buy and develop existing ones.'

Sloan and his managers proceeded as one might expect. They

decided to go ahead and produce in Europe – rather than export cars
from America – but they would build their European manufacturing
base through acquisition, rather than by developing new plants. Ford
took the opposite route, starting up their own plants in Britain,
which may be one reason for Ford's eventual dominance of the UK
market.

GM's first target for acquisition was Citröen of France, in 1919.
The deal could have been made: Citröen was willing, although the
French government was reluctant. But Sloan felt uneasy with the
Citröen management – he felt they were weak and that a GM
executive should take the helm – and neither of the two possible
candidates, Sloan or Walter Chrysler, wanted to leave Detroit. A few
hours before they were scheduled to sail to France to close the deal,
they decided to call it off. 'I sometimes wonder just how different the
history of the industry would have been if either Mr Chrysler or I had
offered to operate Citröen for General Motors,' muses Sloan.

Next, GM turned its gaze to England for a likely candidate and,
in 1924, set its sights on the Austin Company. It was a successful
manufacturer, and its Longbridge plant (near Birmingham) was producing about 12,000 cars per year, 'which in England at that time was
fairly substantial production'. (GM, by contrast, sold nearly 600,000
cars in 1924.) Sloan had reservations about Austin, as well, because
it had 'the same disadvantages that had bothered me about Citröen
six years earlier; its physical plant then was in poor condition and its
management was weak.' The Austin deal also fell through, and GM
stopped looking for a large producer to buy in England. Instead, as
Sloan puts it, 'We entered into negotiations to purchase Vauxhall
Motors Ltd, a much smaller concern in England. This acquisition in
the latter part of 1925 was a much less controversial matter in General
Motors. It was in no sense a substitute for Austin; indeed, I looked
on it only as a kind of experiment in overseas manufacturing. The
experiment seemed appealing, however; and the investment required
of us was only $2,575,291.'

In other words, Vauxhall was available and the price was right, but
it was hardly a big purchase. In 1925, Vauxhall built 1,398 motor
cars. GM built over 790,000.

                                    *

Vauxhall's roots are very different from those of its parent. GM's 'overseas experiment' was founded in 1857 as the Vauxhall Iron Works by Alexander Wilson, a Scottish engineer. Its initial business was the production of high pressure marine engines, donkey pumps, cranes and various equipment for the Admiralty pinnaces, tug boats, launches and pleasure steamers that plied the rivers of England.

Wilson established his company on the south bank of the Thames and named it after the Vauxhall district of London where he was located. The name Vauxhall derives from Fulk's Hall, the house of Fulk le Breant, a thirteenth-century mercenary soldier and aide to King John. Fulk's heraldic emblem was a griffin – the mythical half-eagle, half-lion – and Wilson adopted the griffin as his company emblem. Vauxhall may have, therefore, the oldest corporate symbol in the automotive business.

Wilson had left the company by the time Vauxhall produced its first automobile, in 1903. This was a five-horsepower open car, available with two or four seats, and powered by an engine originally designed for river launches. By 1905, Vauxhall was doing well enough to warrant moving the car operations to a small building in Luton, where the company has been based ever since.

At the time of the GM purchase, Vauxhall was a luxury car maker which built expensive models – with prices up to £750, in comparison to the £250-£300 for humbler makes – and competed with upmarket producers such as Rolls, Bentley and Sunbeam. Vauxhalls were sporting machines, purchased by the wealthy. Photographs from the period show that the owners included Burmese film producers and well-to-do Japanese businessmen.

During its early years, the company had a number of successes with technology as well as several firsts in various motoring trials. The Prince Henry model, first shown at the 1911 Motor Show, was a version of racing models which had performed well in the Prince Henry trials in Germany the year before. The sharp-beaked Prince Henry has been called the first 'true' British sports car, and led to the development of Vauxhall's most famous car of the period, the 4.5 litre 30/98.

For several years after the purchase in 1925, General Motors waffled about their commitment to the European market and their relationship with Vauxhall. Sloan admits that 'although we had made the gestures I have described toward producing abroad, and had taken on Vauxhall, the Executive Committee had not yet crystallized an overseas policy.' There was even talk of abandoning the whole effort: 'Should we expand Vauxhall, or should we write it off as a bad investment? Was it really necessary to manufacture in Europe?'

Eventually GM decided that since 'the British Empire covered 38% of the world markets outside the United States and Canada' it was worth some time and attention. The emphasis, however, would no longer be on the upper end of the market. The first issue of the GM/Vauxhall marriage was the Cadet, launched in 1930 and priced at just £280. From making sports cars and powerful saloons, Vauxhall gradually fell in with the general market trend towards less expensive, more modest family vehicles. It was like an orphaned royal being married off into a huge family of 'regular folks'.

Generally speaking, Vauxhall prospered under GM's ownership. It began producing the Bedford range of commercial vehicles in 1931; pioneered integral construction techniques in Britain in 1937; built Churchill tanks in record time during World War II; greatly expanded production facilities at Luton; and produced a number of models remembered more or less fondly by the British motoring public – including the Cresta, the Victor, the Viva (which had achieved sixth place on the list of the UK's all-time best selling cars by the time it went out of production in 1979), the Firenza, the Chevette and, in 1975, the Cavalier Mark I.

In 1929, General Motors extended its commitment in Europe by exercising an option to purchase a controlling interest in Adam Opel AG, based near Frankfurt in Germany. Opel was a family-owned company, founded by Adam Opel in 1862 to produce sewing machines. Number one son Carl got the company into bicycles around 1887, and in the 1890s the Opel sons – all five of them: Carl, Wilhelm, Heinrich, Fritz and Ludwig – showed terrific prowess as bicycle racers. By the mid-1920s Opel had become the world's largest bicycle manufacturer, capable of turning out 4,000 bikes per day. In association with a pioneering engineer, Friedrich Lutzmann, Opel had begun car manufacturing in 1899.

In 1928, Opel was (as it still is) a much larger company than

Vauxhall, producing about 43,000 cars that year. It was, in fact, the largest car manufacturer in Germany, with a 44% share of domestic models sold in the German market. Of course, that was still a puny output in comparison to GM. In fact, at the time of the acquisition, a GM newsletter *General Motors World* reported that 'in so far as the automotive industry is concerned, Germany's present position is now somewhat analogous to that of the United States at the beginning of the development of the industry.'

Although Alfred Sloan believed that buying Opel was a smart move, and regarded the company as well-equipped and staffed, he evidently had little faith in any managers who were not his own: he reports that, while Opel was a well-run company, it – like Austin and Citröen – 'was not without management problems, especially at the top policy level.'

Soon after the acquisition, Sloan spoke to a gathering of some 500 Opel dealers and distributors in Frankfurt and '. . . observed to them that, while Germany was a highly industrialized country, its automobile production was very low by American standards, and that I anticipated Opel production might one day run as high as 150,000 vehicles per year. When the statement was translated into German, it was received with a good deal of derision.' Of course, Opel eventually achieved that mark (producing 167,650 cars in 1954) and then vastly exceeded it (with nearly 570,000 cars produced by Adam Opel AG in Germany in 1989).

The Opel acquisition cost GM a total of $33 million, as against the $2.5 million paid for Vauxhall. It gave GM not only a strong production base but an extensive dealer network as well. It was inevitable that the American parent would pay more attention to its powerful German subsidiary over the years than its experimental little outpost in the UK.

J'89 was a product of these automotive genes, certainly, but was just as strongly influenced by its environment. The development of any new car is affected by dramatic external events, as well as by the personality, background and relative success of its competitors. The volume manufacturers are, arguably, reactive rather than pro-active in nature – to oil shocks, foreign incursions, a competitor's good idea.

The history of the auto industry is like a long chain reaction, each new model ricocheting off competitive models that have come before. And, knowing this, manufacturers are constantly trying to anticipate the direction of the next ricochet. If they get it wrong (as the American manufacturers did after the '70s oil shocks, when they assumed that the demand for big cars would not be affected), it can take two or three product cycles to get back on track. If they get it right, they may accomplish a leapfrog – they may land in a clear spot just ahead of the competition and find that they are being reacted *to*, rather than being the ones to react.

But achieving a leapfrog is difficult to do in the car industry, because of the long lead times involved and the crowded field of competitors. It was easier when each company and each model had its own favoured and well-defined competitor, by which it could measure its success. Traditional two-company rivalries – such as Mercedes versus BMW or General Motors versus Ford – are becoming huge, multi-national battles with five, six, ten combatants, all fighting over smaller and smaller bits of turf. But there remains at least one extremely clear-cut automotive rivalry in the UK: Ford versus Vauxhall in the intermediate segment of the market. And, ultimately, Ford against Vauxhall in the total UK market.

The roots of this rivalry go back some forty years. In the mid-1950s the British Motor Corporation (which, at the time, included Austin, Morris and MG among others) was still the leader of the UK market (although slipping) with about a 39% share, and Ford came second with about 27%.

In November 1956 came the first oil shock – the blocking of the Suez Canal as a result of the dispute between the Egyptians and Israelis, with Britain, the US and eventually the UN all embroiled. It was April 1957 before the canal reopened and, while it was closed, oil shipments from the East were delayed, causing shortages and petrol rationing in the UK.

People in Britain reacted predictably to the crisis: they wanted cars with greater fuel efficiency that would allow them to travel as far as possible using their measly ration of six to ten gallons per month. One answer was to buy the tiny, three-wheeled, fuel-efficient bubble cars being built in Germany. British car makers were enraged at this defection. According to Andrew Nahum in his book *Alec Issigonis*, Leonard Lord, who was then head of BMC, swore at the 'bloody awful bubble-cars' and vowed to 'drive them off the streets by designing a proper miniature car'. In 1959, BMC introduced the Mini, designed by Issigonis.

This was a radically different small car from any that had been seen before in Britain with front wheel drive, small wheels, rubber springs, a transverse engine and sliding windows. Although it had some build problems at the start, the Mini became the most successful British car ever built, with over five million sold by 1990.

The Mini had, in short, achieved a leapfrog. It became so popular that Ford, of course, had to respond. But rather than compete with the revolutionary Mini head on, Ford looked for a gap in BMC's line-up and found one: above the Mini and the larger, also very popular, 1100 model.

They aimed the Cortina Mark I directly at that gap, launched it in 1962, and it soon became the frontrunner in its category. Vauxhall brought out its own new model a year later – the one-litre Viva. It too was successful by Vauxhall standards – it sold over 100,000 copies in 1967 and '68 – and gave both Ford and BMC (or British Leyland, as it soon became) some respectable competition.

While these cars were duelling for market share, a new phenomenon was emerging: the fleet market. This grew rapidly, particularly from the mid-1970s, when the Labour government imposed a variety of wage restrictions and employers found a practical way of getting round them: offering a company car as compensation.

The UK is unique in Europe in the size and influence of its company car market. Today, fleet sales account for about half of all car purchases in the UK, in comparison with the 12-15% share in most other European countries. And the growth of the company fleet has directly benefited the UK manufacturers (some say, kept them afloat) because of a general policy on the part of UK companies to buy British.

The heart of the fleet market is the intermediate car – used by legions of middle managers, sales people and company reps – accounting for about 25% of total sales. Car makers may sell their smaller models in greater volumes, but the profit margins are also smaller. The luxury models have higher margins, but sell in very low volumes. So, the intermediate model offers the best combination of volume and profit margin.

As the company car market grew, the Cortina happily sailed through three new editions, or marks, in 1966, 1970 and 1976. It sold well throughout the '60s, was the best-selling car in the UK market in 1967, and was unbeatable during most of the 1970s – the best-selling car in the UK from 1974 to 1981. The Cortina gradually came to define the intermediate company car, growing in size and improving in specification as the fleet car gradually left behind its image as company workhorse and took on new life as company status symbol. Over its twenty years of existence, the Cortina ceased to be just a car and became an institution. It helped Ford become and remain the dominant UK manufacturer, even as the industry was going through a period of general decline.

Throughout the General Motors empire, including Vauxhall, many people who have joined the company early in their careers will stay through to retirement. Sons will follow fathers into the business, siblings will join siblings. And so there still are many people at Vauxhall who remember the grim years that began in the late 1960s. John Butterfield, for example, joined Vauxhall in 1955 as a young man directly out of university and at the time of the launch of J'89 had risen to become Manager of Marketing Communications.

'There was a time, in the fifties, when if Vauxhall sneezed, Luton caught cold,' remembers Butterfield. But, although the Viva did well for Vauxhall and the company was profitable through the mid-1960s, it began to suffer at the end of the '60s. Sales drooped, and in 1969 Vauxhall recorded a loss for the first time since 1957. It lost money again in 1970 and in 1972, '73 and '74.

In 1975, Vauxhall production was a paltry 98,000 cars and, with no competitor for the Ford Cortina in the burgeoning fleet market, everyone knew that 'the marque of Vauxhall wasn't exactly the brightest and sharpest,' as Butterfield put it. But, in that year, Vauxhall brought out two new models. The first was the Chevette which, Butterfield remembers, was 'accepted tremendously well'. But the problem was that the 'intermediate group was expanding dramatically. And we didn't have such a car at all.'

At the same time, 'We, as Vauxhall, were undergoing a dramatic change. Up to 1975, we did everything ourselves. We designed the car. We engineered it. We brought it to production. We built the engines here. We were a very integrated manufacturing unit.' The then Chairman of Vauxhall, Bob Price, decided that an intermediate model was needed.

According to Butterfield, Price 'was a tremendous guy for making things happen. He took the Opel Ascona and put the sloping front of the Opel Manta on it. The Manta had two slats on it, and he took those slats out.' This was accomplished in an unprecedentedly short space of time. When Price presented the concept for the car to the appropriate committee, Butterfield reports that he said, '"Gentlemen, it comes to the market in nine months time." And it did. It was a fantastic thing.'

The Vauxhall design staff (including Wayne Cherry, who became Director of Design for Vauxhall in 1975 and would later become design chief for J'89) worked with Price on the new Cortina-fighter. It began life as a cluttered sheet of paper, with components and personality traits borrowed from various members of the GM family. The designers used the floor pan and rear end of the Opel Ascona model, borrowed the basic front end of the Opel Manta and made the new car their own, primarily through the addition of the sheet metal nose in place of the slatted Manta grille.

'We couldn't decide on a name for the car,' recalls Butterfield. 'We had a terrible time. We thought Cavalier was a good name in so many ways and there were all sorts of arguments. Bob Price didn't like it. We'd have battles royal and in the end we agreed to call it Cavalier.' The new car was introduced in October 1975.

At first, the Cavalier was built at the Opel factory in Antwerp, which meant, in effect, that it was an imported car. That a British company would sell foreign-made cars under their own domestic badge caused great consternation on the part of Vauxhall dealers and the motor industry in general. 'Stop This Foreign British Car' led the story in the *Daily Mail* of 10 October 1975. 'Vauxhall Cavalier is further evidence of Opelization,' reported the *Financial Times* on the same day.

Butterfield was involved in the launch of the Cavalier at Elstree film studios. 'We were very nervous because at that stage it was wholly an import. You couldn't imagine it now, but thirteen years ago for a British manufacturer to be importing a car, oh! it was not done. We made a big point of the whole presentation: now we're part of Europe. In fact the phrase was, "We're all Europeans now."' Vauxhall fleet managers were 'dead scared' that fleet operators would not buy the car because it was imported. 'But the Vauxhall badge bridged that. And it took off.'

The Cavalier Mark I did well (selling over 50,000 cars in its best year, 1978) and was the competitor Vauxhall needed in the intermediate sector. It did well enough to warrant Vauxhall beginning assembly of the car at Luton in 1977. Even so, the Cortina seemed to be untouchable. In 1979, it sold 199,280 copies, three times Vauxhall's total domestic production of just under 59,000.

Sales of the Cavalier might have been better, however, if Vauxhall hadn't been discovering the downside of importing: they couldn't get enough cars to sell. 'The real tragedy was that right through the '70s we didn't have the availability,' says Butterfield.

Things looked grim for Vauxhall. It didn't have the volume of sales or profits to support the increasing cost of developing new models, and although GM invested in Vauxhall, they paid more attention to Opel. Beginning in the mid '70s, GM began shifting design and engineering operations from the UK and consolidating them at Opel. From being a complete auto manufacturer – capable of designing, engineering and manufacturing a car from scratch – Vauxhall became an assembly and marketing operation only.

The company couldn't stop losing money: in 1975, '76, '77, '79. Then the general market downturn in Europe led to an increase in supply of Cavaliers. 'Right at the end of 1979,' says Butterfield, Cavaliers 'suddenly became available. We had tummies bigger than our ability to digest. We took thousands of them. And we got buried. We ended up with fields full of the things. The run-out of the first Cavalier was not a happy event.'

In 1980 Vauxhall posted its worst loss ever, £83 million. Butterfield puts it plainly: 'In '81, the Vauxhall name was very, very sick. There were all sorts of rumours around. Will Vauxhall continue in this country? Will General Motors pull out? Bedford [the commercial vehicle division of GM in the UK] was making all the money, Vauxhall was losing it all.'

To make matters worse, Opel was competing with Vauxhall in its own domestic market, at the same time relying on Opel for some production. This made for an extremely messy situation, where brand identity was confused – and confusing – and loyalties were divided. 'We were fighting against Opel,' says Butterfield. 'We spent as much time worrying about Opel as we did about Ford. It really was a state of war between us.'

Of course, 1980-81 were bad years for the industry in general. In the US, General Motors suffered its first loss in sixty years in 1981. For the US manufacturers, one answer to the problems in the domestic market seemed to be to broaden their operations, consolidate production and create fewer car platforms that could be sold, with minor variations, in many markets. Ford introduced the first 'world car' – the Escort – in 1981. It was the fruit of a mammoth development programme, costing about $1,076 million.

General Motors introduced its own version of the world car a year later and at an even greater cost, estimated at about five billion dollars. In the US, the first J car appeared under the badges of three GM divisions, as the Pontiac Sunbird, Chevrolet Cavalier and Buick Skyhawk. The cars were considered underpowered in the States, and some customers were unhappy because the models looked so much alike across the divisions, but the car did reasonably well. In Europe, however, the new J car – the Cavalier Mark II in Britain – was extremely successful.

Eric Fountain, another Vauxhall veteran (he had joined the company in 1954), was Public Relations Director at the time of the launch of the 1981 Cavalier. 'It was the regeneration of Vauxhall,' he says. 'Even we didn't perceive the tremendous value it had for the customer. We didn't realize it was as good as it was. It was the most exciting thing we'd been involved in.'

The new car competed in size with the Cortina Mark IV, but, in comparison to the twenty-year-old Ford, the Cavalier was modern and exciting. It featured front wheel drive and a transverse engine (just like the leapfrog Mini, which had led to the reactive Cortina in the first place). This made it roomier inside. It had quick and responsive Opel-made engines. It was fuel-efficient, had good aerodynamic efficiency for the time, had a lot of the features and interior equipment that UK customers love, and it was reliable and economical to run.

The car was immediately successful. 'It was a driver's car, a fast lane cruiser,' says Fountain. 'It was perceived to *be* Vauxhall. It had an image stronger than any car we've had.'

Best of all, Vauxhall's timing was right. The Cortina was due for replacement in 1982, and Vauxhall had beaten them to the market by a year – a crucial year in which to establish an identity and win conquest sales. They'd been a year behind with the Viva, several years behind with the Cavalier Mark I, but this time they had landed in the clear. 'The Cavalier was coming in brand new,' as Fountain puts it. 'Ford allowed themselves a one-year hiatus when they had nothing, before the Sierra came in.'

Of course, good as the Cavalier was, it seemed likely that the all-new Cortina, once it appeared, would continue its indomitable leadership. Vauxhall expected a year-long breathing space before Ford came roaring back with an even more popular replacement to their most successful car of all time. Says Fountain, '[The new Cortina] should have been, let's face it, so *new* that it knocked the Cavalier back where it belonged, in Ford's mind.'

But that is not how it happened. The new Cortina, launched in September 1982, was not a Cortina at all. It was called the Sierra and it had a strange new shape, smooth and rounded and a little droopy. Although it was well received by the press, the Sierra reminded people of a soap dish in appearance, or perhaps a jelly mould. Or was it a fuselage, or a pudding basin? There were no visual vestiges of the old Cortina.

'We couldn't believe our luck,' says John Butterfield. 'They dropped the name Cortina, which was a household name.' It seemed that Ford had wantonly killed a national institution, the second most popular car of all time in the UK. To some this was shocking. In addition, the Sierra had some problems. It tended to be unstable in crosswinds and to wallow in the corners. Butterfield remembers that 'there were all sorts of rumours and rumblings about, "You have an accident in the Sierra, the front deck crumples." All in all it was bad, bad news.'

And, despite its radical exterior styling, some of the Sierra mechanicals were old-fashioned. It had rear wheel drive, ignoring the trend toward front wheel drive in many European models, including the Cavalier. It used the same old iron engines as the Cortina, and the basic suspension and chassis. In fact, it seemed like an overly modern body on an antiquated skeleton. To make matters worse, there was no booted version offered at all, just a hatchback. Hatchbacks are fine for families, but the middle manager wants a boot – it's considered more dignified and serious.

It looked as if Ford had committed the worst possible error: they had destroyed the car's character, negated its heritage, confused its bloodlines. They had taken a huge gamble on a futuristic car and lost. The rumour began to circulate that even Henry Ford II, son of the founder, didn't like the car. Apparently he was touring a design studio when he saw a model of the new Sierra. He remarked to a designer, 'I hope I'm dead before that one comes out.' 'I hope not, Mr Ford,' the designer replied. 'It's coming out in six months.'

The press reported that fleet buyers weren't buying. Under a headline in *The Mail on Sunday* on 16 November 1982, 'Well, have *you* seen a Sierra?' Mr Peter Judson, General Manager of Hertz UK car leasing, was quoted as saying, 'People are nervous about the Ford Sierra. They're tending not to give orders.' In the space of a year, Hertz had gone from a fleet dominated by Cortinas, to one where five Cavaliers were leased for every Sierra. Mr Judson wondered if Ford might 'have to go back and redesign the Sierra'.

Vauxhall was ecstatic, and taken aback by its own success. Over 100,000 Cavaliers were sold in 1982. But Ford had initiated a new price policy in March of that year – before the Sierra was released – slashing prices on all models, except the Cortina. Their goal (they said) was to help fight the rise of imports, and to rationalize the UK prices of their products in comparison to lower Ford prices on the Continent. But, whatever the reason, the Sierra was launched into a blizzard of discounting. No manufacturer wants to discount prices on a new model as it enters its first year of life.

Soon, there was a price war which consumed the entire UK car industry. '**Car Wars**!' declared the *Daily Express* on 30 March 1982, relating that 'Ford is cutting prices drastically – threatening a new battle in the car market.' The *Daily Mail* of the same day reported that 'Ford announced a "Sale of the Century" yesterday which is certain to spark off a car price war. The move by Britain's top car maker is a bold attempt to stem the rising tide of imported cars from Europe.'

The Sierra benefited from the discounting, and surged ahead of the Cavalier in 1983. But then, according to Butterfield, 'We stole the march on them again with a simple thing: updating all our audio in the car, putting stereo radio cassette players in. I don't think we quite realized what we were doing at the time. But we were trying to get at the [fleet] user-choosers. Ford never knew what hit them.'

The audio upgrade helped Cavalier bounce back in 1984, taking the sales lead in the intermediate segment and becoming the second best-selling car in Britain (after the Ford Escort) with a healthy 26.8% of the intermediate market. It repeated the performance in 1985.

In the UK, Cavalier was voted Fleet Car of the Year three years running, from 1985 to 1987. It was awarded First in its Class by *Autocar* magazine in 1981, and named Tow Car of the Year in 1982. It won Holiday Car of the Year in 1986, and, in Europe, the car won everything from the Hertz 'Most Reliable Car' of 1986 to the 'Most Rational Car of the Year' from the German magazine *MOT*. Cavalier sold so well that, virtually on its strength alone, Vauxhall's total market share in the UK nearly doubled, from 8.5% in 1981 to 16.5% in 1987. This kind of performance was unheard of – a Vauxhall outselling a Ford? As Butterfield puts it, 'The main springboard for that growth was Cavalier.' Vauxhall was often referred to as the Cavalier Car Company, and consumers confessed to a much stronger name recognition for the child than the parent. The rumours about the demise of Vauxhall died away.

Even as the Cavalier was improving the company's fortunes, General Motors was undergoing a restructuring throughout the world. Vauxhall trimmed costs and reduced employment. From an average of 33,000 weekly employees in 1978, the number was down to 11,132 by 1989.

In 1981, the dealer network was merged as well. In that year, Butterfield relates, the corporation 'sent a fellow over here called John Bagshaw. He came in as Director of Marketing to pull the two organizations together. In March of '81, both dealer organizations, Vauxhall and Opel, were invited to the Metropole in Birmingham. And he stood up and told them, "As from tomorrow morning it's one organization. Vauxhall/Opel." Bagshaw was the architect of the merger. And there's no doubt he became the sort of focal point in the dealers' eyes, the eyes of the press, the industry itself. It was Bagshaw that merged the company, that really brought Vauxhall forward.'

Of course, Ford applied its considerable marketing and technical expertise to the Sierra. According to Eric Fountain, 'Ford bolstered the Sierra by throwing money at it, literally, and got us all a bad name.' The Sierra's stability problems were solved. Ford used their large dealer network and price advantage to push the Sierra past the initial reluctance to buy. 'They really got their act together,' says Butterfield. 'They poured millions into marketing the Sierra, putting the job right.'

In 1986, the Sierra sneaked slightly ahead of the Cavalier in sales, with an edge of about 400 cars. Ford successfully introduced variants and special editions that kept the Sierra fresh. The booted version, the Sapphire, appeared in 1987. And the performance Cosworth variant came out in 1988, with its great rear wing and engine power that the trade press called 'shattering'.

At the end of the '80s, the Sierra was going strong, darting back and forth among the top three positions of the sales chart – exchanging places with its Ford stablemates, the Escort and the Fiesta. Even so, the Sierra never regained the dominance of the Cortina, and the Cavalier had won an acceptance for Vauxhall the company had never before enjoyed.

Cost-cutting continued at Vauxhall. Bagshaw, who had been posted to Germany as marketing overlord in 1983, came back as MD in early 1986. His job, says Butterfield, was 'to get the ship ready for the competitive battle of the future. Costs were the main problem. He started a massive cost-cutting exercise, going right back to the bedrocks of the job. He literally ripped millions of pounds out of our spending costs. We had to learn to live with a much slimmer organization. We had to learn to do things in different ways.'

Finally, thanks to the Cavalier, thanks to the new organization, thanks to reduced costs, Vauxhall turned a modest profit in 1987, for the first time in nine years.

The Cavalier Mark II had achieved that wonderful, rare and unbelievably gratifying business ambition: it was a runaway hit, a leapfrog.

3 · PLAN

'The question is: what does the customer need?'

Friedrich Lohr, GME Technical Director

Of course, there are always different interpretations. To many, the Sierra represented a bold move for Ford at a time when the market demanded a bold move – in response to the oil shocks and to rising Japanese imports. Despite its early problems, the Sierra gradually regained the Cortina's title as the leader in the intermediate category.

But even in 1989, the Sierra's best year to date, its sales of 175,920 were well below the Cortina's record of 193,784 in 1979 – and in a market that had grown in volume by over 25%. Yes, there were many more worthy competitors in the market during the '80s. And yes, the Sierra certainly has had longer legs than the Cavalier – maintaining sales over a greater number of years. Even so, the Sierra has not taken over the Cortina's role as a British motoring institution.

In an age of multi-national companies and global marketing, perhaps no car can or should achieve such status again. But the way the Sierra failed – and the way it succeeded – presents one of the clearest illustrations of the fundamental nature of the development process for a new volume car.

A bundle of often conflicting objectives – design, engineering, financial and marketing – all strain to exert an influence on the new car. The end-product itself must be a well-balanced package that offers styling, features, performance, reliability and value in the proper measure to attract the largest number of customers. If any

one of the objectives overshadows the others, the car may emerge
out of balance in some way.

For the designers of J'89, the example of the Sierra was often
in their minds. Had it really gone wrong and, if so, how and why?
Could they avoid the same mistakes?

Robert Lutz was Chairman of Ford of Europe when the Sierra was
developed. He had formerly been with Opel, then with BMW, and,
after leaving Ford, he became President of Chrysler in the US. Lutz
clearly articulated Ford's objectives for the Sierra in a *Financial Times*
interview of 21 September 1982: 'My product philosophy is to get
Ford cars out there that people desperately want, rather than cars
they will buy because they are the lowest price on the market. The
Japanese have taken over the efficient, no-nonsense, no-frills, high
value-for-money, reliable transportation part of the market. My goal
is to be a mass producer of the type of cars BMW and Mercedes
have a reputation for making. We are moving up in technology and
credibility so we get the same price elasticity as they have.'

In other words, Lutz wanted to differentiate Ford cars from the
bland, but practical, Japanese models. He was looking for an 'added
value' that would help Ford avoid the nasty and tedious business of
competing on price alone.

At the time, sales for the luxury makers – BMW and Mercedes –
were growing steadily, and it seemed they were able to charge any
price they liked and get away with it. Their added value was based
on two elements: superior engineering (at least in perception) – and
an intangible *image*.

Ford couldn't really add value through image – it takes time to
create one, and it is difficult (if not impossible) for a volume
manufacturer to create an exclusive, upmarket image at all. And,
the value had to be added without substantially increasing the price.
The Sierra was to be, after all, a competitor in the very middle of
the market. So Ford seemed to settle on design as the most effective
way to distinguish the Sierra from the rest of the pack.

In 1986 the Vice President of Design for Ford of Europe, Uwe
Bahnsen, decided that it was time for a change of career. He

had always been interested and involved in education for transport designers, and had helped establish both the transport programme at the Royal College of Art in London and The Art Center College of Design (Europe). The latter was to be an associate school to the Art Center College of Design in Pasadena, California, which has trained a good percentage of the world's automotive designers since its founding in 1930 (including the chief designer for GM Europe, Wayne Cherry).

Bahnsen, having been involved in automotive design for nearly thirty years, accepted an offer to join the Art Center College (Europe) as Education Director. The school sits atop a gentle hill overlooking the village of La Tour-de-Peilz, near Vevey in Switzerland. The village comes to an end at the edge of Lake Geneva. To the south, there is a suggestion of the Alps shooting up into the clouds and at the far end of the lake lies the city of Geneva.

Bahnsen inhabits a quiet corner office in the administration building, a renovated nineteenth-century château, the Château de Sully. He is a tall, slender man with a precise manner that suggests his German background and an articulation of speech, in English, that seems at once both scholarly and executive.

Bahnsen is one of the chief advocates for the role of design in the automotive industry, and industry in general, in Europe today. He was trained in the fine arts, worked in advertising and window display design and joined Ford in 1958. He worked for Ford in Germany and then the States, and became Chief Designer for Ford of Britain in 1967. He rose to be Head of Product Development for Ford of Europe, and, finally, to Vice President of Design.

As a designer, that is about as high as one can go in the hierarchy; designers may achieve director status in the big multi-national firms but have not ascended to the position of managing director. Over the years, Bahnsen was involved in the design of the Cortina, the Fiesta, the new Escort of 1980, the Sierra, Scorpio and the Cargo and Transit vans – in short, the backbone of the successful, current Ford range.

Bahnsen freely expresses his beliefs about the importance of design. For years, he says, car designers were thought of as mere

stylists. Engineers created the car and the stylists were called
in later to drape some sheet metal around the mechanicals and
decide which colour to paint it. This attitude was strongest and
most prevalent in America and Bahnsen believes that 'American car
design contaminated the idea of design'. Car design was generally
held in low esteem in art schools and, as a profession, was about
on a par with one of Bahnsen's former occupations – shop window
display.

The 1980 Escort was the first expression of the phenomenon that
became known as the 'world car', and it was the first Ford model
of the new line-up to be created in direct response to the events of
the 1970s. Something radically different was called for, and Bahnsen
and his team believed that one of the answers was to be found in
aerodynamic styling. Ford invested about a billion dollars in styling
and engineering the new, front-wheel-drive Escort. It proved a huge
success – and has been the best-selling car in the UK every year
since 1981.

Similarly, when the Cortina was due to be replaced, the basic
approach did not change, but the aerodynamic look was extended.
There was a surprisingly hostile reaction in the UK to the new shape,
since the basic styling approach that characterized the Sierra had been
shown at the Frankfurt Motor Show in 1981 in a well-received concept vehicle called Probe III. And the Audi 100, introduced the same
year, had already broken new ground in terms of aerodynamics.

Bahnsen echoes his former boss, Robert Lutz, when he describes
why the Sierra was the way it was. 'The 1974 energy crisis changed
our emotional relationship to cars. The Japanese had pulled the rug
out from under the European maker's feet. Big cars became socially
unacceptable. Ford decided to take a bold move.'

In the Sierra, Ford wanted to achieve its bold commercial objective
with an unmistakably new design approach. It was the exterior shape
that would be the clearest signal to customers that this was more than
a new model, it was a radical departure from the old.

The Sierra was unusual, says Bahnsen, not only because it was
a bold design but because it was a bold design that was not
substantially altered during the development process. Before the
days of supercomputers and an integrated design process, it was

not unusual for designers to create an innovative new design and then watch as the engineers and manufacturing specialists modified, re-interpreted and simplified it to death. Bahnsen, having suffered through that process in the past, did not allow it to happen with the Sierra and 'the production Sierra looked just the same as the first clay models'.

In other words, the *art* of car design was becoming more successfully integrated into the *business* of car development.

For Vauxhall and the developers of J'89, the Sierra had to be seen as a mixture of mistakes and successes – just as most cars are – but it was the exceptionally high visibility of the model it replaced that brought the Sierra under such extreme scrutiny.

The car was initially criticized for its old mechanicals, carry-over engines and traditional rear wheel drive. Although Ford engineers say the reason they chose rear wheel drive for the Sierra was that it is more appropriate for a larger car, there are others who argue that Ford had spent so much money on the Escort that they weren't prepared to make another huge investment in a front-wheel-drive system for the Sierra. The primary advantage of a front-wheel-drive car is in packaging. Because of the configuration of the engine and the lack of a drive train to the rear wheels, the front wheel configuration generally allows for more interior space than in rear-wheel-drive cars.

So the newness of the Sierra lay mostly in its exterior shape and interior appointments – rather than the mechanicals. As a result, the styling did not seem as well integrated into the whole car as it should have been.

Some competitive designers also believe that the Sierra design did not reach the market in quite so pure and unaltered a state as Bahnsen suggests. The rounded shape designed to express what Bahnsen calls a 'totality of volume' was compromised by the late addition of a drip rail that arched from the A pillar (between windscreen and front window) to the rear window pillar.

The drip rail stood up high enough and was pedestrian enough in appearance to interrupt the sculpture and confuse the eye. Although it sounds like a minor detail, it is often just such minor details that make or break the total look. Thus the car earned the epithets 'soap dish' and 'jelly mould' rather than 'spacecraft' or 'birdlike' that it might otherwise have deserved and would certainly have preferred.

Finally came the corporate marketing decision to drop the Cortina name. It was twenty years old and too closely identified with the UK market for a pan-European car. It was linked with an Italian ski resort, which was no longer appropriate to the product. The product was different enough from its predecessors to warrant a whole new persona, but while the word 'sierra' may mean both a mountain range and a type of Spanish mackerel, to the UK market it didn't mean much of anything.

So there were nagging inconsistencies in mechanicals, design and marketing with the Sierra. If the new car had attempted just one or two of these changes, it might have been more successful earlier on. But changing the name, changing the look, and disregarding a current hot technology trend – front wheel drive – constituted too much change in one package, and may have stepped over the boundary that separates 'new and exciting' from 'radical and dangerous'.

It is a truism in the motor industry that the buying public, particularly of the intermediate, volume car, is conservative. They want a certain amount of change in the new model, but not too much. Determining just where the line is drawn is what the development process is all about.

But the Sierra design has exhibited remarkable longevity. Not until the end of the 1980s did the car begin to show its age. The shape seems bulky now, its streamlining surpassed by newer models. There is a definite crease in the sheet metal at the waistline, rather than a smoothly rounded curve. The headlights look too big and chunky. The window treatments (not flush) and the windscreen wipers (sticking up rather than concealed) are clues to its age. But, if the car had a slow start, it's had a long, strong finish. Which makes sense – if you take the risk of leading the market, it may take a few years to catch up with you.

For the developers and marketers of J'89, the Sierra was everything a chief rival should be. It was a reminder of their greatest opportunity: the moment when Ford seemed to stumble and let Vauxhall surge ahead. It was also the spectre of what could amount to their worst mistake: in redesigning its most popular model, Vauxhall was in danger of stumbling too.

Overall, the Sierra was simply the Cavalier's greatest sales challenge, the epitome of the best-selling intermediate car. It was the car that Vauxhall had knocked out once, but had come back to regain the title – the car Vauxhall had to beat once again.

One of the first steps in the process of designing any new model is to decide just how new it will actually be. In the 'all-new' model, the platform dimensions and structure are redesigned, the exterior is completely restyled, the interior is redesigned and the mechanical and electronic systems are thoroughly updated.

In a 'facelift', the platform is not changed, the exterior styling is freshened by the restyling of the front and rear end sheet metal, one or two new mechanical elements may be offered and usually the equipment specification is upgraded or at least repackaged. A special edition is usually a reshuffling of some of the elements of the car for a short-term promotion – a sports package or a special colour combination. Facelifts and special editions are tactical weapons in the battle to keep the model exciting and new over the course of its life.

Currently, the life span of a new model is roughly linked to the length of the development process. Because it takes a European or American car manufacturer about five years to develop a new car today, that is roughly how long it stays on the market. The cost for the totally new model can be anything from £300 million to £3,000 million, to develop the designs, engineering and tooling. The investment the company will make and the price it will charge for the car are both geared to this five-year cycle.

During the first two years of development, the key design decisions are made. Given the average five-year life of the new model, the designers are working to develop a car that will look good for as long as eight to ten years after they have completed their design work. All these timings are acceptable, so long as everybody plays the game the same way. But the Japanese have demonstrated an ability to get cars to the market faster, in as little as three or four years. Now the talk throughout the industry is of greatly reducing the development cycle, and bringing out new models every two or three years.

The lumbering nature of the car development process amazed Ross Perot when he first encountered it. Perot is the maverick entrepreneur who sold his computer company, Electronic Data Systems, to GM in 1984 for $2.55 billion and a seat on the GM board of directors. He found that car makers were disastrously slow to market – in comparison to computer companies – and saw this as a result of their vast and clumsy organizational structures.

Soon after that, Perot told a reporter for the *Wall Street Journal*, 'It takes five years to develop a new car in this country. Heck, we won World War II in four years. We are spending billions to develop new cars. This isn't a moon shot, it's just a car.' Perot was probably right, but he did not have a chance to affect the GM car development process – his disagreements with Chairman Roger Smith became so acrimonious that GM finally bought Perot's and his close associates' shares of EDS in GM in 1986 for over $700 million.

The process has steadily grown more complex and expensive over the years. As far back as 1963, Alfred Sloan reported that the cost of developing a new GM model was $600 million. Today, the volume car manufacturer is faced with keeping up with an accelerating spiral of increased competition, more sophisticated consumer expectations, more expensive technologies in every phase of development, and ever stricter legal and safety restrictions.

The costs and pressures are such that only the big car makers can shoulder the burdens of creating and marketing new cars. That is one of the reasons why so many of the smaller makers, like Saab, Lamborghini, Lotus, Aston Martin, Maserati and Jaguar, have joined forces with one of the multinationals.

Given the high costs and long lead times involved in development, the number of vehicle platforms any one company can produce is limited. A platform is the basic chassis and underlying structure of the car, which is usually identified by a letter. Just as Henry Ford introduced the A and T models, among others, the GME Cavalier/Vectra is known as the J car, the Carlton/Omega the V car, the Astra/Kadett the T car, and so on.

GM Europe has five basic platforms and uses them to create

many variants – hatches, notches, estates, convertibles and special editions. With just five basic platforms, each one involving hundreds of millions spent in development, the manufacturer cannot afford to get one platform wrong. Seven years in the market is not so long a time to recoup a big investment – a commercial aircraft model may have a life of twenty to twenty-five years – and it means that the car manufacturer has to define the market correctly, understand the competition and get its forecasts right.

If it fails to do so, not only may profits be disappointing but a competitor may be provided with its opportunity. Witness the Sierra.

Imagine that it is early in 1982, and you're trying to predict the changes that will occur in the marketplace by the time your new product will be introduced in 1988 or 1989. In five or seven years, anything could happen. Some major, unforeseeable event could change the nature of the game significantly.

During the development of J'89, this is exactly what happened: the whole world, including the world of GM, has shifted since planning began.

First, General Motors was entirely reorganized. In the States, Roger Smith had taken over as Chairman in 1980 and almost immediately launched into a programme of reorganization, consolidation, new plant construction and joint ventures that was expected to cost tens of billions of dollars by 1990. In Europe, GM finally saw the wisdom of the kind of pan-European organization that Ford had created in 1967, and established General Motors Europe (GME) in 1986.

Formerly, the centre of GM European activities had been at the Opel facility in Rüsselsheim in West Germany, which had jurisdiction over Vauxhall Motors and its two plants in the UK, the Opel plants in Germany, and others in Europe. With the reorganization, Vauxhall and Opel became the producing subsidiaries, along with the National Sales Operation which co-ordinates sales in the other European countries. GME, with its European marketing and administrative personnel, is based in a geographically and politically neutral location – Zurich in Switzerland.

The inauguration of GM Europe was a big change for the better for the development of J'89. For years, Vauxhall and Opel had wrangled with each other and the parent company for power, financing, recognition and resources. Opel, being larger and more successful, generally received more attention and money. With the reorganiza-tion, Vauxhall gained a stronger voice in new product decisions.

On a broader scale, in the early 1980s the world car market was suffering. The European market was shrinking. Sales and new registrations declined seriously in 1979 and did not really start picking up again until 1984. Manufacturers worked hard to decrease capacity, reduce production and cut costs and, in those years, the future of the European market looked dismal. But then sales picked up, and the European market started to grow rapidly, even overtaking the American market to become the largest in the world. This surge in the European market still has analysts puzzled. But, as a result, J'89 was elevated in status from being an important car to Vauxhall and Opel, to being an important car for General Motors worldwide.

Given the limping history of the European Common Market, it was difficult to predict that an EC Summit would take the recom-mendations of a 1985 report called 'White Paper on Completing the Internal Market' so thoroughly to heart, and that suddenly there would be a milestone called 1992 looming ahead. Now J'89 would face the prospect of even greater competition, and would have to be successful not just as a British but as a European car – and during its most difficult, mid-life years.

Finally, the emergence of a powerful 'green' movement was hard to foresee in 1982. Although in the US, much stricter tailpipe emissions standards were prompted by the Clean Air Act of 1970, the European market had been slow to follow. But at the end of the 1980s, partly as a result of political movements in Germany and Holland, concern for the environment became a major corporate issue, with self-regulation regarded as better than governmental restriction. General Motors found itself well placed on the green issue, because its models had been designed to run on lower octane fuels and therefore could operate on unleaded petrol.

None of these things could the GM marketing and product people predict as they set about developing J'89.

The headquarters of General Motors Europe is not the looming, corporate edifice one might expect. In fact, it consists of six floors of modern but relatively nondescript offices in the same building as the Zurich Novotel (one of a chain of business hotels), not far from the airport. In both Luton and Rüsselsheim, no administrative office is very far from a plant, and the heavy drabness of traditional manufacturing sets the tone.

But at GME there are no manufacturing facilities. The Novotel is just off the motorway and is a popular meeting spot for international business people. In this setting, GM looks less like an industrial dinosaur and more like a modern corporation. The visitor recognizes the signs of a company that is focused more on the outer world of customers and competition than on its own internal organization. The staff work in sunny offices. They seem to care about clothing and appearances. There are no pin-ups of either girls or cars on the walls.

Dieter Krocker, a German Marketing Strategy Manager for GM Europe, is straightforward in his discussion of the marketing objectives for J'89, and only occasionally lapses into the incomprehensible jargon that characterizes theoretical marketing: words like softnomics and syntetics now and again slip into his conversation.

He explains that with the establishment of GM Europe in 1986, a fundamental change took place in the entire development process. Pre-GME, the key functional disciplines worked sequentially. Management and engineering developed the basic specs for the new model – wheelbase and cost parameters. Styling created a body, and handed it over to engineering. Engineering created specifications for every component. Manufacturing wrestled to build it. Marketing was only called in at the very end of the process, and had to figure out how to sell whatever it was that came out at the far end of the assembly line.

In the past, 'the engineers developed, and marketing sold. But today, marketing has much more influence than in the past,' says Krocker. New car development at GM Europe has become a more integrated process – with give and take among marketing, engineering, design, manufacturing and finance all the way along the line.

The production and registration statistics which the auto industry loves so much allow marketing people primarily to look backwards – seeing trends after they have happened and getting a view of markets after they have already changed.

Perhaps the most appealing aspect of market research and a marketing strategy based upon research is that it makes one feel as if
the world is truly quantifiable. Research often confirms the obvious,
sometimes reveals a hidden trend, but at least it is in numerical form
and is therefore hard to argue with. At the same time, collecting and
interpreting market data is a fascinating pursuit in itself, regardless
of what its final use might be.

One major market trend was becoming obvious to volume manufacturers like GME during the first half of the 1980s: they were getting
squeezed at both ends of the market. At the low end, Japanese cars
offered high build quality, good reliability, low running costs and
decent specifications at reasonable prices. The import penetration of
Japanese models was felt more strongly in some European countries
than in others. In West Germany, Japanese market share grew from
about 2.5% in 1977 to 15% in 1987. It also grew in Switzerland,
Sweden, Austria and the Netherlands. But in other countries, the
Japanese invasion was more of threat than an actuality, often averted
by import quotas. In the UK, Japanese penetration changed very little
from 1977 to 1987, hovering around 11% as a result of a gentlemen's
import agreement.

Not only were the Japanese stealing sales away in the lower price
categories, but their cars were redefining what quality means in a
motor car. For many car buyers, quality has long been equated with
luxury and high price. The Japanese approach is that quality has
nothing to do with luxury, and everything to do with 'fitness for
purpose' and 'meeting customer expectations'. In other words, an
inexpensive car need not and should not be a cheap and poorly built
car. Everything about it should work properly and meet expectations
for functionality, reliability, durability and safety. The ability of the
Japanese to build high-quality cars at reasonable prices has changed
customer expectations in the American and European markets. Car
buyers are less tolerant of cars with parts that don't fit, bits that fall
off, mechanical faults, patchy paint jobs.

At the high end of the market, the volume manufacturer was
being squeezed by the advent of the compact high-technology car,
specifically the BMW 3 series four-door saloon and Mercedes 190.
Although the German models could not compete in the middle of

the J'89 price range, there was disturbing evidence that people who might have bought at the top end of the J'89 range were now being attracted to the low end of the luxury market.

Despite the fact that GME engineers insist there are few mechanical advantages in a BMW or Mercedes, there is a vast difference in the image of the cars. Both makes, and BMW in particular, are perceived to be the leaders in technology, driving excellence and style. If customers have a choice between a Cavalier CD with a 2.0 litre engine at £13,000 and a BMW 320i at £14,000, there is a good chance they will choose the BMW.

Even as the volume maker was being squeezed, the centre of the market – the intermediate group segment – was also being eroded throughout the 1980s, primarily as a result of the continued 'downsizing' caused by the 1970s oil crisis. The intermediate market is strongest in four European countries: Germany, the United Kingdom, France and Italy. These four countries represent 71% of the total European market for intermediate cars, with Germany and the UK accounting for about 45% of the total. The J car, in particular, sold 69% of its models in those two countries in 1988.

According to Dieter Krocker, there are four intermediate sub-segments. The traditional saloon is primarily purchased by families, with or without children. Estate cars are bought almost exclusively by families with children and, probably, dogs. Coupés are purchased by single men and young couples without children. The fourth segment is the compact, high-technology car which is generally bought by men, who are mostly unencumbered by large families and have a high disposable income.

In each sub-segment, the typical buyer is in search of some rather obvious qualities in his or her car choice. The estate car buyer, for example, is thinking of practical matters – how wide is the cargo opening, how stain resistant is the seating material – but does not expect much in the way of sportiness or performance. The traditional saloon buyer, perhaps a weary middle manager embarking on a long journey homewards at day's end, is mostly interested in comfort equipment and ease-of-use features such as electric controls and adjustable seats. The coupé customer wants sportiness, individuality and good performance. The compact high-tech buyers are in the market for the prestige afforded by the latest in technical wizardry such as four wheel drive, four wheel steering, an anti-lock braking system (ABS), the latest in high technology engines using electronic controls and featuring lots of cylinders or valves; to this buyer, image is a strong buying factor.

Of these sub-segments, the traditional saloon is the biggest seller – with about 65% of the intermediate segment – but it has lost a few points over the past few years. Estate cars have gained a point or two, coupés have lost a few, and the compact, high-tech sub-segment has jumped by about five percentage points.

In a particularly revealing piece of statistical analysis, Krocker compared the sales of J'81 in each price category to total car sales in the UK. Except at the high end, the Cavalier exactly matched the market. For example, 30% of all sales in the UK market were of cars in the £7,001 to £8,000 price range, and the percentage of Cavalier sales in that range was 33.7%. But the percentage of Cavaliers sold in its top category – over £10,000 – was half that of the total market.

In other words, Cavalier did not offer a strong competitor at the high end of the market. This confirmed what everybody in the organization and throughout the UK already knew: the Cavalier is a repmobile.

Predicting what the competition will do in the coming years is much trickier than studying what the consumer has done in the recent past. But here the traditional, cyclical nature of the business helps. Looking forward from 1982, GME could reasonably assume that the next generation Sierra would appear a year or two after J'89. They could also predict that Ford would probably apply all its vaunted marketing skills to keeping the Sierra fresh and on the market as long as possible, as they had done with the Cortina.

This is exactly what they did, and by 1986 it looked as if the second generation Sierra would not show its face until 1991 or 1992. If that were true, J'89 would have nearly two years of potential supremacy, with their new model up against a severely aging one. A new Volkswagen Passat was due for launch in the late 1980s (it emerged in 1988), as was a new intermediate Peugeot (the 1987 405).

There were several major competitive developments, however, that could not be predicted. In 1981, British Leyland was still a national-ized company, and, as such, General Motors Europe could expect it to sell cars at discounted prices, going for volume and market share. It did. They could not foresee the effects of the partnership with Honda (leading to a whole new series of intermediate cars, the 200 series); nor the eventual privatization of the company through sale to British Aerospace in 1988; nor the sell-off of Jaguar in 1989.

By 1981, there were rumours and false starts that presaged an even more worrying competitive development. The Japanese company Nissan was talking about building a new assembly plant somewhere in Britain. This it eventually did, announcing plans in 1984 for production to begin by 1986: fast work, indeed, and nerve-wracking for the local UK producers.

Production of the intermediate Nissan Bluebird began in 1986 in a brand new plant in Sunderland. The biggest worry for Vauxhall and General Motors Europe was that Nissan cars produced in England would not be considered imports. There would be no quota restrictions.

In short, from the time GM began planning the 1989 J-car to the time it was announced, an entirely new competitor appeared on the scene complete with assembly plant and new model.

Based upon their research, corporate gut feeling and initiatives from design and engineering staff, GM could have outlined the key tasks for J'89 as follows:

- It shouldn't grow much, if at all, in size. This reflected the influence of the 1970s oil crisis, the Japanese competition and the power of the green movement.

- It should incorporate as much new technology as possible, but still be affordable, to compete with the BMW and Mercedes incursions.

- To compete with both low-end and high-end quality, J'89 would have to exhibit excellent build quality and finishing.

- J'89 should have a high-end variant, like the Sierra Cosworth, to lend prestige to the entire Cavalier range.

- And, one final objective: after years of selling cars at a loss

in the UK, despite strong gains in market share, let's make
some money.

The city of Rüsselsheim lies about 25 km west of Frankfurt. The
main Opel manufacturing plant occupies the heart of town, a great
conurbation of buildings, warehouses and offices, punctuated by gates
and encompassing a network of internal streets. At the perimeter is
a stolid brick building of five storeys that appears to be as much a
fortification as a place of business.

The main gate, through which workers and visitors pass under the
inconsistent scrutiny of uniformed guards, leads off a town square
that is also faced by the Rüsselsheim railway station. Here, a giant,
grey statue of Adam Opel presides. A few blocks to the north is the
River Main. There is an air of order and control in the town that
may stem partly from the looming presence of the great plant, partly
from the basic nature of a small German town.

The main plant is clearly identified with the Opel name, painted in
bold white block letters across a brick tower that constitutes its highest
point. The southern perimeter of the plant is bordered by the railway
tracks, which one must cross to reach the Technical Development
Centre (TDC). The plant may be strictly Opel territory, but the TDC
belongs to General Motors Europe and it serves Opel, Vauxhall and
the countries of the National Sales Operation.

If a new GME model can be said to be 'born', this is where the
birth takes place. The TDC comprises three buildings, facing three
sides of a grassy open plaza. The largest building towers above the
other two and houses nearly 8,000 employees who are involved in
car engineering, manufacturing engineering, testing, and the development of new technical systems.

Set at a right angle to the TDC is the Design Centre, which
contains the design studios and craft workshops that support the
design process. Tucked away behind an unmarked, high white wall
is the two-storey home of Electronic Data Systems, the GM computer
systems subsidiary bought from Ross Perot, the man who railed
against the length of the car development process. In this building
the Cray supercomputer does its work of high-speed, high-volume
number crunching.

To achieve the 'integrated development process' that Krocker describes, the TDC was reorganized in 1984. The key to the reorganization was the establishment of a new position, that of Technical Director, to whom would report the heads of engineering, design, manufacturing and finance.

The Technical Director would oversee a process in which the needs, priorities, concerns and idiosyncrasies of engineering, finance, manufacturing, marketing and design services were all included and considered from the very beginning. This is a demanding task, not only because of the complexity of the project itself but because of the vastly different mentalities, interests and working methods of the people involved in these disciplines. The man chosen for the job was Friedrich W. Lohr and he assumed the title of Executive Director of Technical Development in 1986.

Fritz Lohr appears to be a good man for the job. He is one of six members of the Opel board of managers, which means he has clout within the organization, both up and down. He comes from an engineering background – he was once in charge of shock-absorber development and is known for his work in front-wheel-drive pack-aging – so he understands the technical issues. The design staff also feel he is sensitive to their aesthetic and sculptural concerns.

This is the man who must weigh the importance of conflicting views, who must mediate when a discussion turns into a fight, and who ultimately makes the decision if a fight turns into a stand-off. He is keenly aware of the tension inherent in the process. 'On the one side, you are looking for simpler pieces. On the other side you are looking for a nice design. The designer is coming up with a complicated shape, but the car looks good. Then you're in a battle. What should we do? Should we support the manufacturing area, to make it easy? Or take over the more complicated but nicer looking design concept? Sometimes there is a compromise. The key thing is we work very closely together.'

Whoever you talk to, on whichever side of the grassy square or however lofty the floor, the discussion again and again comes back to the operative word behind the integrated process: compromise. Any car, every car, is a package of compromises.

No one at the TDC is willing to claim the title 'Father of J'89'

for himself, nor assign it to anybody else. But the popular idea of the
lone designer who conceives of the new model whole – in a flash of
inspiration – and then drives it singlemindedly through to completion
is a misconception, particularly for the volume manufacturers. Uwe
Bahnsen says it very clearly, 'Car design is not a profession for
soloists.'

The process of development is reasonably well controlled as corporate processes go, and proceeds through a series of well-defined
steps. At the same time, it is such a sprawling activity and such
an overlapping way of life that those involved have a hard time
remembering exactly when this or that project began, when this or
that event took place.

But it was definitely in the middle of 1982 that everyone instinc-
tively knew it was time to start work on the new J car. The Advanced
Development Group had been collecting data about the marketplace
and competitors and about the acceptance of J'81 since its launch.
Everyone who would be involved in the new model had read the
press reports about J'81 and had, of course, driven the car themselves. It wasn't hard to define what was right with it and what was
wrong with it.

According to the Master Timing Schedule, which measures all
events in terms of weeks before the pilot programme begins, it was
233 weeks (four and a half years) prior to pilot that a group of about
six people, including representatives from marketing, manufacturing,
design, engineering and packaging, began to hold regular meetings.

The purpose of the meetings, which continued over a period of
three to four months, was to establish a set of the most basic objectives
for J'89, define the preliminary package programme based on those
objectives and work up some preliminary cost estimates. Coming
up with the objectives 'was almost an automatic process,' recalls
Peter Döring, a staff engineer at TDC responsible for European
J car co-ordination. If Fritz Lohr plays the role of tie-breaker and
ultimate authority, Döring was on the J front lines, helping to make
or delegate the thousands of decisions that constituted the day-to-day
process.

First, the basic package dimensions – the proportions and package
'architecture' – were agreed. The new J car would stay in the same

size class, in terms of both physical dimensions and weight. However, one of the major criticisms of J'81 was that it was cramped inside, and that, in particular, it was a tight fit getting into the rear passenger compartment. The Advanced Development Group followed a design recommendation to remedy this by lengthening the wheelbase of the car just a bit – the 'bit' ended up being 26 mm – so that the rear wheels could be moved back and the rear door enlarged.

J'89 would also have to fit into the GME range of cars, which over the past eight years had been totally restyled. To this end – and in keeping with the corporate objective – J'89 would stay in its current position, in terms of size. Although the wheelbase was to be slightly bigger, it would not be so much larger as to push J'89 into competition with its big brother, the V car, the Carlton/Omega. Nor would it move so far away from the T car, the Astra/Kadett, as to leave a hole in the range.

There was also the elusive matter of pedigree to consider. From the designer's point of view, pedigree came down to finding ways to provide J'89 with a fresh design with an identifiable GME heritage. The car should not, of course, look like a Ford or a Peugeot or a Volkswagen.

Keeping the Sierra example in mind, it was decided to offer J'89 in two styles – hatchback and notchback (or saloon) – from launch. The two variants had to resemble each other, yet retain an individual character of their own.

And, of course, the car had to be developed as both a right-hand-drive and left-hand-drive version. Engineering a left-hand-drive and then 'flipping' everything is not an acceptable way to create a right-hand-drive car. The driver controls and foot pedals, in particular, need to be placed differently for right-hand-drive countries. In fact, the 1981 Cavalier had been criticized for its poor pedal placement – with the accelerator too far away from the side wall.

In November 1982, the preliminary package – described in just a few pages and including first dimensions, costs and package descriptions – was complete. The next milestone was the Official Product Programme, to be ready in twelve to eighteen months. It would contain all the engineering parameters of the car, including programme timing, physical dimensions, features and costs.

Any major changes made to the car after the official release of the Product Programme would have to be approved by the Director of Engineering and would be likely to lead to fights and headaches, cost overruns and other problems.

It would be in everyone's best interests to do what the quality consultants preach: get it right first time.

4 · DESIGN

'When you're replacing a successful car you build on its strength, eliminate its weaknesses, incorporate the latest engineering and manufacturing technology and add the marketing request all within the agreed investment and cost consideration, then you add character, flair and excitement. Sounds easy, doesn't it?'

Wayne Cherry, Director of Design for GM Europe

In the motor industry, the term 'designer' is an imprecise one, and whom you apply it to can reveal your feelings about the true nature of the automobile. Some people consider a car's true designers to be its engineers – people with engineering degrees, who deal with numbers and technical specifications. Just to confuse the issue, these people are sometimes called design engineers.

Then again, the 'designer' may be used as a replacement for the old term 'stylist'. This is usually someone with a background in the fine arts or graphic design, with or without a formal degree, but who may also have an engineering background. These designers are the ones who deal in forms, shapes, colours, textures, cosmetics and human factors. Within General Motors, the official term for this second discipline is 'designer', and all designers have a formal degree.

In fact, the two disciplines overlap. Designers – the people who are primarily responsible for the visual and tactile aspects of the car – are strongly constrained by the mechanical and functional requirements of the car (no matter what the engineers say) and cannot ignore them. And the engineers are not insensitive to the cosmetics (no matter what the designers say) of the systems they develop. As technology has come to play a greater role in the development process, the disciplines have come to overlap even more.

But design remains an elusive quantity to many business people who would prefer to focus on issues that are supposedly more quantifiable, such as manufacturing, forecasts, financial results, investment. It is virtually impossible to make a direct correlation between the particular curve of a rear quarter panel and the car's monthly sales results.

As with advertising – another profession that cannot ultimately quantify its results – many corporate executives consider design to be slightly mysterious, lightweight, not really a profession at all. Such executives wonder: how can drawing shapes and choosing colours be anything more than fun? It certainly can't be as serious a pursuit as, say, engineering a camshaft or crunching the numbers.

And yet, throughout the motor industry, everybody knows that the surfaces of the car – including exterior and interior design – are what attract customers and sell cars. It is also well known that designing a car intelligently for manufacture can have a tremendous and positive impact on the success of the model. The easier the car fits together, the happier and more productive the assembly operation will be. The cost of rectification and reworking will be lower.

Expensive as the design process may be, it is nothing in comparison to the phases of development that follow. It costs very little to change a pencil sketch or clay model, but a great deal to make an engineering change after the Product Programme freeze. It costs a fortune to make a change after tooling has been completed.

So the designer occupies an extremely important, even privileged, but often difficult, position within most large companies. Some great companies are known for being design-led, with senior managers who believe profoundly in the importance of good product design – IBM, Philips, Sony, Braun, Bang and Olufsen, Apple are examples – and their attitude shows not only in their products but also in the image and identity of the corporation as a whole. Alfred Sloan recognized the importance of appearance to sales early on. In 1927, he wrote: 'I think that the future of General Motors will be measured by the attractiveness that we put in the bodies . . . the degree to which they please the eye, both in contour and in colour scheme, also the degree to which we are able to make them different from the competition.'

But the fact that GM developed a reputation in the US for being the styling leader does not mean it is a design-led company. Sloan made that very clear as well: 'The primary objective of the corporation [is] to make money, not just to make motor cars. General Motors is an engineering organization. Our operation is to cut metal and in so doing to add value to it.' These are words to make a designer wince inwardly.

The roots of GM as an organization – Durant, entrepreneurship, the conglomerate approach – and the roots of GM design are, of course, intertwined. It was through another of Billy Durant's acquisitions that Lawrence P. Fisher came to General Motors, and became, along with Sloan, a prime advocate of styling.

Fisher was one of several brothers who owned and managed the Fisher Body Company, also based in Detroit. Sloan refers to them as 'skilled artisans with a background in the carriage industry'. Fisher Body had turned from carriage making to producing car bodies, and GM acquired a 60% share in the company in 1921, bringing the brothers into management positions. They purchased the remaining shares of the company in 1926.

In 1927, Lawrence Fisher, who was then General Manager of GM's Cadillac Division, went on a nationwide tour of dealers and distributors and stopped in at the Don Lee Corporation in Los Angeles, California. This was a sales operation with an interesting sideline – a custom body shop which fitted special bodies to existing chassis for clients who were, in Sloan's words, 'Hollywood movie stars and wealthy people of California'. Don Lee's chief designer and body-shop director was a young man named Harley J. Earl.

Fisher was intrigued by Earl for many reasons. For one thing, he was using modelling clay to help him develop the flamboyant styles of his custom bodies, rather than the unwieldy wood and metal that GM and the other big companies were using at the time. The malleability of clay allowed him to work with complex curves and to develop fine detailing, to create cars that had integrity of form, were sculptural and not just sheet metal enclosures for seats and engines.

Earl was creating unified, integrated bodies – from the bumpers to the running boards and the tail-lights – 'blending them together into a good-looking whole', according to Sloan. He was well-educated (Stanford University) but also had experience in a profession dear to Fisher's heart: he was the son of a successful carriage maker. Fisher enticed Earl to come to Detroit and, within a year, a whole new department called the Art and Colour Section had been formed around him.

Until the mid-twenties, engineering had been the dominant activity in the auto industry. With the establishment of the Art and Colour Section at GM, the tension between art and commerce, styling and engineering, instantly surfaced. 'The automobile stylist,' wrote Sloan, 'is an advocate of change to a degree that was at first somewhat startling to production and engineering executives.'

Earl was fortunate in that the first model with which the Art and Colour Section was involved, the 1927 La Salle, was a great sales success – particularly because the first model they had *complete* design control over, the 1929 Buick, was a flop. This was partly because of that systemic affliction: lack of integration between design and engineering.

Earl had designed the new car with a slight body curvature both above and below the so-called 'belt-line', the horizontal crease that usually continues the line of the bonnet into the passenger compartment body surface. But, Earl said, 'Unfortunately the factory, for operational reasons, pulled the side panels in at the bottom more than the design called for. In addition, five inches were added in vertical height, with the result that the arc I had plotted was pulled out of shape in two directions, the highlight line was unpleasantly located, and the effect was bulgy.' The public was not pleased either, and dubbed the car 'the pregnant Buick'.

Over some thirty-three years, during which GM produced fifty-five million automobiles, Earl helped make General Motors the US styling leader. Earl, says Sloan, always worked to one clear purpose: 'To lengthen and lower the American automobile, at times in reality and always at least in appearance. Why? Because my sense of proportion tells me that oblongs are more attractive than squares.' One can still see this influence in the current GM models in the US. The fussy grilles, long sweeping lines and low profiles retain some of the influence of Earl's movie-star days, and embody an idiosyncratic, American idea of grand style.

General Motors may have set a precedent for the industry by installing Earl as head of styling, because many of the men who influenced car design came from non-engineering pursuits, disciplines devoted to surface appearance and immediate visual effect.

Raymond Loewy, who designed early models for Hupmobile and later for Studebaker, became one of America's most visible industrial designers. He was trained as an engineer in France in the early 1900s, but emigrated to New York in 1919 where he had a one-day career as a window dresser, before working as a free-lance fashion illustrator.

Norman Bel Geddes, who was involved in the design of the famous but commercially unsuccessful Chrysler Airflow of 1934, began in advertising and went on to a successful career in theatrical set design and also – like Loewy and Uwe Bahnsen – shop window display. But these two, and others, were independent designers who were called in by the manufacturers for specific projects. None had as great an influence over such a long period as Harley Earl, who is best remembered for his role in pioneering the annual model change and for the invention of the most outrageous example of flamboyant American styling, the tail fin.

This American approach to automobile design comes close to being anathema to the European designer. With roots in architecture and handicrafts, European designers tended to think in terms of the design maxim: form follows function. A seminal influence on European industrial design was the German Bauhaus, the art school which operated from 1919 to 1933 and which sought to bring the fine arts and crafts together in architecture, the design of furniture and other practical products.

As General Motors established their operations in Europe, first with Vauxhall and then with Opel, Sloan writes that the corporation was aware that 'basic differences in utility cause the difference in appearance between the European and American car designs'. And within General Motors Europe, even today, there is a sense of tension among the different design traditions.

But internationality is typical of the multi-national corporation and probably contributes as much energy to the process of design as it does discord. The real issue is how the role of the designer is defined and valued within the company. At GM, the designers are supposed to be the ideas people. They are the ones who ask the 'What if . . .?' and 'Why not . . .?' and 'Wouldn't it be terrific if . . .?' questions. Or, in the words of one former GM designer, 'We throw our hat in the door, and see if it gets shot off.' That may not make much literal sense, but the idea is clear: the designer, in terms of the product itself, is supposed to be the bell-wether, the futurist, the adventurer and, sometimes, the fall guy.

Although more and more designers are highly trained in industrial and transport design, with bachelor and master degrees in science or fine arts, they are still considered to lack the technical basis of the engineer. Not everything the designer does can be measured, quantified or even explained once it has been accomplished. The designer relies on pictures and models and talks of forms and colours and emotions, while the engineer speaks in equations and co-efficients and can 'prove' things. The fact that most engineers will concede that their numbers are not as precise as one might believe – that test conditions are highly variable and interpretations vary – doesn't lessen the power and effect of those numbers, particularly in a numbers company like GM. It is no wonder that engineers often describe designers – not without affection – as the 'nuts', the 'crazy' ones.

If the size of your facility reflects the importance of your position within a company, the designers lose out to the engineers at General Motors Europe. The Technical Centre where 4,000 engineers' labour dominates the troika of buildings that form the Technical Development Centre. However, what the designers lack in size, they compensate for in terms of style and atmosphere.

There is always an array of gleaming Opel cars parked along a small macadam strip in front of the Design Centre: a big, black, powerful-looking Omega 3000; a calm, silvery-fawn, top-of-the-range Senator; a couple of 1989 J cars – new Vectras. Rarely do you see a Ford or Volkswagen or Mercedes parked there, and if you do, it is probably for evaluation by the design staff. Concrete steps take the visitor up over a bright blue-bottomed pool complete with fountains, then through glass doors and into the peaceful reception area.

On the lintel above the double doors leading from reception to the interior of the building are inscribed the words, 'Quality Begins With Design' like a maxim on some public monument. Pass under the lintel and you are in the inner sanctum. People scurry quietly about. At the end of the corridor, a cloth is being pulled over something that must be a scale model of a new car. There are several full scale models parked along the corridors, each one covered with a cloth. Outsiders must not glimpse the new designs, and this is no joking matter.

There are six studios in the Design Centre. Four are car line studios, for the V car (Omega/Carlton), the S car (Corsa/Nova), the J car (Cavalier/Vectra) and the T car (Kadett/Astra), each with its own chief designer and staff; two are combined interior, colour and trim studios. J'89 was the first GME model to be developed with one chief designer overseeing both interior and exterior design – an innovation that would lend consistency to the final product. The studios have an atmosphere similar to any artist's studio. They are quiet, light, airy, spacious, yet cluttered and littered with drawings. Each one is equipped with a computer screen. The business here is to think, to sketch, to render, to imagine, to work out the details.

The studios are supported by a number of workshops, including fibreglass modelling areas and a computer-aided design facility. There is also a show-room where clay models, fabrics and partial interior mock-ups, called seating bucks, are displayed. During the year of developing the Official Product Programme, it is in this showroom that the J'89 committee would often meet to work on interior and exterior concepts.

The atmosphere in the corridors and studios is mostly what you would expect in any design shop, but tempered by the fact that this is a large corporate design centre, and the corporation is General Motors. It is an international place. Working in the J car studio, Studio 3, the head designer Erhard Schnell is a German, and six other designers represent the United States, Japan, China, Indonesia and Germany. You can tell that style and appearance are important – in the colours and furniture, in the clothes people wear, in the way they move – which you will not find to be true in the world of the engineers.

Yet there is a boxiness about the interior, a feeling that many features are slightly out of date, which reminds the visitor that a design studio within GME cannot – and probably must not – move with the times as quickly as a small design shop in, let us say, London. You have the feeling that the designers here may be tempering their wilder instincts with the acceptance and knowledge of the realities of the business they are in. It is just not possible to go mad with the exterior design for a high-volume, high-ticket, long-cycle product like a car. These are not clothing, or packaging, or media, or graphics, or appliance designers, although, in many ways, they are all of those things.

Leading off an interior corridor, beyond a reception area presided over by a secretary, is Wayne Cherry's office. There is something about the atmosphere here reminiscent of a 1960s James Bond film-set vision of the future. It may be the obviously 'designed' look, with exterior windows along one side, all of which are covered with black, thin-slatted blinds kept three-quarters closed. The wall meets the floor, not in a right angle, but in a soft, sculptured curve.

On the broad, low desk the Car of the Year trophy, received in 1987 for Cherry's first GME assignment, the Carlton, is proudly displayed in a pool of lamplight, although bright sunlight can be seen behind the blinds. Two rows of chairs (by the designer Harry Bertoia) face each other across a large perforated metal coffee table. In a corner is the ubiquitous flip chart, filled with hurried black marker lines.

Wayne Cherry is the Director of Design and, as such, presides over design for all the car lines for General Motors Europe. He is tall, dark, quiet, well dressed and well groomed without being flamboyant. His American accent seems unaffected by almost twenty-five years of living in Europe. In appearance, he strikes a balance between the artistic and the commercial: no exaggerated suits, shirts with unconventional closures, hand-painted ties or motorcycle boots, but you would never mistake him for the typical corporate financial officer either. Cherry is to be found in double-breasted jackets, well-cut grey or blue suits, the occasional yellow cashmere V-neck on a cool day.

Because he is American and has almost seven years under his belt as chief designer for General Motors Europe, you might reasonably assume Cherry will be moving on to some new assignment soon. The studio heads have become quite used to the regular changing of the guard at the top.

As Director of Design for GME, the fastest-growing division of the largest car manufacturing car company on earth, based in the largest car market on earth, Cherry is an influential person – in a class with perhaps a dozen other car designers around the world. He is not, however, one of those designers (like Bahnsen, perhaps) who might have become a designer of something other than cars. He always wanted to design cars, and only cars.

Born in Indiana in 1937, he is now in his early fifties, but he could just as well be forty, judging by his dark, well-groomed looks. Or, judging by his enthusiasms, fifteen. He was brought up in Indianapolis and, like so many other members of the huge GM community, his father worked at the Allison division of General Motors in Indiana. From an early age, he was 'crazy about cars. Obsessed with them. Ever since I was a little kid. And I was always a GM guy. When I was a kid in the US even before you started driving – particularly before you started driving – you formed an allegiance with different brands. And you'd fight about it. One guy's a Ford guy. One guy's a Chevy guy.'

In the midst of the Great Depression, GM mounted a science and technology display, masterminded by industrial designer Norman Bel Geddes, at the 1933 World Fair held in Chicago. The exhibit was so successful that GM decided to enlarge and package it as a travelling exposition called the Parade of Progress. They created a caravan of eight custom vans, each with 'GENERAL MOTORS, Parade of Progress' in big letters on the side. They were extremely successful, too, and travelled across America, visiting hundreds of small towns between 1936 and 1956, with a pause during the war years.

GM complemented the travelling shows with a series of expositions known as Motoramas. The first was an extravaganza called 'Transportation Unlimited' which opened at the Waldorf Astoria Hotel in New York in January 1949. It featured new production models as well as lots of the experimental cars that were being produced by the Art and Colour Section, all presented with displays and stage settings and live performances featuring plenty of costumed girls and boys dancing and singing to the accompaniment of a live orchestra.

GM found these events were not only good publicity, they helped the designers get a feel for public reaction to new styling ideas before they went into production. The use of such experimental vehicles – today called concept cars – continues to be a key method of testing the waters of public opinion before actually diving in.

Although exactly when and where he saw one of these extravaganzas is a bit uncertain, Cherry remembers the effect of the Motorama vividly. 'You know those travelling shows of the future? As a kid . . .' He whistles softly. 'Perhaps because of those, perhaps because of other things as well, I was just a GM guy.' In this way, futurism becomes a self-fulfilling activity: the young boy glimpses a conception of the future and is drawn in to making it reality.

In 1958, Cherry left Indianapolis to attend the Art Center College of Design in Pasadena, just outside Los Angeles – one of the few colleges at the time with a curriculum in industrial and transport design. It was founded in 1930 by an advertising man, Edward 'Tink' Adams, who saw a growing need for professional designers but no school to train them.

When Cherry went to Detroit to join General Motors in 1962, GM was at the peak of its reputation as the American styling leader. It was the only place Cherry wanted to work because 'GM was always the place. It was the most difficult. When I graduated and was hired by General Motors, that was a dream come true.'

As a boy, Cherry had heard all about Harley Earl, and now he was working for Earl's famous protégé and successor, William Mitchell. To be working in the studios where Earl had virtually created car styling, and on the staff of the man who had worked with Earl for over thirty years (he'd retired in 1960) was exciting stuff. As a junior member of the design team, Cherry contributed to the first Oldsmobile Toronado, an early front-wheel-drive model, and, as part of the advance group, he helped develop futuristic concept cars to be shown at the 1965 World Fair.

After just three years in Detroit, he was offered the chance to work in England, at Vauxhall Motors. He decided to take the opportunity to visit the land of the Hillman Minx and Austin Mini for the first time – and stay in the UK for just a few months. But Vauxhall proved a good place to work, and he stayed on, gradually rising through the ranks until he was named Director of Design for Vauxhall/Bedford in 1975.

Cherry's work for Vauxhall is still remembered for the development of concept vehicles and for the 1973 Firenza, a powerful two-door coupé which he developed with Geoffrey Lawson, who went on to be head of styling at Jaguar. The greatest distinction of the Firenza was its front end – all glossy fibre-glass, enclosed headlamps, and no grille above the bumper. The Firenza was quickly dubbed the Droop Snoot, and today there is a fan club called the Droop Snoot Group which keeps track of some ninety existing Firenzas, a development that amazes and amuses its designer. Cherry and his colleague, John Taylor, also experimented with aerodynamics, creating a series of functioning cars as efficient as most on the road today.

By 1975, when the decision was taken to centralize all GM European engineering at the much bigger and better-equipped operations at Opel, it was clear that the days of passenger car design at Luton were numbered. Many of the design staff continued working within Bedford for another decade, however, as part of the World Truck and Bus Group.

In 1978, Cherry helped develop a concept for a Vauxhall sports car, called the Equus, which was never produced. Bill Mitchell, then GM Vice President in charge of design staff worldwide, promised (probably ingenuously) that Vauxhall would remain strong in design. On a trip to London in October 1975 Mitchell told the press, 'I have put the best people up there and they have got some good ones. Wayne Cherry is one of our top boys.' Cherry ascended to be the very top boy in Europe in 1983, when the Director of Design at Opel, Gordon Brown, was killed in an accident.

That is how a tall American came to be running the design department at the heart of one of Germany's oldest producers, and creating one of the most important cars to be sold in the United Kingdom. World cars, world companies, world people.

In Rüsselsheim, the pace is quicker, the volume of work much greater than in Luton. When Cherry arrived in 1983, the staff were working on the new V car – the Omega/Carlton – which was the first of the 'new look' GM Europe cars. It was an expensive project, costing about

2 billion DM, including new production factories and product development costs. It involved some new technologies and was designed to set a new standard for aerodynamic efficiency. Until it was bettered in 1990 by its stablemate, the new Opel Calibra, the Omega held the record as the most aerodynamically efficient production car in the world.

The development process was still in its early stages – far from Official Product Programme freeze that would be reached some two years later – so Cherry could have an influence over the development of J'89. And, with eighteen years of experience in the UK, he understood the role of the Cavalier in that market very well.

For the design staff, the challenge of a new car tends to be expressed differently from the Product Programme objectives. Cherry saw the primary challenge in designing J'89 very plainly: 'It was the problem of replacing a successful model.' J'81 had been the saviour of Vauxhall, and the J car had helped revitalize GM's fortunes in Europe in general. Despite the changed market conditions, and the generally much stronger GM product line, the new car, J'89, represented an excellent chance for failure. So 'you have to be very aware of what the strengths are of the car. You want to keep those strengths. And, to me, the strength of the Cavalier is that it's very much a driver's car.'

But what does this mean? Isn't every car a driver's car? 'From the design side, I believe it's the way the car relates to the driver. And the driver to the car. Part of that is size, part of it is proportion. One of the important things about the Cavalier is that the size is just right,' says Cherry. And here you begin to see how often the objectives for a new car model are contradictory or conflicting. If the major strength of J'81 was as a driver's car, and that quality comes from its size – well, one of the package objectives for J'89 was to increase its interior roominess, and one of the ways to achieve this was through increasing the length of its wheelbase slightly. How to make a car roomier and yet keep that feel of the 'right' size at the same time? 'A longer wheelbase does not have to make the car longer overall,' says Cherry. 'The objective was to get more interior room and achieve the right visual proportions.'

Although the J'89 programme began with the interior dimensions, the first and major design task was the exterior form of the car.

Developed in 1983, it would have to stay reasonably fresh until the mid-1990s. The challenge, therefore, was to create a form that looked modern and new without being so radical as to alienate the generally conservative public that buys the mass-production, intermediate size car.

'It is important when you're designing cars that you're going to sell hundreds of thousands of to have a design that a wide number of people appreciate,' says Cherry. 'My personal feeling is that you want to avoid a controversial car, without losing the style, the flair or the character of the car. Without losing that, you want to extend it to the widest number of people possible. That's part of our responsibility.'

J'89 also had to be designed to fit within the entire GM Europe model range. In terms of size, that meant it had to stay in the slot between the smaller T car and the larger V car, so that it wouldn't be a competitor for either one. In terms of appearance, it meant incorporating the most identifiable GME characteristics – sharp nose, wedge shape, U-shaped grille and particularly the aero look of the new V cars and Senator. And, most complex, it meant communicating its own brand character through the shape and style of the car.

'The shape of the car communicates values. In your smaller cars you want something that has more personality, looks friendly. You know, people smile when they look at it, and say, I'd like to drive that little car. When you get to the top of the range, you want people to look at it and say, that's a serious car. And that's part of our responsibility, too, to communicate those values to the customer.'

The J'89 range would include two models, a notch and a hatch. In some new car programmes, one will be developed first – usually the notch – and the hatch will be developed from it. With J'89, the goal was to create the two simultaneously and develop a similar, but individual, look for each.

Part of looking modern, and communicating the proper values, is to incorporate the best of current trends, so the designers are voracious trend watchers. In the early 1980s they saw rounder shapes, less chrome, more body-coloured details, flush exterior hardware (windscreen wipers and door handles), more steeply angled

windscreens, tinted glass and, in general, the continuation of aerodynamic styling.

It was Raymond Loewy who coined the MAYA maxim for industrial
design – that to be successful, a new product needed to be the Most
Advanced, Yet Acceptable – and it is a maxim volume car designers
tend to follow whether they articulate it in those terms or not.

From the very beginning of the process, the experienced designer
remains acutely aware of the limitations and responsibilities of his
role as a 'visionary'. He knows that he is not an illustrator or graphic
designer, that, ultimately, his product is not a drawing or a model –
it is a car that must be forged and shaped and welded out of metal
and plastic and glass.

So one result of the integrated development process is a greater
emphasis on design for manufacture or 'forgiving' design – design
that takes into account the difficulties that engineering and manufacturing face. Rather than ignore them and invite disappointment,
design-for-manufacture finds ways to overcome the difficulties.

One other objective seems distinctly American: 'Design creates
love at first sight,' says Wayne Cherry. Whether or not that is possible
in today's crowded marketplace, and with cars meant to be as middle
of the road as the intermediates, is arguable, but it is certainly an
objective that reflects the influence of marketing in the integrated
development process.

With these key design objectives in mind for J'89, 'You say, okay,
that's pretty straightforward, every car company in the world wants
to do that. But what happens in the design and development of a new
vehicle is that every day you're making decisions. You know, maybe
one day there's a few, and the next day there are a hundred little
decisions. Each one of those decisions is ultimately biased in one of
those directions. You can have cost, you can have styling, you can have
engineering, you can have manufacturing, each decision is biased one
way. And at the end of it, you have a package of compromises. Every
car in the world, whether it's a Yugo or a Ferrari – there's no such
thing as an uncompromised car.'

Cherry smiles. 'The idea is that your package of compromises
appeals to a greater number of people than your competitors'.'

*

The process begins with scribbles, which evolve into sketches, which become full-colour, full-scale renderings. The car designer thinks with a pencil or a marker in his hand. He may start a conversation about some new idea or possible shape, try to explain it with expressive hands and language, but the moment always comes when he is brought up short by a question or comment – and he must lunge for any scrap of paper he can lay his hands on. Designers, in general, tend to be aficionados of writing instruments, carrying the most striking examples of marker, lead-holder, pencil, roller-ball or fountain pen technology.

They also tend to think of paper in unconventional ways, using gridded pads, translucent sheets, rolls of tracing paper – and making their marks on them in the landscape format if the paper is ordinarily configured for portrait, and vice-versa, or at a steep angle, or in circles, or from top to bottom. They love to grab cocktail napkins, old notebooks, discarded memos, bits of board, polystyrene trays, the proverbial envelope – the more asymmetric and unusual the better – and cover them with quick, sure, dashing strokes. Newspaper and magazine accounts will report – often with a slightly sarcastic or ironic tone – that some momentous project was begun 'as just a sketch on the back of an envelope'. Well, where does any project begin? How else *could* any project begin?

The first J'89 sketch is dated 5 November 1982. At that time, just about everybody made sketches and scribbles of what they thought the new car should look like. George Gallion, the chief of exterior styling. Gordon Brown, the former Director of Design, before he died. Wayne Cherry, when he arrived. And Erhard Schnell, chief designer.

As head of Studio 3, the J car studio, Schnell was closer to the total process than anyone else. They were looking toward an exterior that was rounded in shape. J'81 had been a sharp-lined, squarish-looking car. 'The direction was soft, round shapes. We felt after so many years of strong shapes – edgy and boxy shapes – the time was coming for more soft shapes.' Gradually, a series of ideas evolves, and one begins to see what the new car will probably look like: the operative word is smooth. But these early sketches are meant for designers only, not for engineers. 'We don't show them sketches,' says Schnell. 'They wouldn't understand.'

What is it the engineers wouldn't understand? They would certainly understand the idea of soft, round shapes and a smooth slippery body. What they probably would not understand is why designers persist in creating sketches with the same old impossibilities – yes, the same old lies – in them.

For instance, the wheel openings. One thing designers hate is the ugly, yawning space between the opening in the fender and the tyre itself. It is a negative space that breaks the fluid line of the car. What's more, you can look right into it and see crude interior surfaces, usually dirt encrusted. 'What we are after all the time is a wheel arch that is not too big, that is filled with wheel. A wheel-oriented shape.'

And so, in most early sketches, designers succumb to their desires – although they know perfectly well that it cannot be in the final result – by drawing wheel openings that fit the tyres snugly. This is such a passion at the Design Centre that the wheel/body relationship even has its own acronym, coined by Cherry: WOD, for Wheel-Oriented Design. Wheel openings tautly filled with tyre contribute to shapes that appear more powerful, more consistent – a solid 'stance'.

Peter Döring understands this very well. 'Every project has this discussion. The stylist wants to have it closed. But the wheels have to move! They [designers] don't want to look into the opening. There's a saying, "You could throw a hat in there!"' It's not that the designers don't realize that wheels in such tight openings would never work, and that the unfortunate car would be unable to turn left or right. What the engineers might not be willing to admit is that the designers are there to provide a vision, because visions excite people, and visions are often exaggerations.

Early sketches show greenhouses – the glass that wraps around the passenger compartment – with no structural support. Bonnets slope at angles that would not accommodate an engine. Windscreens slope at angles that would not accommodate a passenger. There are doors without handles, fenders without side lights, bodies with no grilles at all. Peter Döring laughs. 'Styling always wants to eliminate the openings. Just eliminate the openings!'

Then there is the question of movement. A car is a kinetic sculpture, not a static one. The GME designers work to make the car look as if it is moving, even when it's not. In a sketch, and in the real thing, suggested motion is certainly a matter of the shape itself. Raymond Loewy says that there are three possible 'movements' that can be suggested by the form of a car. One is the wedge shape we've become accustomed to, that appears to sit back on its hind wheels and attack the road with its nose down. The second shape suggests the full-bonnet style of the 1950s and 1960s, with its nose in the air, a style that to Loewy seemed to have a 'conflict between forward and rear motion'.

The third possible shape is one with no suggested motion forward or backward, a shape of immobility, but stability – the shoebox. 'This is the approach used for the highly popular Mercedes Benz,' wrote Loewy in 1979. 'Its highly conservative look, almost an anachronism, apparently appeals to many.'

J'89 followed the first configuration. The wedgy bonnet, swept back windscreen, sloping rear window, rising tail all suggest the shape of a creature in flight, head down and legs bunched up behind. But a subtler suggestion of motion – and one that you don't get with feathers or fur – comes from the reflection of light off the surface. Horizontal reflection lines that are smooth and unbroken, with a steady rise to the rear, provide an unmistakable, although unconscious, signal that the car will move.

Once the basic direction has been agreed among the designers, the next step is to create full-scale drawings. This process involves fitting the car to the theoretical driver.

On 14 March 1988, Peter Negus, Product Planning Manager for Vauxhall Motors in Luton, received a letter from Mrs M. Garner of Broadstone, Dorset. She wrote, in part: 'I am the reasonably proud owner of a Nova 1.2L purchased in February 1986. I state "reasonably" because although the car is completely reliable, beautiful to drive and a joy to behold, it's a real pain to get in and out of the driving position because I am only just over 5 ft tall. Unless I buy an automatic next time I shall have to consider having my left leg stretched four inches to enable me to operate the clutch without having the steering wheel in my lap and my right knee knocking on the bunch of keys. The Nova is an almost perfect little car, but there is no way I can get out of mine without immodestly showing my knickers!'

Mrs Garner is unlikely to receive much satisfaction in her search for a comfortable driving position because she is up against the tyranny of the 95% Oscar. The 95% Oscar is a model of the human being – available in either two or three dimensions – that is supposed to represent everybody except the 5% of the population that comprises the tallest (usually men) and shortest (usually women). Oscar's exact dimensions change as the dimensions of the population change.

During the early stages of design, several full-scale drawings are made of the most promising new shapes and a two-dimensional Oscar is used to establish the driving position and the relationship of the driver to the interior of the car. The side-view Oscar is a flat template of transparent plastic, usually in yellow or orange, and hinged in all the places people are naturally hinged. Most of the interior package dimensions relate to a single point on Oscar, called the H-point – the theoretical pivot point of the theoretically average person, somewhere around the hip. On the 2-D Oscar this is a brass-coloured ring, and using that point the designers determine chair height, ankle angle, leg angle, knee clearance, headroom – the critical dimensions that define the relationship of the driver to the landscape of the car that surrounds him or her.

Because a major objective for J'89 was to improve interior roomi-ness, developing the interior dimensions was particularly critical. The major problem with J'81 was with the 'rear entry' dimensions. The rear passenger door did not swing open wide enough, and, once you squeezed in, there was less knee room and head room in the rear compartment than most people wanted, and found in some other makes. It felt cramped.

At the same time, a major plus point of J'81 was its capacious boot, which was deeper than the Sierra boot, and with the spare tyre mounted at the side it seemed to swallow up just about anything a normal person would carry. So the designers had to enlarge the interior space without stealing capacity from the big boot.

The 26 mm that had been added to the wheelbase was not suf-ficient to provide the total amount of additional interior room. The challenge, therefore, was to squeeze more room out of the passenger compartment and to make it appear bigger than it actually was.

This was accomplished by moving the position of Oscar's H-point. The front passenger H-point was moved forward and upward. The steering-wheel position was moved forward slightly, along with the dashboard and the foot pedals. The H-point of the rear passenger was moved back and up as well. This led to gains in rear leg room, knee clearance (distance of knees from back of front seat) and couple distance – i.e. how far apart the two rear passengers are from each other at shoulder height. But the key dimension for rear entry was the increased width of the rear door, allowed by the increased length of the wheelbase. With these dimensions incorporated, the full-scale drawings could now serve as guides for the clay modellers.

At the Design Centre, clay models are created in one-third-scale size. Since the car is a three-dimensional sculpture, in order to evaluate it properly, you have to be able to see it from every angle – from the front, the side, the rear, from above and below. Sketches and renderings can only offer a few views, and the renderer will always choose to draw the car at the most appealing angles. The clay model reveals the awkward areas, as well as the most successful ones. The designer studies the car under different lighting conditions, takes it outside to look at it under the sun and – working with the sculptor – can make dozens of changes to a model in a single day.

It is extraordinary how different the form of a car can look, depending on the angle of view, quality of light and the colour of the surface and surroundings. Often, the clays are made with two different halves, with slight variations in the roof line or front end graphics. This is where the form and visual personality of the car are really born – in the sculptor's studio.

Personality and character are concentrated in a few key areas, with large expanses that look pretty much like every other car. The front end of a car is a key part of its signature: a face with two headlamp eyes, grille nose and grinning bumper mouth. The front end is what you see the most often, as cars come toward you on the street – the most complicated and detailed portion of the car.

Think of the great marques, and you think of the front end: Mercedes and its famous grille and three pointed star; the double

kidney grille of the BMW; the softened oval grille and hooded headlamps of the Jaguar; the massive triangle-top, vault-like Rolls-Royce
grille and flying lady hood ornament.

The makers of these marques may modify the look of the front
end over the years, but they are careful to retain a recognizable
character, no matter how vestigial. The kidney grille of the BMW
850 introduced at the Frankfurt Motor Show in 1989, for example,
has been reduced so much that it has almost become a symbol of a
symbol, rather than the symbol itself.

There has been a continuing discussion at GME about front ends:
should there be a standard front end that becomes the GME look?
For J'89, the front end retains the basic shape of J'81, particularly
in the modified U-shape of the grille opening. But there are some
innovations. The headlamps are slim profile, much narrower than
the current standard, which makes the front end seem sleeker and
smoother than its predecessor whose headlamps really are ugly, great
staring bug eyes, out of proportion with the size of the car's face.

As a demonstration of the kind of detail that can lead to controversy
in the design phase, the designers specified a slim strip of sheet metal
that would separate the headlamps from the bumper. Why did they
consider this so important? Because, if you think of the car as a form,
that form is primarily defined by the painted sheet metal, and the
so-called daylight openings, or DLO's. Many of the other exterior
elements interrupt the basic form.

If you interrupt the form often enough, it ceases to be a form at
all and begins to look like an oddly-shaped cover. That little strip
of metal reassures the eye that the form is continuous, although
accented above by the headlamps and below by the bumper. It's
the difference between a well-fitting suit of clothes and a clumsy
ensemble of shorts and jumper, the difference between an egg and
a discarded eggshell.

The front end was further distinguished by the addition of a new
badge – a glazed griffin in a circle flush-mounted on the nose. It is
an improvement over the old griffin applied to the grille of J'81, but
it is similar to the BMW badge in size and style and placement and
seems to imitate it.

One of the most important reasons for producing clay models

is for presentation to management. There is no substitute for a tangible, three-dimensional representation of the new car to help top executives – who are very often from the sales, marketing, finance or engineering side – get the idea. They need a model they can touch, walk around, show colleagues. They need a model to make this act of the imagination seem real.

The clay studio represents a link to the early days of car design, when car manufacture was a craft – when it had to do with coach-work and hand finishing. In a world of technology and booming assembly lines, the quiet studio and its products seem comforting and reassuring.

Now, based upon these third-scale clays from design, one-fifth-scale models are developed by engineers in the Technical Centre for aerodynamic testing.

On the first floor of the Technical Centre is a locked door, marked with a single bold word AERODYNAMIK. Behind it lies the tiny kingdom of the clay modellers. The keys to the kingdom belong to Joseph Schulze, a voluble, energetic man who talks tirelessly about aero values, past Opel events and about clay and design in general.

Four blocky stands fill the modellers' room and on each rests a one-fifth-scale model at varying stages of completion. Each is about a metre long, and the finished ones look like the most wonderful toy cars you could imagine – perfect in every detail, complete with mirrors, wheels, handles. The clay is a dirty reddish-brown colour, the same as fine artists use, and the odd instruments of the clay sculptor are evident here and there – little goose-necked tools with wooden handles, smoothing tools of wire stretched across what appears to be the doctor's end of a stethoscope, pokers and edgers.

The far end of the room is filled with a glass-doored case, and inside it several more models are displayed, some of which have been finished with a plastic skin material so they can be painted with full colour. They look as if they are patiently waiting for some enthusiastic young boy to take them home.

It is like Santa's workshop after the elves have gone home, and Santa (Schulze) is our host. As he proudly, carefully takes model after model from the display case, each one more precious than the next – and with a longer story attached – you almost expect the models to awaken slowly, blink their headlights and dance groggily around the studio.

For J'89, eight fifth-scale models were made for aero development, the first one completed within three weeks of the initial sketch. It is possible to create a fifth-scale clay in as little as a week and a half, if pressed.

The fifth-scale models can easily be transported to the wind tunnel for testing. If a fifth-scale model is well made, the results in the tunnel will be almost identical to those of the full-scale model and, finally, the production car. The principal measure of aerodynamic efficiency (as we shall see in the next chapter) is the co-efficient of drag, or Cd. The J'89 package objectives called for a Cd of .30, down from about .34 for J'81. Wind tunnel tests of the fifth-scale clays showed that the smooth body might even exceed the target.

After a glimpse of the Aerodynamik clay modelling studio, Schulze has a surprise for us. He crooks a finger in a conspiratorial sort of way and leads us, not quite surreptitiously but not quite boldly either, out of the model shop door – a quick glance in either direction– along another corridor and then he halts outside a door that does not appear to lead to an office at all. He unlocks it as quickly as possible and lets us in. It is dark inside, some sort of mechanical system rumbling away. He finds the light switch. We are in a furnace or mechanical room. It is very warm, and nestled on makeshift pallets around the furnace are six or seven shrouded shapes – more fifth-scale clays.

Schulze is speaking quickly now, with great excitement. These clays are for future models, he says, and they have been delivered to this room to dry. Suddenly, with a look of daring combined with love, expectation laced with mischief, he whips the covering off one of the models.

It is a clay in natural colour, difficult to see clearly in the poor light. Schulze explains that he is giving us a special treat: this is the 1990 coupé – what became the Calibra – an all new sports model based on the J'89 chassis. We stare appreciatively at the model for no more than five or six seconds, and then he re-drapes the model with the cloth.

The model will soon feel the rush of wind over its clay body.

5 · AERO

'The Audi 100 had the nickname: the fastest sauna on
the road.'

Hans-Joachim Emmelmann, Opel staff engineer

The strange thing about a wind tunnel in operation is that nothing
appears to be happening. A car is parked on a square section of very
flat floor positioned at the intersection of painted cross-hairs. There
is no one inside the cockpit, no driver, no passengers. The car appears
to be on a short length of road between two tunnel openings. A sharp-
cornered rectangular opening ahead is no more than $2^1/2-3$ metres
away, with a softer-edged opening an equal distance behind.

Peer into the throat of either opening and you see a quick fade
into darkness, a closing down into a sleek, metal epiglottis: from one
the wind is disgorged, into the other it is gulped. You can make out
a thin incision that describes a circle in the floor around the car,
and is, in fact, the circumference of a turntable. There is nothing
much else in the room – some large lamps overhead, windows into a
dimly seen control room beyond, a heavy hinged door large enough
to accommodate the passage of a car.

Here, at the University of Stuttgart wind tunnel, a bright red
Cavalier is being prepared for test by four technicians in red overalls.
They apply sticky tape to the gaps around the headlamps – tape, it
seems, is one of the most important tools of aerodynamicists in the
wind tunnel. They check tyre pressure. They tape ventilator inlets
and outlets shut so that only body drag will be measured. The fuel
tank is filled. The height of the wheel arches is measured against
design specification. Standard 70 kg weights are placed in both front

seats to simulate passengers. The handbrake is applied. A final bounce
to free the springs, and everyone retires to the control room. The
test begins.

From inside the control room, bristling with computers and other
electronic equipment, you can safely watch the car, patiently waiting
for the 220 kph torrent of wind. But when it comes, nothing seems to
happen. There are no streams of smoke to make the air layers visible,
the car does not buck or sway, the sound of the wind is muted by
the soundproofing door. The only visible evidence that something
has changed is on the computer screens, where data and graphics
are displayed.

But, step from the calm and quiet of the control room into the test
section itself and you might as well be opening the door of a mountain
cabin and stepping into a force 17 hurricane. The test chamber is
wider than the tunnel itself, so it's possible to be in the chamber but
out of the flow of air. When the huge, unseen fan (which is over seven
metres in diameter) is activated there is an almost instant acceleration
of wind, accompanied by a tremendous whining roar. It is the same
sound you hear at the top of a mountain in a high wind, the sound of
a hurricane screaming through a ship's rigging. If you gingerly stick
your hand out from the safety of the sidelines into the airstream, it is
instantly torn backwards. Just as great height beckons you to jump,
the wind urges you to throw yourself into it. You wonder: how would
it feel to be carried away into that huge, sucking hole?

As laboratories go, automotive wind tunnels are magical. They're
large, expensive to build, extremely complex, wonderfully specialized,
and there are only nineteen of them in the world. General Motors,
true to form, operates the largest one, in Warren, Michigan. Although
the tunnel at the University of Stuttgart where J'89 was tested was
only completed in 1986, the Institute has been in existence since
1930, making it one of the oldest wind tunnel/vehicle development
centres in the world.

The intrigue of the wind tunnel is not only due to its complexity and
rarity – there is something mystical about it as well. At the centre of
all this technical resource is an ineluctable, poetic quantity: wind.

The wind tunnel is the temple of what has become, in the past
decade, a kind of technological cult: aerodynamics. In addition to

road vehicles and aircraft, designers have applied the principles of streamlining to almost everything that moves – bicycles, skis, helmets – and some things that don't, such as buildings.

Aero design became so prevalent in the 1980s that Fulvio Cinti, editor of *Auto and Design* magazine, railed, 'This has been an important yet controversial decade for the car, whose chapter in history could only have been titled "the tyranny of aerodynamics".' He ascribes 'the general flattening of the appearance of the modern car' to this tyranny which was 'imposed by the energy crisis'. And, further, he blames car makers' marketing departments, which 'for mere promotional ends, in a certain period of the decade forced designers to take part in a kind of "Cd" Olympic Games.'

The 'Cd', for co-efficient of drag, has become a key number in marketing jargon. It has a pleasing ring of high technology about it and at the same time, offers a quick index for comparing competitive models – the lower the Cd number, the more aerodynamically efficient the car.

The phenomenon is reminiscent of a scene in the film *This is Spinal Tap*, in which one of the musicians in the rock band called Spinal Tap (the loudest band in England) is showing off his Marshall amplifier to an interviewer.

'This is a very special one because as you can see the numbers all go to eleven,' he says proudly. 'Does that mean it's louder?' asks the interviewer. 'Well, it's one louder, isn't it?' responds the musician. 'What we do is if we need that extra push over the cliff, you know what we do?' 'Put it up to eleven,' guesses the interviewer. 'Exactly – one louder,' says the musician. 'Why not make ten louder and make ten be the top number?' persists the interviewer. The musician cannot believe the man is so unable to see the benefits. 'These go to *eleven*,' he repeats, as if no further explanation could really be required.

The automotive Cd number is about as well understood by car buyers. The lower the number the better, but exactly what it means and why it's better, few people are sure.

Hans-Joachim Emmelmann is a staff engineer at the TDC. He oversees body development, including the Aerodynamics group, and he has been a major proponent of aero design at Opel. After nine years at Volkswagen, one of the industry pioneers in aerodynamic development, he came to Opel for a change. 'The drag co-efficient represents the aerodynamic *quality* of the body,' he explains. 'It doesn't say anything about aerodynamic drag. One very simple example: the drag co-efficient of the fifth-scale model and of the production car is approximately the same, so they both have the same aerodynamic quality, of course, because they are the same shape. But the *drag* of the full-scale model of the same car is twenty-five times bigger because the frontal area is twenty-five times bigger.'

In other words, two cars can have the same Cd number, but may have a different amount of drag acting on the body, depending on the frontal area. One motoring writer, Bill Amos, in an article in *Scottish Field*, vented his rage about how this truth is regularly overlooked: 'The strange thing is that the PR people who yack on about "lowest ever drag factor" claims are never able to quote frontal area figures.' The point to remember, he says, is that 'the so-called drag factor (Cd) is *meaningless* unless the frontal area of the car is also known'.

GME aerodynamicists, of course, know very well the frontal area of their new models – and the effects of length and wheelbase and dozens of other factors – in relation to *all* the aero forces, of which there are six. But the aerodynamicists still use the Cd number as a useful guide to a car's behaviour in the wind.

The major reason drag is such an important factor in car design is because a large amount of the car's energy is expended working to overcome it, especially at high speeds. The automobile is not a terribly efficient machine for converting chemical energy (petrol) into mechanical energy – specifically, forward motion. In fact, in an average mix of city and motorway driving, the petrol-powered internal combustion engine converts only about 35% of the chemical energy of the petrol into mechanical.

Of that amount, 30% goes into acceleration, 30% into overcoming rolling resistance, and 10% is lost due to friction and the operation of accessories, such as the heater and air conditioner. The remaining 30% is consumed in overcoming aerodynamic drag. So, if you could reduce drag to zero, you'd increase your fuel efficiency by almost a third. Which, of course, you can't.

Drag is caused by turbulence in the air behind a moving body. As any form moves through the air, the air resists it. If the form is driven by sufficient power to overcome the resistance, it pushes the molecules of air out of the way. As it does so, the air has to go somewhere and so it flows around (or through) the form in reasonably predictable ways. A smooth flow of air is actually composed of parallel layers, or streamlines, and is therefore called 'laminar'. The layer closest to the form is called the boundary layer and, in a laminar flow, is said to be 'attached' to the surface of the form.

If the flow encounters something unexpected – a gap, protuberance, obstruction, irregularity, bend – the boundary layer may separate from the surface and cause turbulence in the flow. It essentially 'trips' and tumbles into eddies or vortices, just as a stream of water forms whirlpools and confused ripples as it flows past a protruding rock.

The turbulence creates a partial vacuum behind the separation point, and this causes a drag on the forward motion of the form. The more turbulence there is around a form, the more energy is required to move it forward. The less turbulence, the more aerodynamically efficient, or streamlined, it is.

The amount of drag on a form can be determined by taking a variety of measurements, including the frontal area of the form, speed of the air, speed of travel and relative pressures of the air – and inserting them into a mathematical formula that yields the co-efficient of drag number, the Cd.

The Cd values for some basic, non-automotive forms are well known. The flat face of a half sphere, for example, has a Cd of about 1.4. A complete sphere moves through the air far more efficiently, creating very little turbulence, and has a lower Cd number of .10. An aerofoil (such as an aircraft wing) is one of the most efficient forms, with a Cd of approximately .05. Today's cars hover around the .30 mark.

The relationship between Cd and fuel economy is directly measurable. A car with a Cd of .46, driven at 90 kph, consumes approximately six litres of fuel for every 100 km driven. A car in the same weight and size class, but with a Cd of .30, will consume 5.5 litres in the same distance – for an improvement in fuel economy of about 10%. That fits roughly with the generally accepted formula that a 10% reduction in aerodynamic drag equals 3.5% to 4% reduction in average fuel consumption, and a 15% reduction in drag can improve fuel economy by as much as 10%. Other estimates, however, put the advantage much lower – and very dependent on the wind direction and driving speed.

But there is no question that there is greater potential for improving fuel economy through aerodynamics than other means. 'Engine people have always had problems getting fuel consumption down one per cent or two per cent, only with aerodynamics we have the potential of ten, twenty or more per cent,' says Hans Emmelmann.

That translates into a great deal of fuel. Geoffrey Howard estimates, in his book *Automobile Aerodynamics*, that if two million cars in the Audi 100 class 'on the roads of Britain covering 10,000 miles a year each could reflect these improvements overnight, 100 million gallons of fuel per year would be saved'.

Although drag is the principal concern, there are other aerodynamic forces that affect the car's performance, the most important of which are lift and side force. Lift is created when air passes over an aerofoil, which is a shape with an upper surface area greater than its lower surface area. When the air parts around the aerofoil, the flow travelling over the upper surface of the aerofoil increases in velocity. This reduces pressure on the surface, and when the pressure is reduced enough to overcome the force of gravity, the aerofoil starts to rise.

The basic shape of a car is that of an aerofoil – the bonnet, windscreens, roof and boot-lid have far greater surface area than the underbody. So, if you were to accelerate to a speed of about 240 kph your car would actually start to take off. 'Of course, it would come down quite quickly,' says Emmelmann, 'because there is no propulsion, no propeller.' You'd lose power and come back down again, making for a very bumpy and unstable journey. Many automotive racing pioneers found this out the hard way when they experimented with aerofoils that were incorrectly configured.

Drag and lift, along with side force – airflow that pushes the car sideways – are the three so-called parallel forces that act on the three axes of the car. In addition, there are three moments that operate in rotation around these axes. The location of the pitching moment determines a car's tendency to rock back and forth lengthwise. The yawing and rolling moments affect the sideways movements of the car. Calculation of how these forces interact, and how they are measured and how the form reacts to them is the basis of the science of aerodynamics.

The widespread popularity of aero is new, but the discipline is not; experimentation with aerodynamic styling and design has been going on since the beginning of the century.

Through studies of hydrodynamics, aerostatics (lighter-than-air aviation) and aeronautics made in the eighteenth and nineteenth centuries, the early car makers had some understanding of the principles of the science of 'moving air'. Many also had an intuitive understanding that some forms moved more gracefully through the air than others. They looked to natural and organic forms – birds and fish – for models and clues to the secrets of streamlining. They also studied man-made forms: airships, boats and torpedoes. The ideal aerodynamic form was identified as the teardrop: a smooth, rounded front with a long, tapering tail, like the body of a bird, a dolphin, or a seal.

Aerodynamics in the service of fuel efficiency is a 1980s phenomenon. In the early days, the goals were improved performance, greater speed, better stability. Speed trials were held as early as 1898 (a measured kilometre race outside Paris) and continue to this day. Racers found that more powerful engines were not the only way to make a car move faster. By making their cars longer and lower and by smoothing the front end (often into a bullet or torpedo shape) they found that cars were both more stable and faster.

The underbody – with all its juttings and cavities created by mechanical components – was also found to cause drag, and was enclosed. The spokes of wheels and the heads of drivers caused drag, too. Wheels were covered, and drivers scrunched lower and lower into their cockpits.

Opel prides itself as being a leader in aerodynamic development. In 1927, Fritz von Opel, the fourth son of founder Adam Opel, embarked on an aero adventure that a company publication calls 'one of the most bizarre episodes in the history of any of the world's automobile companies'.

Von Opel was approached by Max Valier, an Austrian-born rocket enthusiast, who wanted the Opel firm to fund and help him develop a rocket-powered car. Valier saw it as a first step towards the development of a space ship, von Opel saw it as an interesting opportunity for spectacular publicity. During the years 1927-30, they built and tested three rocket-powered cars, Raks 1, 2 and 3, each more aerodynamically efficient than the one before.

The Rak 2 looked like a large bullet with stubby wings and was powered by twenty-four rockets, whose exhausts formed a fearsome ring at the tail. Von Opel drove (piloted?) this vehicle himself and, although he couldn't beat the land speed record of 333 kph, he recounted that the drive was an exciting experience: 'On either side everything disappeared and I saw only the wide stretch of concrete road in front of me . . . The acceleration was intoxicating; I ceased to think, reality disappeared and with this raging power behind me my actions became purely subconscious.'

Von Opel was a victim of the car's natural urge to fly – the front end of his Rak 2 began to rise dangerously as the racer reached top speed, primarily because its wings were too sharply angled.

In the 1920s and '30s, the leading experimenters in aerodynamic design for automobiles were aircraft designers. Few of their designs were realized as production cars, but their findings and ideas were influential. Paul Jaray was chief designer of the German Zeppelin airships during World War I. The only one of his many prototype designs that reached commercial production – manufactured by Tatra of Czechoslovakia in 1934 – had a smooth nose, enclosed rear wheels and an upright, dinosaur-like fin arching down its back.

Dr Edmund Rumpler, another designer of both aircraft and cars, developed a teardrop car – the Tropfenwagen – which was produced as a prototype in Germany in 1921. Tested at the VW wind tunnel in 1983, this extraordinary car recorded a drag co-efficient of just .28 – as low as the most efficient of today's production cars. And, by modern standards, it doesn't 'look aero' at all.

In America, Chrysler began experimenting with aerodynamic design in the middle 1920s and introduced the famous Airflow model in 1934. The Airflow had a curved front end, partially flush headlamps, integrated front fenders and semi-wraparound windscreen. In his book *The Streamlined Decade*, Donald J. Bush quotes the copy from a 1934 advertisement for the car: 'Old mother nature has always designed her creatures for the function they are to perform. She has streamlined her fastest fish . . . her swiftest birds . . . her fleetest animals that move on land. You have only to look at a dolphin, a gull or a greyhound to appreciate the rightness of the tapering, flowing contour of the new Airflow Chrysler. By scientific experiment, Chrysler engineers have simply verified and adapted a natural fundamental law.'

The 'scientific experiment' referred to was wind-tunnel testing but, unfortunately for Chrysler, aerodynamics didn't have the legitimacy and cachet then they have now. In addition, the Airflow looked wimpish, homely even, and therefore seemed to make a mockery of its chief asset. The car failed Raymond Loewy's 'Most Advanced, Yet Acceptable' test, and, although it remained in production for four years, it was not a big seller.

Aero forms were also copied purely for novelty in styling. An extreme example was the General Motors tail fin that first appeared on the 1948 Cadillac, designed by Harley Earl. Alfred Sloan relates that 'the story of the tail fin began during the war when an air force friend of Harley Earl invited him to see some new fighter planes. One of them was the P-38, which had twin Allison engines, twin fuselages, and twin tail fins. When Mr Earl saw it, he asked if he could have some of his designers look at it . . . They were just as impressed as Mr Earl, and a few months later their sketches began to show signs of fins.'

Although later wind tunnel tests have shown that these tail fins may have had a small stabilizing effect in crosswinds, the tail fins were primarily a marketing craze and had very little to do with aerodynamics.

Despite the advances in the understanding of aerodynamics over the years, they weren't applied in great earnest until the post oil-shock days. The typical European saloon of the 1960s and early 1970s was pretty inefficient, with a Cd above .40. The Ford Cortina, for example, had a Cd of .44. The Volkswagen Beetle (a 1940s design) looked to be aerodynamically efficient, but wasn't – with a Cd of about .48. But, in the mid-1970s aerodynamics came of age dramatically, primarily because improved aerodynamic design meant increased fuel efficiency. As oil became scarcer and more expensive, fuel efficiency suddenly became terribly important.

The 1981 Ford Escort was marketed as having aerodynamic styling (with a 17% reduction in drag over its predecessor, from a Cd of .46 to about .40), but the manufacturer that really inaugurated the 'Cd Olympic Games' and set the standard for the 1980s was Volkswagen. Their Audi 100 Mark III, introduced at the Paris Motor Show in 1982, was the first production car with a Cd of .30 – an improvement of about 28% on the .43 Cd of the Mark II. Not all of the aero improvements were beneficial to the passengers, however; its poor ventilation earned it the 'fastest sauna' tag. The Ford Sierra was also launched in Paris, and had a respectable Cd for the time – .34.

Although GM Europe ran slightly behind, they achieved lower numbers in the long run, and now consider themselves to be a leader in aerodynamic design. The 1984 Astra/Kadett GSi reached .30. J'89 achieved .29. The 1986 Carlton/Omega set a new record for production cars of .28. And the 1990 Calibra coupé, based on the J'89 platform, boasts the lowest Cd of any production car in the world – .26.

One of the main challenges for automotive aerodynamicists is that the bulk of aerodynamic study has been done for aircraft, and cars and aeroplanes behave differently in the wind. The major difference is the proximity of the ground, which creates separation lines that are not caused by the form itself.

Real driving conditions are, of course, much more complicated and less consistent than those in the tunnel. In the wind tunnel, the car doesn't move. The wind flows steadily over it, always in one direction and at a constant speed. There are no other vehicles on the road, overtaking or being overtaken, to disturb the wind and create turbulence. There are no trees or buildings at the verges.

Although some tunnels have moving platforms so the tyres can roll, and others conduct tests with several cars in line to simulate traffic (and GM has developed a new, on-site, computerized measuring system), the basic test is of a single car moving straight ahead into a steady wind.

The reason there is nothing to see when the test begins is that the real work of the wind tunnel is done with the balance, an electro-mechanical weighing mechanism installed beneath the test section. It contains five strain gauges – one beneath each wheel and one forward of the car – that work not much differently from the weighing mechanisms in domestic scales.

The car rests on a platform which in turn rests on top of the balance; the gauges measure the changes of weight that occur – in comparison to the weight without wind – when wind begins to flow over the car. The data are delivered directly into the computer system, and, through a variety of different programs, the computer can express what's happening in the form of equations, charts or graphics. The basic measurement from the tyre transducers is lift: how much heavier or lighter does the car become in a wind flow? The five other aero forces can be calculated using these measurements in various formulae.

Because a car sitting alone in an empty room is visually unexciting, typical photographs of the wind tunnel show streams of smoke arcing over the form, or pieces of string attached to the body. These methods are secondary to the work of the balance, and are simply used to make the windflow visible and give a quick visual understanding of where and how turbulence is occurring.

There are many such methods, including smoke (which is actually heated oil) emerging from a pipe, helium bubbles, wool tufts attached to the surface of the car (which themselves create turbulence) and long pieces of string trailing out from a fixed point. Where there is a separation, the smoke will eddy or the string will tremble. Of course, you never see any eddying or turbulence in public relations photographs – that would imply a less than optimum form – and so it seems the only thing that happens in the wind tunnel is that serious-looking engineers watch as perfectly smooth streams of smoke flow over their cars.

There are many types of wind tunnels. Some test aerodynamic forces only, some can be used to test climatic conditions (heat and humidity) and some, general purpose tunnels, do both. All aerodynamic tunnels are composed of a large fan (rather like an aircraft propeller) which creates the wind, a tunnel to direct it, a test section where the car sits, the balance and a control room.

The tunnel and fan can be configured in two basic ways. The Eiffel type tunnel is named after Alexandre-Gustave Eiffel, the French engineer who designed the Eiffel Tower in Paris. The Eiffel-type wind tunnel is of the open circuit, straight flow type, which means that the air is drawn in at one end, flows through the test chamber and vents out the other end.

The Göttingen-type tunnel (named after Göttingen University in West Germany) is a closed loop, and the wind races continually around inside it. Göttingen tunnels (Stuttgart's is one) are more complicated to construct and take up more space than the Eiffel type, but have some advantages – including better control over the temperature and humidity of the airstream, and reduced energy usage because the wind is recycled.

The Stuttgart facility contains two tunnels – one for testing full-size models, and another for testing fifth-scale clays. Testing begins in the smaller tunnel, because the fifth-scale models are cheaper to make, easy to transport (Stuttgart is only about two hours south on the autobahn from Rüsselsheim), quicker to test and easier to change than full-size models. And a well-detailed fifth-scale clay, with all shut lines and an articulated underbody, will yield test results that are almost identical to those of the full-sized model.

For J'89, GME aerodynamicists spent some 760 chilly hours in the full-sized tunnel, wearing their anoraks or winter coats, testing and refining nineteen different full-sized concept models. Eight fifth-scale models spent a total of over 700 hours in the smaller tunnel.

Hans Emmelmann remembers that 'in former times, the stylists created the car and it had a Cd of .45 or so. Then we took the car into the wind tunnel, and we did some refinements but, of course, they were limited, because otherwise we would spoil the whole styling concept. We could fair [smooth] the leading edge of the hood, or round the headlamps, and could maybe reduce the Cd to .40.' In other words, minor aero adjustments were not enough to show big reductions in drag, and, by the time clay models were being produced, it was too late for major adjustments.

Now, as part of the integrated development process, the aero-dynamicists are involved from the very beginning. In fact Emmelmann explains, 'We start very early, sometimes ahead of the first styling sketches. We know the main dimensions of the car and during the aero concept phase, we carry out studies of fifth-scale models which have these main dimensions to find potential [for aerodynamic improvements].'

Most of the aerodynamicists at the Technical Development Centre are engineers. Some of them are 'vehicle' men, trained in applying aerodynamic principles to car forms. Some of them are aero specialists, who understand lift and drag and the workings of the wind tunnel but would not presume to call themselves car experts. The vehicle aerodynamicists are constantly creating and testing concept cars, working on new aero refinements that could be applied to any new model – J'89 or the new T or future V.

With ideas in hand, 'We try to influence the first styling sketches,' says Emmelmann. 'We talk to the studio heads of styling and say, okay, if you do that and that – in the rear end this, in the front end that – you'll have a better drag co-efficient.' Another Opel aerodynamicist, Chris Makepeace, says the process can be politically tricky, because they're often involved before they're officially supposed to be. 'We have to tell the stylists what they should do without them knowing we're telling them. We're not allowed to work on a project till it comes to us.'

Hans Emmelmann knows quite well how to design and build cars with exceptionally low drag. 'Okay, if I'd like to build a car of .15 or something like that, that is not really a problem for the aerodynamicist. He takes a pencil and draws a nice shape and it's close to .15'. In fact, GM's own experimental, solar-powered car – called Sunraycer – has been reported as having a Cd somewhere in the range of .099 to .12. Most engineers agree that the 1990s generation of cars will have an average Cd of .25 or so.

'Most people get the impression that the only task for the aerodynamicists is to reduce aerodynamic drag. We have a cigar on wheels and people lying down inside and that's it. But we have a lot of legally conflicting goals and functionally conflicting goals. The problem is to optimize a real car.' So the question in aerodynamic development is not 'Is it possible to go lower?' but 'How much lower should we go?' How much aero will the public pay for and how should we compromise when aero objectives come in conflict with comfort, legal, functional or cosmetic objectives?

The lower the height of the car, the more aerodynamically efficient it will be. But, for J'89, a key programme objective was to improve interior comfort and entry conditions, and the lower the car the harder it is to get into. Similarly, cavernous wheel openings create turbulence, but once again there must be enough clearance for a range of tyre sizes. A sharply sloping bonnet is best for wind flow, but not so convenient for fitting engines in.

Then there are legal specifications – for the position of the number plate, the surface area of the driver's mirror and width and angle of window pillars – that may conflict with the optimum aero design for these elements.

The simplest, cleanest, cheapest and best way to achieve aerodynamic efficiency is to get the basic forms right rather than fix details later, adding strakes or spoilers. Here again, the Ford Sierra represented the example not to follow for the J'89 aerodynamicists. Despite a great deal of wind tunnel testing, the Sierra, on the road, suffered some problems with stability in crosswinds.

The cause was found to be the airflow pattern around the C pillar, where a separation point caused turbulence. The problem was eventually fixed by the addition of two plastic fittings called strakes, affixed to the edges of the rear windscreen on the saloon and a protruding window moulding on the trailing edge of the rear side window on the hatchback.

Both solutions are relatively unobtrusive unless you really look for them, and then the strakes, in particular, seem odd and unnecessary. This constituted aerodynamic patching-up, and the J'89 team were after a body form that created no such problems, required no such fixes.

Marketing needs also sneaked into the early aero development phase. The visual language of aerodynamics has become so familiar to car buyers in the 1980s that it was necessary for J'89 to 'say' it was an aerodynamically efficient design as well as actually to *be* one. The shape would have to satisfy the public's perception of what aerodynamics is all about. The problem, of course, is that the public has only a limited understanding of aero design, much of it gained through the car makers' advertising and public relations efforts. In this way, the car maker is both tyrant and slave.

The aero design process involves more than simply developing a slippery shape. The total discipline, often called airflow management, entails creating a car that not only minimizes the negative effects of drag and lift and side force, but also controls airflow for all kinds of positive uses as well: stabilizing the car, cleaning the surfaces, reducing wind noise, cooling the engine and passenger compartment. Airflow management involves three key areas of development: the basic body form, the protuberances from the surface, and airflow through the car.

The teardrop form is still considered the aerodynamic ideal, but the interpretation of the ideal has changed a bit from the dolphin and bullet days. Dr Wunibald Kamm, an aero pioneer working at the Stuttgart wind tunnel in the late 1930s, discovered that the long teardrop tail could be truncated – cut off sharply at the rear – with no great increase in drag. Also, a truly rounded front end was found to be impractical and inefficient for a number of reasons.

So, all that's left of the true teardrop is a front end that is as rounded as possible – from bumper up into the bonnet, and from bumper into the fenders. And a shape that, in plan view, gradually widens from the nose to the B pillar and tapers in again to the boot. J'89 follows this modern teardrop form exactly. From above, it looks like a well-proportioned lozenge, almost identical to the shape of a typical rear-view mirror. The rear end, true to Dr Kamm's model, cuts off sharply.

Now, think of the most basic automotive saloon shape as three boxes, or volumes, of different size – engine compartment, passenger compartment and boot – welded together. All surfaces meet at right angles, as they often do in a child's drawing of a car, and every join represents a point of air separation. To avoid separation of the boundary layer, all the surfaces of the boxes need to flow into one another smoothly. The sharp edges must be planed away, the surfaces melted into one another. Nose into bonnet, nose into fenders, bonnet into windscreen, bonnet into fenders, windscreen into roof, windscreen into side windows and so on. This is relatively easy when you're working in clay, but when you're bending metal and forming glass and creating a structural framework it becomes much more difficult.

Just exactly how and where the sheet-metal segments join to create the form is critical. The narrower the gaps between sheet-metal pieces and the more gracefully they follow the basic line of the car, the greater the visual integrity will be. The idea for J'89 was to make all the shutlines into design lines, with the boundary of each sheet-metal piece to fall at a functional shut line – the natural meeting-places of door and fender, for example, or bonnet and fender. The upper edge of the fender would end at the bonnet opening, the trailing edge of the front fender at the door opening, the leading edge of the fender at the margin of the headlamp – and so on with every sheet-metal section.

This approach caused problems at two tricky junctures. The first was the so-called three countries corner, the place at the lower corner of the front windscreen where three sheet-metal components meet – fender, bonnet and front door. But it is even more complicated than that, because the windscreen wiper, the windscreen, usually an air intake grille and the A pillar are also involved.

In many cars, the A pillar is covered by a sheet-metal segment that ends at the base of the pillar, and there may be a separate piece containing the grille and wiper housings. But, with J'89, the idea was to create a smooth curve – an unbroken line along the trailing edge of the bonnet, around the three countries corner, up along the front door shut and into the door shut line into the roof. Bonnet, fender and door fan out from the corner like three slices of pie.

This scheme would require complex engineering and manufacturing, particularly for the doors. To accomplish this smooth line, the doors would have to be the aircraft or wraparound style – a single sheet-metal stamping that would overlap and shut into the roof. The shut line would actually be facing up, rather than to the side. The front segment of the door would completely cover the A pillar, which is a critical contributor to the strength and rigidity of the entire car, and there would be no place for the traditional (ugly) drip rail. Although the designers agreed that this made for a smooth and appealing line, they also knew it would make for controversy with the engineers and difficulties in manufacture.

In addition to the basic form a second cause of drag comes from all the protuberances and aberrations that sprout from these surfaces.

THE VAUXHALL CAVALIER J'89

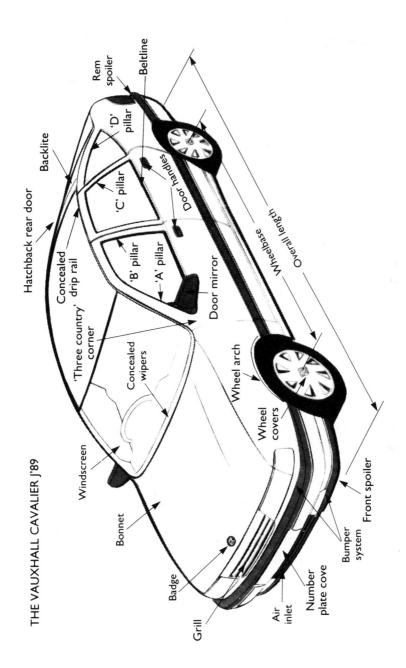

Rem spoiler

Beltline

'D' pillar

Backlite

'C' pillar

Door handles

Hatchback rear door

Concealed drip rail

'B' pillar

'A' pillar

'Three country' corner

Door mirror

Wheelbase

Overall length

Concealed wipers

Wheel arch

Windscreen

Wheel covers

Front spoiler

Bonnet

Bumper system

Badge

Number plate cove

Grill

Air inlet

Grille, headlamps, number plates, badge, sidelights, windscreen wipers, wheel arches, door mirrors, window mouldings, drip rails, radio aerials, door handles – anything that sticks out into the flow of the air causes drag. Flush mountings, smooth fittings and concealed fixtures can help here.

Depressions and gullies cause drag, too. Sheet-metal gaps need to be as tight as possible. And then there is the underbody, the unloved, undesirable, problem zone. The exhaust system, fuel tank, sump and engine components hang down below the plane of the underbody and cause airflow disturbances which are aggravated by the proximity of the road.

Various concept cars have been used to demonstrate that an enclosed underbody can significantly reduce drag. But an enclosed underbody is expensive to manufacture, it would also be heavy and would make maintenance difficult. Besides, most customers have no interest in the underbody and the glories of a completely enclosed one would be difficult, if not impossible, to promote – and sell.

J'89 cost constraints called for carrying over most underbody components from J'81. But the J'89 team explored another solution to underbody drag. Simply reducing the volume of air flowing under the car reduces the potential for drag, and so they sought a solution in a front spoiler with a 'tuned lip' that would direct much of the onrushing air over and around the car, rather than under it.

The third major source of drag is the airflow through the car. Air has to flow into the engine compartment for cooling, and must also be directed into the passenger compartment for ventilation, defrosting, heating and cooling. But as it flows into the grille, the air meets the radiator and then the engine components head on – and their shapes have very little in common with the teardrop. The best answer to date is to tailor the grille openings to the size of the engine, so that only the necessary amount of air flows into the engine compartment.

The final result is a smooth car, with a Cd of .29, beating its target of .30. Smooth roof transitions, curved surfaces, tapered pillars, flush fittings, integrated spoilers, hidden mouldings, concealed drip rail – all these details add up to substantial aerodynamic improvements: a 21% reduction in drag over the previous model; a 40% reduction in lift for the saloon, 60% for the hatch;

a reduced plume of spray behind the car when travelling along wet roads.

The contribution of each area of improvement could be measured as follows:

Rear end	50%
Front end	15%
Flow through	15%
Side airflow	10%
Details	10%

Once the car is on the road, however, there is an endless number of factors that the aerodynamicist has no control over, which can further increase drag, affect lift and generally negate the aerodynamicists' careful work. These include a roof-rack, an open window or sun-roof, a hand out the window, dirty surfaces, dents, windscreen wipers in operation, a heavy load in the boot that brings the nose up too high, rear seat passengers. In everyday life, the Cd number is a highly variable quantity.

Fromund Kloppe had wanted to be a designer, but found it was too subjective a discipline and turned to engineering instead. 'Two plus two equals four in engineering. There is no discussion about it.' But on the walls of his office in the Numerical Control Systems area of the Design Centre where he is Studio Chief, there hangs evidence that he has not completely left the fine arts behind: three framed images of a woman's torso, each rendered in a three-dimensional grid of fine lines. These images seem accurately to symbolize the role of a relative newcomer to the design process: computer-aided design, or CAD.

The transition from the vision of the new car to a functioning road vehicle is a long slow one, and, before computers came on the scene, it was plagued with tension and imprecision. But now, along with the aero concept cars, sketches, full-size renderings, third-scale and fifth-scale models, computer technology is making its contribution, helping to provide an interface between the fluidity of the idea and the inflexibility of the number.

Five full-scale models, some in clay, some in fibre-glass, were made for J'89. Unlike the charming fifth-scale clays, the full-scales are massive and brutal-looking. They are covered with a thin plastic material called Di-Noc, which simulates a painted surface, so the surfaces, graphics, colours and reflections can be evaluated.

The windows are left black and the various grilles and openings do not penetrate completely into the body. The models look heavy and brooding. Interior bucks are also constructed to various stages of finish – to evaluate seating dimensions, seat size, fascia layouts, fabrics and trims.

The pivotal moment arrives when management reviews the programme (usually about a year after the process begins) and the full-scale clay sculpture is finally approved for digitization. It is the symbolic handover point from art to technology. Digitization is a method of measuring the clay model precisely using an electronic measuring system. The model is positioned on a gridded surface plate and then, using an electronic probe attached to an upright, a technician begins a three to four day process known as point taking. This involves touching the probe to the surface of the model at 10-15,000 different points. The distance of each point from the surface plate is measured and recorded, each with its own reference number.

Although point taking can be done automatically, it is not the preferred method. The automated scanning method will take a standard concentration of points over the entire body. In some places where the geometry is complex, there will not be enough points to create an accurate picture of the form. In other places where the form is simple, there will be more points than are necessary.

The skilled measuring technician has something of the artist in him, and will compensate for the shortcomings of the model itself. The clay modeller may have trouble getting edges or corners exactly right, or may scrape away more clay than he means to, leaving a hollow place where none is meant to be. The good measurer will avoid the mistakes and help compensate for rough spots.

The interior models are digitized separately, and are the most complex of all. Kloppe tells a story that sounds as if he has impressed many visitors with it before. The Statue of Liberty was designed in

France by the sculptor F.A. Bartholdi in a fashion similar to that used for cars today. A scale model was made, from which points were taken – manually – and used to create the full-sized version. 'We take more points,' says Kloppe, 'on the interior of the J'89 door panel than were taken for the whole of the Statue of Liberty.'

The point information is broken into a series of surface areas called patches and fed into the computer. Fresh from the digitizer, the data are not perfect yet. Now the computer operators work with the designers to smooth out and refine the surfaces in a process called sweetening. This is done through two-dimensional and three-dimensional computer modelling, which uses the points to create a graphic rendering of the car on the computer screen. In the cool light of the technical support area there are nine CAD stations, large flat computer screens with keyboard and keypad attached. It takes a year for an operator to learn the language of the CAD station but, once it is learned, he can perform mesmerizing tricks on the screen: calling up a three-dimensional image of the car, zooming in on a section, shading it in any colour, rotating it, representing it as a wire frame image.

In addition to sweetening the surfaces, the operators perform a number of other operations. For example, the sheet metal flutter test allows the technicians to check the stability of the surface: will it bend or cave in on itself? The designers sit quietly before their screens, staring steadily at them, eyes seldom moving to the keypad or keyboard. There is something eerie about the scene – a row of silent men, completely in the thrall of their giant screens, tapping away like blind men, seeking a clue as to their whereabouts or directions.

The perfected surface information now forms the database that will govern the rest of the process: this series of mathematically defined points is now the car. The points do not change, and the database is accessible to all the engineers and designers that need it. This brings a great deal more consistency into the process.

'In the old days,' says Kloppe, 'you had various drawings and you always had an excuse that the copy machine wasn't copying it properly – for example, putting tolerances in the dimensions. Now there is no excuse any more, because we mathematically define the surface or engineering construction work. And all the people in the production work are not using the line, they are using the number.'

In addition to the consistency, it also leads to greater accuracy. 'You cannot say two is 1.9999. It means you must be very accurate, cannot negotiate about tolerances. They are there and everybody can measure it. They can tell you precisely, no, this point is off twelve hundredths and we needed nine hundredths because that is our tolerance. Suddenly all this appreciation of millimetres is coming up which was impossible before. We feel both constrained, but also confident. Now they all know this is what they have designed and established. It goes unchanged through the process of development.'

The consistency and accuracy afforded by the computer, in turn, have an effect on the people that use the data. 'It puts a great responsibility on people – responsibility for what they have done and there is no cheating. The people are proud. It is a human mentality to look for the perfect. And this is one way to support them.'

The computerized digitization and sweetening process is a key element in a longer term, industry-wide move towards computer-integrated manufacturing or CIM. The next step in the evolution of computer-aided car design is to go from computer sketch to small-scale model directly. The sketches won't be eliminated in the near future; they are the easiest, quickest method of jotting down new ideas. Nor will the third and full-scale models disappear because people, particularly management, will always want to touch the new model, see how it looks from different angles, in different lights.

But Fromund Kloppe has plans to install a new system in the technical support area. From a preliminary sketch, the computer can generate a surface database that can be translated into instructions to a new, automated cutting machine capable of sculpting small-scale models in a wood-like material. No need for studios filled with sculptors. No give and take between designer and craftsperson. No cabinet filled with lovely models. Just a computer controlling a whirring blade and presto, a computer-generated model.

6 · 4,000 ENGINEERS

> 'You have a lot of targets: a target on size, a target in weight, a target in finance, a target in time. You have to do the best compromise at the time. Then later on, once in production, we will get criticism and try to improve what we have done.'
>
> *Peter Döring, Assistant Staff Engineer responsible for European J car coordination*

Dietmar Pfeiffer was talking about his speciality, brakes, and particularly anti-lock braking systems (ABS), and the ABS system he helped develop (based on Bosch technology) for J'89. Talk of wheel slippage inevitably led to a question about traction and how much tyre area is actually in contact with the road at any given time. 'Oh!' said Pfeiffer, looking a bit surprised. 'You'll have to talk to the tyre guys. I don't know anything about tyres.'

Pfeiffer undoubtedly knows a great deal about tyres, but what he meant was that tyres were not his speciality, and GM has plenty of people whose life's work it is to think about the nature of tyres and how they meet the road. In fact, Dietmar Pfeiffer is one of about 4,000 engineers and technicians based at the Technical Development Centre and engaged in vehicle design and in the development and production of tools and equipment. Virtually every bit of J'89 was redesigned, and each one had a project engineer to oversee its creation.

Nobody can really say how many parts there are in J'89, partly because it's difficult to define just what a part is – is a screw a part, or is it just part of a larger part? – but there are somewhere in the range of 10-15,000 of them. A large percentage of them were redesigned for the new car, not necessarily nuts and bolts but all the components that matter – down to the switches on the fascia – and every one has a project engineer.

In contrast to the cloistered, even secretive, atmosphere of the Design Centre, the TDC is organized with open floor plans, so in some places you can see from window wall to window wall, and as far as you can see there are rows and rows of desks and technical drawing tables. Hundreds and hundreds of men (and only a few women) are labouring over their tables, working on one of the details that make up the new car. Here and there are examples of the finished work: here, an entire engine block sits on top of a cabinet like a meteorite that has just crashed through the ceiling, here a clutch mechanism or a few gears.

The atmosphere is bustling and jovial, down to earth. The floors are filled with light, and the few managers are enclosed, for the most part, in glass-panelled outer offices. The place has the feel of a giant schoolroom, with thousands of desks and not enough teachers; the teachers who are present are overly busy and tolerant of their students' misdemeanours because they know they are sufficiently devoted to their work.

In their hearts, engineers believe that they are the ones who truly create the new car. Take away the structure, remove the chassis and drive train, engine, suspension, steering, controls, wheels and all the other functioning components – and you wouldn't have much left. Just a thin metal skin, some fabric and a few colours. If you abolished the design department, the engineers could still create a functioning new car. How it would look, and whether it would sell, is a different matter. But fire all the engineers, and the designers would be back where Harley Earl was when he started – sculpting forms on to existing chassis.

Although there may be no identifiable father of J'89 (or mother, for that matter), Peter Döring was definitely the attending nurse. As assistant staff engineer with responsibility for European J car co-ordination, he was involved in the project, not just in the development of the preliminary product programme, but all the way through to start of production and introduction.

At first glance, Döring looks like a good-natured but slightly harassed plumber in a well-cut suit and tie. He has a distracted air, emphasized by his penchant for running a hand through his already neatly combed hair as if trying to keep everything in order against impossible odds.

The engineering of a new model seems never to end, nor even to begin. There are the major new model programmes such as J'89, which was preceded by the Senator, and before that the V car and before that the T car. At the same time, there are a number of engineering development programmes that are not necessarily linked to a specific model. Four wheel drive, four wheel steer, advanced chassis technology (ACT), ABS systems may début on a particular car but don't belong solely to that model.

And, even when the new model has been launched, it is constantly being refined throughout its life. It is as if the technology inside the outer skin evolves at its own pace and that the designation 'new model' comes at an arbitrary moment, mostly dictated by marketing and corporate requirements.

For the engineers, the process of developing the new model involves building dozens of test cars, each one containing more and more new components until, finally, it *is* the new model – and then they fit some more new components, and those become the engineering refinements of 1992, or 1994.

The first of these test vehicles are called component cars, and are simply the old J'81 model with a new component fitted – a new engine, a new sub-assembly of some type. The engineers can take these out on to public roads for testing and evaluation, because there is nothing that the inquiring press or observant members of the public can see yet.

The next stage is a set of cars called pre-test. These still have the old J body, but it's attached to a new chassis and complete drive train. These cars, too, are tested on public roads. Then come the prototypes, which are completely hand-made cars with the new body shape and mechanical components. The first one is the most expensive – costing as much as 1.5 million DM, or about £540,000.

Many prototypes are built, some are crashed against test walls and others are tested at private proving grounds. As the manufacturing tooling is completed, the hand-made parts are replaced by production parts. The differences between the final prototype and first pilot car are therefore minimal. Meanwhile, the members of the cost research group are eviscerating another whole set of cars – those of the competitors. They take everything apart, price every component, find the clever innovations and identify the areas where the solutions were unsatisfactory.

It takes at least eighteen months from the beginning of the engineering process to arrive at surface release, and another year or so to reach engineering release, when technical drawings are delivered to manufacturing so that tooling design can begin. It is prior to surface release (represented by digitization of the full-scale clay) that the most heated design and engineering discussions take place. The nub of the issue comes back to the relationship between form and function. To a degree, function dictates certain automotive forms, but there are few instances where function is absolute. Wheels must be round. There must be an enclosed passenger compartment. Headlamps must point forward. There must be openings for air intake and exhaust. But even in these places there is plenty of room for function to be reconfigured to follow form. But totally rethinking the automotive form is the task of the advance groups and concept car designers. In the day to day process of developing J'89, the form/function sticking points seem to have been quite familiar.

Peter Döring chuckles. 'We had big discussions on the rear roof line, from the windshield to back line. On the hood line. Head clearance. Wheel-housing. Every project has similar discussions.' The designers wanted a steeper angle for the bonnet, for example, because they thought it looked better. Hans-Jürgen Pache, one of the engineers involved in advanced product study, says there are a few very clear-cut situations: '. . . for example, the engine sticks out of the hood line by 20 mm, so that's a clear situation. So styling will accept we can't do it. But before they accept, we have to look clearly into alternatives. Can we turn around the engine? Can we tip it to the back? Can we lower the engine?'

In this case, the engineers did accommodate the designers, to a point – going so far as to develop a whole new arrangement of front-end components, including radiator, hood latch and reinforcement. Another engineer recalls, 'We have a lot of problems with wraparound doors – you get marks on the outer surface. You can see you don't have a flat surface. You need a reinforcement piece to weld on to the one piece sheet-metal. There is a lot of investment involved.'

Money, of course, keeps entering into the equation. The Official Product Programme lists every component, every new element of J'89, with costs of production and cost of investment estimated for each. In the spring of 1984, after the Product Programme had been fully estimated, the cost was found to be 35% too high in investment, and about 250 DM (£90) too high per unit for production. Now the real negotiation begins.

'I guess we have to talk about the system we use,' says Pache. 'We have a lot of items that are musts. A lot of items that are wants, or "nice to haves" as we call it. Styling, their wishes are very strong for a time.'

A rear-lit instrument panel, at 10 DM, was taken out of the programme, (although the designers prevailed and it was later put back in). There were agonized discussions over the underbody. With new exhaust emission regulations expected in Europe, it was likely that the fitting of catalytic converters would eventually become standard for some models, and that would require a specific underbody design.

For J'89, the engineers had to decide whether to create a single underbody that could be used for cars with and without catalytic converters, or whether to go with two underbodies. To create one new one would increase the product cost now, and would be of no clear benefit to the customer without a catalytic converter. Eventually, however, it would make manufacturing simpler and more cost-effective. Should the 20 DM per unit go into some other component that the customer could see and appreciate immediately, or into something that would be a benefit the company in the long run? The J'89 team opted for the long-term benefit, in this case.

Another continuing debate is over something called deproliferation. The more tailored various components are for different models, the greater number of combinations are possible. The greater the proliferation of combinations, the more complicated everything else becomes: production, assembly, stocking, advertising, selling. For example, at the beginning of the J'89 programme, eighteen exterior body colours were specified, with body-coloured bumpers on the higher spec models and different types of bumpers that could accommodate the different air openings specified by the aero people for optimum cooling of different-sized engines.

'You cannot imagine how many different bumpers you get, with exterior colours, open and closed grilles, yellow fog lights, white fog lights. We came up with 256 different bumper variations. This was crazy. So we proposed to go down to ten colours and to reduce the number of bumpers. We finally compromised with fourteen colours,' says Döring.

Rounded wheel arches or squared? How steep can the windscreen angle be? Wraparound doors, or conventional doors? Wraparound doors mean semi-flush glass, rather than fully flush, how does that affect aero performance? These are issues that are answered partly by the demands of engineering and manufacturing, partly by the needs of form and the total sculpture. But some are issues purely of taste or personal preference. What will appeal to the market, the potential customer?

It is the clinic which provides a way to bring the customer into the design process, and to do it early enough so that changes can be made based on what is learned. The objective of a clinic is to show the new model, along with current and competitive models, to a cross-section of a specific segment of the general public – people who are current owners or likely future buyers of intermediate cars. Clinics are primarily marketing exercises, and not so different from the advance showing of concept models at motor shows, only more controlled and more focused on a specific new model.

Two J'89 clinics were conducted, the first in the spring of 1984 in Duisburg, just as the Product Programme was being solidified; the second was in June 1987 in Düsseldorf. In Duisburg, 600 people from the UK, Germany and France were invited to view nine cars. Two were J'89s, a hatch and a notch. Seven were competitors: a Ford

Sierra, Volkswagen Passat, Mazda 626, Audi 80, BMW 3, Citröen and Austin Rover Montego.

The two J'89s were mocked up showing different window treatments, as well as different door construction. On the driver's side of both models, the doors were framed; on the passenger side, they were the stamped, wraparound style. The attendees know this is a new model and, although it isn't badged, often people guess who the manufacturer is. They respond to a questionnaire which helps quantify their reactions to specific aspects of the interior and exterior design. In general, the new cars were well received. People liked the wraparound doors, but they didn't like the wheelcovers, and of the two front end treatments, most preferred one with a large grille.

Marketing prepares a report that summarizes the results of the clinic. The results are discussed with design, with the engineers and then presented to management. Now a third viewpoint is added to the discussion of how J'89 should look. The problem is exactly how to incorporate this information.

For Wayne Cherry, favourable response from a customer clinic is a mixed blessing. 'The clinic is only as good as the effort that goes into it, and the understanding and ability that you have to process the information in an intelligent way. And the whole argument is that people don't know what they want five years from now, until somebody shows them. And a lot of people will be showing them between now and the mid-nineties – in other words competition – will show things that then will set the standards or the needs or the wants, or create the need.'

In other words, people expect that a car will be and should be based upon past history. Is it possible for them to understand what the new model is all about, based on a rather unceremonious exposure to it during a short clinic? Why should the first reactions of a group of unknown people, who feel coddled and important and may think it is necessary to make judgements whether they have an opinion or not – why should these reactions be considered more valid than the best judgement of designers and engineers who have spent many successful years in the business? Yet, from the marketing point of view, although negative reaction to one specific element may not turn the customer away, why risk it?

And so the clinic results become part of the process. For J'89, the positive reaction from the clinics helped keep the wraparound door concept alive and stimulated a re-design of both the front end and the wheel covers.

When J'89 was launched in Germany as the Vectra, the launch presentation to dealers and the press focused on a rather different aspect of the development process: the technology used to create the car. Vectra, the dealers were told, was 'born in the computer'. And the machine that received star billing in the show was the mighty Cray supercomputer.

This approach did not sit very well with many of the J'89 designers and engineers, because it represented a fundamental misunderstanding of the role the computer plays in the design and engineering process. The computer has many capabilities, but conception is not one of them.

The Cray supercomputer is another glamorous technological marvel, perhaps even more glamorous than the wind tunnel, and even less scrutable. Seymour Cray is one of the most interesting and eccentric computer designers in the US, possibly in the world. He did not design the first supercomputer, but the Minnesota-based company he founded in 1972, Cray Research, has become the world leader in supercomputing.

Cray himself is an engineer who actually designs the machines, working closely with a small team of experts in remote locations in the middle of America. He is currently engaged in the development of a new generation supercomputer, the Cray 3, using a technology based on gallium arsenide rather than the traditional silicon.

Cray is also in a battle to retain leadership in the field, coming under heavy attack from big Japanese computer makers such as Fujitsu, and from a new approach to engineering computing, the minisupercomputer. But, for now, Cray is the supercomputing king. Of the 300 supercomputers in use in the world today, nearly 200 of them are built by Cray Research. The auto industry is one of the principal markets for the machines, and it has grown rapidly. As of 1985, there were just two Crays in use in the auto industry, by 1988 there were fifteen. The country buying supercomputers faster than any other is, of course, Japan.

The Cray supercomputer is tucked away in the Electronic Data Systems (EDS), a nondescript building adjacent to the Design Information Processing Centre where all commercial and engineering data processing for Opel is done and facing the Technical Development Centre. It is surrounded by a chain-link fence and the entrance is protected by a locking gate of stainless steel worthy of a prison.

Once through the gate and into reception, you are stopped by a uniformed guard and required to sign in and go through a variety of formalities designed to let you know this is not a place to fool around in. All the GM computer systems, including the ones in Rüsselsheim, are linked via satellite to the system in Detroit, and administered by EDS. The Cray at Rüsselsheim is the one GM supercomputer dedicated to production development; a second one, in Detroit, is used solely for research.

Dr Jurgen Lowsky is Manager for Engineering Application Support of the Technical Services Group, and he is an energetic, enthusiastic man in his late thirties, who obviously enjoys presiding over a computer centre that boasts one of the most powerful computers on earth.

The control centre for the computer operations of the entire plant is a film-set vision come to life – new and spotlessly clean, cool, with the kind of cleansed air that you find only in 99% clean rooms and computer facilities like this one.

Along one wall runs a long console with two flanking wings, all embedded with dozens of computer screens, glowing with numbers and text, constantly changing, blinking, rewriting. Also set into the console are many telephone handsets, which buzz with a discreet, understated urgency. The room seems slightly underpopulated, considering the ubiquity of computer screens. Those who do operate there move noiselessly around the room with a singular sense of purpose.

Dr Lowsky leads us to a screen on one of the wing walls. This is devoted to the Cray and displays all the jobs that are waiting to go through the computer, which one is being worked on and which is completed and the number of bits each has required in processing. As we watch, a new job slips into the Cray and, it seems, has been processed almost instantly, and a new one accepted. After allowing us a few moments of hypnosis before this silent screen, Dr Lowsky unlocks another door with his coded card and admits us to the innermost sanctum where the machines themselves quietly do their work.

It is a big space filled with big computers. Off to the left are rows of IBM central processing units, standing like so many buildings along streets of corridors, blue and constantly whirring. Plunked down at some distance from the IBMs, and with nothing much around it but open space, is the Cray X-MP14. It looks like a condensed, computer version of Stonehenge – a series of rectangular shafts, standing nearly two metres high, describing the better part of a circle. They are yellow and plain-faced, with no blinking lights, no buttons. Placed around the outside perimeter of the computer is what looks like a shrink-wrapped window seat, a place where computer technicians might pause for a quick personal chat, or take lunch. Housed in these settees, however, is the Freon cooling apparatus which reduces the furious temperatures generated by the Cray as it works.

Dr Lowsky removes a panel from one of the rectangular shafts. Inside, it seems, there is nothing but lengths of wire. Although you know that each wire must be very carefully connected and perfectly placed, the impression is that some careless electrician, recently finished with a home wiring job, has found himself with far too many short lengths of wire and stuffed them into the nearest cupboard as quickly as he can. The cabinet is filled to choking with wire, and it is wire that does the work. 'If someone were to pull out one of these wires . . .?' 'That is why I am standing so close to you,' says Dr Lowsky, with a slightly threatening smile.

You do not order a Cray from the factory and receive it in cardboard boxes. The computer is assembled by a team of ten Cray people who bring their crates and their wire and their tools with them and spend a week putting the computer together, much of which time is spent connecting the wires. The Cray, in short, is essentially hand made. Once it is assembled, two Cray technicians come to live with you; they are there at all times to attend to the machine.

Promotional writers like to write about the capabilities and speed of a Cray, sometimes comparing its performance to that of a 'regular' or general purpose computer, meaning an IBM mainframe. The Cray is an order of magnitude faster (at least ten times as fast) than an IBM 3090 mainframe, which is considered a big computer. The IBM can perform up to one hundred million floating point calculations per second, the Cray can do up to 236 million.

Dr Lowsky describes it this way: 'A year contains thirty million seconds, which means it would take one technician doing one calculation per second seven years to do what the Cray can do in just one second.' Or seven technicians one year, or 4,000 engineers about two hours.

Of course, these comparisons between machine time and people time are fatuous. If there were no Cray, GM would not hire seven technicians and put them to work for a year on the problem the Cray would have solved. Nor are 4,000 engineers left idle for two hours for every second of supercomputing time. The Cray does not replace any existing effort; rather it allows engineers to do more of what they were already doing – but more quickly, with less manual effort and a great deal more precision. In some cases, it allows them to see what they could not otherwise see (what happens inside the engine during combustion) and simulate events that would be impossible to create in real life (freezing a crash partway through).

In the development of J'89, the major contribution of the Cray – representing about 40% of the supercomputing time spent on the project – was in the area of structural analysis. Another 20% was spent in crashworthiness analysis and 20% in aerodynamic testing.

A supercomputer is basically a monster number-cruncher, capable of performing at high speeds the huge number of calculations necessary for complicated programmes. But the computer does not work the way your desktop PC does. You don't talk to it, interact with it in real time. All the work that goes into the Cray must first be prepared by one of the IBM mainframes, using one of a variety of pre-processing programs. Incorporated into the pre-processing information is the geometry of the car, which comes from the database created through digitization; the characteristics of the materials that will be used (at what force will a piece of sheet-metal of particular thickness start to deform); and the forces and constraints that the body and its materials will be subjected to. Once this information is prepared, then the large body of 'problems' represented by the car is broken down into thousands of smaller problems that the computer can solve. J'89 represented some 14,000 individual problems. The engineers refer to these as 'finite elements'.

The goal of structural analysis is to arrive at a design that has the necessary strength and stiffness required for taut handling and safety in a crash, combined with the lowest possible weight – for the highest fuel economy – and the most elegant arrangement of structural members, for ease of manufacture and ease of use.

The fundamental physical law that applies to structural analysis is Hooke's law of elasticity (named after the seventeenth-century English physicist Robert Hooke who defined it). According to Dr Lowsky, it describes 'within certain conditions, the relationship between a force on a spring and its extension'.

In other words, most solid materials have a certain amount of elasticity: put a stress on one and, up to a limit, it will bounce back. But, when the stress is great enough – when it reaches the elastic limit – the material will be strained, deformed in some way. It will bend, crack, twist, dent. Hooke's law states that the strain will be proportional to the stress, up to that limit.

So the process of structural analysis proceeds by placing a force of a known amount on to a section of material of known characteristics and allowing the Cray to calculate if the stress will cause strain and how severe it will be. Put even more simply, 'If you press here, the computer will calculate what will happen there,' says Lowsky. Once the Cray performs the calculations, the data are returned to the IBM, which post-processes them in forms the engineers can study, primarily graphics.

Because the Cray is so fast and powerful, it allows the engineers to evaluate many more body designs and configurations than they could before (some 120 for J'89). It is a kind of high-speed trial and error process that would be far too cumbersome, time-consuming and exasperating to do in the conventional way – from full-scale drawing to full-scale prototype.

An easy-to-understand example of a tangible result of the process for J'89 is in the design of the saloon's boot lid. The objective was to create a boot lid that opened to bumper height, making it a shorter lift to get packages into the boot. The programme also called for the rear seat both to fold forward and to have a load-through from the boot, and for a rear door of increased size. All these enlarged openings in the frame reduce the integrity, strength and stiffness of the car.

Working with the Cray, the engineers were able to determine how much stiffening was needed to compensate for these features, and where it should go. The result is that J'89 is the only intermediate car on the market with both a bumper height boot lid opening and a load-through back seat.

Supercomputers are being used more and more for crash testing, as well. According to Lowsky, 'You can run a car against the wall without destroying the car and without destroying the computer. And you can do it within the computer as often as you want.' The hand-made prototypes cost from 500,000 DM to 1,500,000 DM (£180,000-£540,000). It costs about 2,000 DM (£720) per hour to operate the Cray, and a crash test takes only about ten hours – a saving of about 480,000 DM (over £172,000).

With the supercomputer, you can send J'89 against a fixed object at a predetermined speed, watch what happens within ninety milliseconds and create a new picture every two milliseconds – which you cannot do even by looking at film taken with a high speed motion picture camera of a real crash. Through colour coded graphics, you can see where and when strains develop in the body, extremely high stress points appearing as bruise-like red patches.

The advantages of computer crash testing are not only the speed and detail with which the information can be delivered. In order to analyse the results of a real crash, you have physically to cut into the structure of the car to look at the internal elements and in doing so it is impossible not to disturb or change the structure. But the supercomputer affords an inside view of what has happened during the crash, with no distortions.

The data and graphics that emerge from the Cray help the engineers assess and analyse many of the characteristics of the car's behaviour. In addition to deformation, they can study vibrations and the effect those vibrations might have on individual components. They can calculate heat transfer from outside the body to the interior through specific components, which is useful in developing heating, ventilation and insulation systems.

But just how much stress is acceptable? How much vibration? How much heat should be allowed to seep through the structural components? 'That's experience,' says Dr Lowsky. In other words, the supercomputer provides the data, but the engineers decide. Another limitation of computer-simulated crash tests is that they are not yet legally acceptable, and so they must be verified by real tests.

We were two minutes late for the crash test because we couldn't find the proper entrance to the crash-test facility. Knowing that Fritz Lohr was waiting – and you do not keep a member of the Board of Managers waiting – we finally ditched the car in what was certainly an unauthorized spot and dashed into the open garage.

We raced past a prototype vehicle, poised on a yellow and black chequered skid, staring towards a blank wall. Three men, one of them Lohr, stood behind a steel barrier running parallel to the track. We joined them. Plastic safety glasses were passed around and we put them on. Without a greeting to us, Lohr raised a powerful arm, pointed a short finger and said 'Okay!'

Immediately, the car on the skid hurtled into motion, dragged forward by cables; it picked up speed and, in less than a second, was in a head-on collision with the wall. Seeing it, you think immediately of those hopeful lies you tell yourself as you drive down the motorway. I'll have time to slip on my seat belt if it's off. I'm alert, I can avoid whatever is going to happen. The speed – this car was travelling at 50 kph – is startling and the damage is all done so quickly and with such a sharp CRACK! The four crash dummies inside are thrown forward with a frightening force, and rocket backwards again. They have no expression and do not complain.

Fritz Lohr smiled. The other members of the party smiled wanly in return, and chuckled a bit. The test was not funny, but smiling and chuckling seemed the only reasonable response. It was such a quick waste of money, for one thing, that it seemed like a rich man burning a £100 note for fun. It was also striking theatre. For a moment we had 'suspended our disbelief' and been fooled into thinking these dummies were real people. For a moment we were imagining the pain and terror involved in such a crash. But then we realized it was an illusion, we felt foolish that we had been so emotionally dragged in, so we felt sheepish, and so we chuckled.

The test car is a handmade prototype, rigged with a variety of sensors and measuring instruments, and, as it crashes against the barrier, it is filmed by a high speed motion picture camera. The test that we have seen is to check the positioning of the rear seat-belts. After the test the technicians rush up to the car and begin removing the sensors and collected data, and we are ushered in to a small room to watch a film compilation of other crash tests.

There are many more types of crash tests performed than you see in television advertisements, and they are filmed from alarming angles that bring the terror and chaos of a car crash vividly to life. And, of course, the tests are shot with a high speed camera which, on playback, produces an eerie, nightmarish ultra-slow motion. The standard 50 kph barrier test – in which a test car is crashed head-on into a fixed wall – is equivalent to a two-car, head-on collision at 120 kph. This test is severe enough to cover some 93% of all accidents that actually occur on the road.

The barrier test is shot from a pit below the track and you watch as that huge chunk of steel or aluminium or cast iron, your engine, and all its connecting bits are skewed and twisted out of place. The test is also conducted with two small child-sized dummies in the back seat without seat-belt restraints and you watch as they fly as if in acrobatic hypnosis out of their seats, perform flips and contortions that you know cannot be possible if bones and flesh are not being torn or folded to accommodate the feats. They crash head-first into the dashboard, or shoot like rockets out through the windscreen.

With the camera mounted inside the car, it is subjected to a roll-over test. Both front seat occupants are clearly visible as the car hurtles along until it reaches a ramp that lifts one of its wheels off the ground – enough to send the car rolling over, down a concrete track. As the car rolls, you watch driver and front-seat passenger, again in ultra-slow motion, as heads wobble, bodies lurch towards the ceiling, then plunge back into the seats, as the driver's arm flies out of the window, in danger of being crushed. At the end of some fifteen minutes' worth of film watching, everyone in the room looks a bit nauseous.

The tests are designed to provide measurements that relate to occupant protection, fuel system integrity, steering penetration (how far into the occupant area the steering column protrudes on impact) and general structural integrity. The modern car is the safest it has ever been in terms of occupant protection, due to a number of innovations including two structural developments we all know about – and which, incidentally, GM, along with several other manufacturers including Mercedes, claim as their own inventions. The first is the crumple zone, the second the collapsible, impact-absorbing steering column.

Here, the role of marketing enters into the development process again, because features that are safety-related often don't look that way to the car buyer. 'It took us years to convince people that the crumple zone was good,' says Lohr. 'They saw crashes with the front end all crumpled up and they thought the car was too weak.'

So it took a great deal of public relations, advertising and other marketing communications efforts to make people understand that the front end of the car was *supposed* to scrunch up like a soft-drink can on impact – that was, in fact, what absorbed the impact. The importance of the impact-absorbing steering column also required extensive communications efforts, but that had a rationale that could be intuitively grasped: no one likes the idea of being impaled by a 10 cm round steel column.

Although GM Europe has not promoted its products on their safety record, as Volvo has, its record is very good. In fact, J'81 – Opel Ascona/Vauxhall Cavalier – was named one of the six best cars for safety in a study carried out by the Swedish firm, Folksam. Their study involved analysis of 700,000 car accidents which involved 34,000 personal injuries. Accidents were rated on a scale for severity from one to six (one being a mild injury, six being immediate death). The results, published in 1987, showed that J'81 ranked with larger models, including the Volvo 240 and 740/760 and Mercedes and VW models, as one of the world's safest cars.

*

Left: Marine engineers of the Vauxhall Iron Works use the river launch *Jabberwock* to test a petrol engine of the type that will power the first Vauxhall car. The photograph was probably taken on the Thames near the original company site in London's Vauxhall district, around 1901.

Right: Carl Jörns, Opel test driver, was a winner in trials at the International Automobile Week held in Nice, France, in 1909.

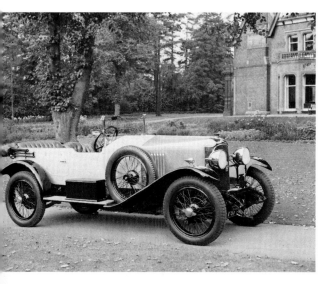

Left: Perhaps the best known of Vauxhall's early models, the E-type, or 30/98, was first developed in 1913 and produced from 1919 to 1926.

William Crapo ('Billy') Durant (1860–1947), founder of General Motors and then President from 1916 to 1920. Alfred Sloan described Durant as being 'very persuasive, soft-spoken and ingratiating'. Durant's chaotic entrepre- neurial style, however, caused him to be forced out of General Motors and, when he died, he was virtually penniless and forgotten.

Above: Alfred Pritchard Sloan, Jr (1875–1966) joined General Motors in 1916, and served as President and Chairman from 1923 to 1946. Sloan (to the right of the man at the microphone) is considered to be the father of many of GM's organizational structures and operating procedures, and led the company into the European market in the 1920s.

Below: A group gathers outside the main factory gate at Rüsselsheim, Germany, to mark the occasion of the purchase of Opel by General Motors in 1929. Son of the founder Adam Opel, Wilhelm von Opel (fifth from right) became President. Fritz von Opel (a grandson of Adam) is fifth from left.

Left: The first Vauxhall Cavalier, launched in October 1975. It began life as an import, being produced in the Opel factory at Antwerp, which brought protests against this 'foreign' car from dealers and the press.

Right: The Cavalier Mark II, the first J car, launched in 1981. The sporty shape, good performance, fuel-efficiency, reliability and front-wheel-drive package made the car a success. The car was responsible for the 'regeneration of Vauxhall' and became the bestselling car in the intermediate segment in 1984–5.

Left: The Ford Sierra was expected to carry on the popularity of the Cortina, one of the UK's most successful and popular cars ever. But its styling was so radical for the time that buyers balked at first, some calling the car a 'jelly mould'. The Sierra and Cavalier have been arch rivals in the intermediate segment throughout the 1980s. The picture shows a 1990 four-wheel-drive variant of the Sierra.

Right: Wayne K. Cherry, Director of Design for GM Europe since 1983. He was born in Indianapolis, Indiana, in 1937, joined GM in Detroit in 1962, and was with Vauxhall in the UK from 1965 to 1983.

Below: Friedrich W. Lohr, GME Technical Director, presides over the development process of new models at the GME Technical Development Centre in Rüsselsheim, Germany.

Above: Joseph Schulze of the Aerodynamic Group measures a fifth-scale clay model of the Calibra, the coupé based on the J car platform. These models are based on third-scale models and full-scale drawings developed by Design, and are used for wind tunnel testing early in the development process.

Left: Erhard Schnell (left) is the Chief Designer of Studio 3 in the Design Centre at Rüsselsheim, where the new J car was created. The development process of each new model begins with sketches that explore a variety of ideas for shape and exterior features.

Left: After third-scale models have been developed, full-scale models are created of both exterior and interior. This J'89 facia is modelled in clay.

Right: Several front ends are developed for the new model. These show differences in grille configurations.

Left: A designer manipulates a two-dimensional 'Oscar', which can be adjusted to simulate the dimensions of about 95 per cent of the population. Oscars are used in developing driver position and key dimensions of the car, including pedal distance headroom and the H-point – the theoretical pivot point of the body.

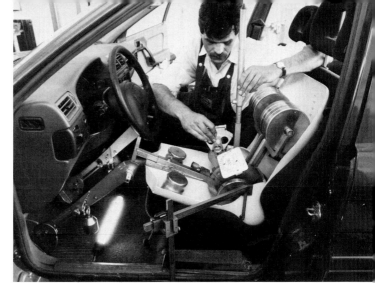

Right: A technician works with an anthropometer, a mechanical measuring device which simulates a human being, to refine such factors as angle of vision and chair position.

Left: A modeller smooths the clay surface of the front fender where it joins the bonnet and door frame in the area known as the 'three countries corner'.

Right: Fifth-scale clay models are based on full-scale, full-colour drawings.

Left: Fritz von Opel at the wheel of the rocket-powered Rak 2, during a demonstration to the press and invited guests in Berlin, 23 May 1928. The Opel firm began experimenting with rocket power at the suggestion of an engineer who saw it as the first step towards spaceship production. The 550-pound-thrust rockets, twenty-four of them, roared von Opel to a speed of about 145 mph – still lower than the land speed record of 208 mph.

Right: Joseph Schulze positions a clay model of J'89 in the fifth-scale wind tunnel at the University of Stuttgart facility, partly financed by Opel. The Institute has been operating since 1930, making it one of the oldest automotive wind tunnel/ vehicle development centres in the world.

Left: J'89 faces a 220 kph gale of wind in the full-scale tunnel at Stuttgart. The car is positioned on a platform, described by the circle in the floor, which rests on a balance. The balance contains several strain transducers that measure the weight of the car at different points. Aerodynamic qualities are determined by comparing the measurements taken with and without wind flow.

Right: The exterior surface of the finalized clay model is digitized. A technician touches some 10,000 points on the car body to define the surfaces, and enters them into a computer database. The surfaces are then 'sweetened' – smoothed and perfected – using computer-aided design programs, and the data become the basis for all future design, engineering and manufacturing work.

Left: The control room at the Information Processing Centre of EDS (Electronic Data Systems). Here the Cray supercomputer is managed and satellite links between other GM computer systems worldwide are maintained.

Right: The Cray X-MP 14 supercomputer is used primarily for structural analysis of new models. The low benches surrounding the towers house Freon apparatus that cools the machine as it operates.

Above: The 50 kph barrier crash test, filmed by a high-speed motion picture camera. The crash test, which is severe enough to simulate conditions in over 90 per cent of all road accidents, is required as part of the Type Approval process.

Below: Dummies representing a female and a male child are positioned for a crash test of seat belts and child safety seat.

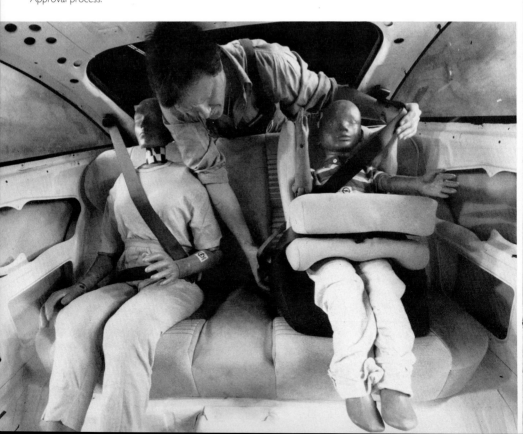

Above: A section of the test track at Dudenhofen Proving Ground, Germany. The irregular paving stone is generally known as pavé, and a drive along this track is part of endurance testing, designed to assess shock absorber, steering and suspension performance.

Below: An aerial view of the Millbrook proving ground, near Luton. The large circle is the five-lane high-speed circuit; the squiggly section in the right foreground is part of the hill route.

Opposite above: Off-line cockpit module assembly was an innovation for production of the new Cavalier. Rather than install the housing, wiring, instruments and controls into the car body as it moves along the assembly line – a tricky and uncomfortable procedure – the components are now assembled as one unit, tested and delivered to the line, when needed, on an automatic guided vehicle (AGV).

Opposite below: Robots accomplish welding operations at the Rüsselsheim assembly line. The plant at Luton is less automated and considerably smaller, producing about 35 cars per hour in comparison to 105 at Rüsselsheim.

Above: Peter Batchelor became Director of Marketing for Vauxhall Motors in 1986, and was responsible for the launch activities of the new Cavalier in 1988–9.

Right: Paul Tosch, Chairman and Managing Director of Vauxhall Motors Ltd (seen here in the passenger seat of a 1904 Vauxhall, now used for rallying), is another long-time GM employee. An engineer by training, he joined the Fisher Body Division (in the US) in 1958. He was brought to the UK in 1986 as head of the Bedford Commercial Vehicles Division and moved to Vauxhall in 1987.

Left: Television commercials were one of the most expensive elements of the most expensive new car launch to date in the UK. The ad opened with a fictional 1950s-style TV programme called 'Step Into the Future', which showed what the 'motor car of tomorrow' might be like.

Above: The new Cavalier was revealed to dealers 'in the metal' for the first time at a special event held at the Royal Lancaster Hotel, London, at the end of August 1988. The elaborate staging involved multiple projections, live singers and dancers and five cars which were revealed at various points on the purpose-built stage.

Left: The symbolic delivery of the new car takes place in an event known as the 'driveaway'. In 1981 about 100 J cars were driven from the Luton plant by dealers.

Above: The lowest specification, standard Cavalier notchback, seen from its most appealing angle. The rising wedge shape, smooth surface, high rear-end, flush fittings, integrated body-coloured bumpers and smooth reflection line make the car look modern, but not radical, in design.

Below: The five platforms of the GM Europe range, seen in Opel badges: from front, Astra/Kadett, Cavalier/Vectra, Nova/Corsa, Carlton/Omega, and Senator.

Left: The solar-powered GM Sunraycer won the 1987 World Solar Challenge, a 1950-mile race of solar-powered vehicles across Australia. Technologies developed for Sunraycer have been modified and incorporated in the GM electric-powered car called Impact. The scales that cover the surface of the tail of the vehicle are solar cells.

Below: GM's Impact, an electric-powered vehicle, is the latest revision in a long line of experimental electric vehicles that GM has developed since 1916. GM announced no plans for production when the car was unveiled in early 1990, but hinted that mass production was a possibility.

The business of testing the vehicle and all its parts is a major part of the engineering and design process. The Cray is just one tool used in the process; there are many others. There is a whole floor at one of the many buildings of the Opel plant given over to various mechanical devices which simulate the wear and tear a given car is likely to be subjected to during its lifetime. Seats are pounded, shock absorbers are plunged up and down, doors are opened and closed endlessly. This is the pedestrian, mechanical and non-glamorous end of the testing business.

The real-life testing takes place outside, both on public roads and at specialized test facilities around the world, called proving grounds. The proving grounds are private and allow manufacturers to conduct a variety of tests that could not be achieved on public roads, primarily because of the speeds, complication and need for consistency and repeatability involved.

They also afford the manufacturer the security which, as we have seen, is a critical issue during the development phase. The major GME proving ground in Europe is at Dudenhofen, just an hour from Rüsselsheim. Taken in short doses, driving at the proving ground is pure fun. Here you are on a system of one-way private roads including hills, rough sections, salt and fresh water baths, a skid circuit and a sloped, circular track. There are no police in attendance, although there are published speed limits for many of the different roadways, and you get the feeling – with safety belt securely fastened and no on-coming traffic or mad drivers around – that no motoring harm could possibly befall you.

The pride of Dudenhofen is called the Big Circuit, a three-lane circular roadway, banked in what is known as a cubic parabola. This shape takes advantage of the various forces working on your car as you drive, so that, according to a promotional brochure, 'the inward and downward gravitational forces are exactly counterbalanced by the outward and upward centrifugal forces'.

What this means to the driver is that, at just the right speed for the given lane you are in, you can let go of the steering wheel and the car will continue blissfully forward in its chosen lane without drifting upward or downward. The track has become an eternal straightaway, the perfect place to test a car for high speed motorway driving capabilities.

As you drive the Big Circuit, you experience the eerie feeling of constantly driving uphill, an optical or mental illusion no doubt caused by the bank of the track. As you drive, you feel slightly timid at first, but gradually come to feel invulnerable to those ordinary plagues of the motorway. There are few cars on the track, the road surface is immaculate, all the drivers who do overtake you are professionals. You begin to realize that most of the hazards of driving have nothing to do with driving itself, but have to do with people and unexpected phenomena. If it were just you and your machine, you'd have to go some really to get in trouble.

Just as you are thinking these calming thoughts, you glance in the rear-view mirror and see a strange black vehicle catapulting towards you at a great rate. You slide down into the middle lane and the car zooms past. You ask, but your guide will not tell you, what the car is. Judging from its curiously lumpy body, it appears to be a component test car.

When testing some new mechanical system or component, the Dudenhofen engineers rig up a makeshift body to disguise the car, and to provide just the requisite protection for the driver. Some of these structures are bizarre in appearance, resembling the homemade plywood boats you often see rotting in suburban back gardens. They tear around the tracks on endless circuits, with drivers working in shifts and sometimes driving through the night.

Within the circumference of the Big Circuit, the Dudenhofen proving ground comprises nearly 40 km of roads and tracks, and on them the engineers spend their time turning, accelerating, braking, rattling the car – trying to establish the limits of its endurance and performance and to find the little 'gremlins' of either design or manufacture.

In the UK, J'89 was tested at the Millbrook proving ground, just north of Luton. Here a staff of some 230 people – including drivers, engineers, mechanics and others – are kept busy twenty-four hours a day in three shifts, helping various manufacturers develop their cars to meet legal standards, realize design goals and satisfy durability standards. The role of the private proving grounds has evolved considerably over the thirty to forty years since their inception.

According to Rodney Calvert, Director and General Manager at Millbrook, proving-ground tests were imprecise in the beginning. 'It seemed like, if you did so many of this test, the incidence of things falling off was less,' he says. Or tests might evolve the other way round. If a production car showed a tendency to a particular problem, a test would be devised that would make it happen so it could be studied. 'Now, what do we have to do in a test to make that happen? Oh, a hundred starts on a steep hill, let's say.'

Testing became even more important with the opening of the motorways in the UK. 'People in motor cars designed to travel at 50 mph were batting down the motorways at dangerous speeds, like 65 and 70 mph. Engines were failing and things were blowing up. There was every problem you can think of,' recalls Calvert.

Over time, the idea of 'equivalencies' evolved – that so many repetitions of a proving-ground test were equivalent to a number of years or miles of motorway driving. But 'it's nonsense to say there's an absolute equivalent,' says Calvert. 'People who quote to you that one thousand miles of pavé [irregular paving bricks] are equivalent to 100,000 miles on the road – it's bullshit. Because 100,000 miles that I drive is going to be different from the 100,000 that you drive. But there's a *feeling* that there's an equivalent. And most manufacturers then drive their cars to those procedures. Recently manufacturers have gone out and actually measured cars in customers' hands. What do they really do? Are we overtesting in some areas, and therefore overdesigning? Are we missing some things out, some things that customers do that we don't test?'

These real-life tests involve attaching electronic sensors and a 'little black box' to the customer's car, and gathering data for some weeks, months or years. This system 'measures all sorts of things that happen. Brakes – how often they're used, how hard they're used. How hard you accelerate, how fast you travel, how fast you stay at different speeds, how long you stay in different gears.'

Whether the traditional method of testing by equivalencies makes sense or not, however, testing has contributed greatly over the years to improvements in the reliability and durability of the car. 'The general product around these days is absolutely astonishing,' contends Calvert. 'And the progress has been the most rapid in the last ten to fifteen years. Not long ago I used to expect something dastardly to happen. I'd travel around with wire and tape. I'd think, oh, it's a hundred mile journey – I'll probably make it. Now I don't even know what a spanner is.'

At Millbrook, as at Dudenhofen, it is possible to simulate driving conditions of almost every imaginable type: country driving and city driving; smooth, bumpy, sandy or wet surfaces. One of the most gruelling tests, for both driver and car, is the Belgian pavé. This is a stretch of road set with chunky paving blocks (which were originally part of the Royal Mile in Edinburgh) set into the earth at heights varying by as much as 6 cm. A ride along the pavé rattles the bones of a car in a way designed to loosen any suspect bolt or weld.

The Millbrook 'hill climb' must rank as the most amusing of all the track routes. It is a course of just under 5 km, with a series of artificial grades of up to 26 degrees. That is an exceptionally steep hill, of the type you would expect to find creeping down the cliffs to some tiny coastal town in the south-west of England, St Ives for example. But here, with the abandon you reserve for when driving a hire car, you can fly up the steepest hills and take the tight corners as sharply as you dare, knowing there are no lumbering beer lorries waiting on the far side. It is, for those whose profession it is not, like a schoolboy's dream holiday.

Testing for J'89 was also carried out on public roads. The estimate is that J'89 was driven millions of km, in countries including Germany, Italy, France, Australia, the United States and Canada, over the course of two summers and two winters. Many kilometres were driven in the fiercely hot roads in Arizona, in the American South-west, where the test is to see how the car holds up under extremely hot conditions. From January to April, the team repaired to Arjeplog, Sweden, about 80 km south of the polar circle, to test the cars on a frozen lake and to see how well the engine starts at temperatures of −35 to −40 degrees Celsius, and to analyse the behaviour of the four-wheel-drive system.

In southern Spain, the engineers check to see how much dust enters the passenger compartment, to see what interior rattles and squeaks develop, how brittle the brakes become. In the Alps, Italy and Florida, they test the paint colours to see how well they stand up to the intense ultraviolet radiation.

Hans-Jürgen Pache, an engineer in packaging, sometimes acted as a test driver. 'Everybody tells me I'm one of the lucky ones. But we've just been through a programme starting at the end of January – ten days throughout the United States and up to the northern portion of Canada, and it is exactly ten days, with 600 miles each day of driving. And if you're not used to driving 600 miles a day, it's not fun.'

The marketing objective for J'89 was to be competitive with the compact high-technology cars. And that meant offering anti-lock braking, central locking, sixteen-valve engines and electronic engine management and – the technology that is currently the fashion – four-wheel-drive.

Switzerland has the highest number of four-wheel-drive vehicles registered in Europe. This makes sense. There are many mountains in Switzerland and it snows a lot. But the United Kingdom with its high concentration of car buffs has, in recent years, adopted four-wheel-drive as the latest and toniest technology to have. For Range Rover drivers, commuting from Buckinghamshire to London, four-wheel-drive is an unnecessary option; in fact, it can cause more problems than it prevents.

The reason is that people driving vehicles equipped with four-wheel-drive feel invulnerable. Because a four-wheel-drive vehicle has much greater traction than a two-wheel-drive car, drivers feel that they can attack any road with impunity – no matter how icy, snowy, muddy – and live to tell the tale. However, four-wheel-drive is no substitute for good driving and prudent judgement, and I have heard at least one tale of a driver manoeuvring confidently down an icy alpine track buttressed against fate by four-wheel-drive and disappearing over the verge.

But the engineers' lot is not to reason why, that is for the marketing men in Zurich and the packagers in the UK and the Product Policy Committee. If it appears that the appetite for new technology is likely to lead significant portions of the buying public to go for four-wheel-drive, so be it. ABS (anti-lock braking system) was one of the recent technologies to create a similar stir: it has become standard on many models, and is bound to become standard on most models within the next decade.

It is also in the nature of the car manufacturing business to continue developing new technologies and technical refinements; that is what the great evolution of the automobile is all about. The good engineers want to keep breaking new ground, finding new solutions. And so, although it may be that most of the public is perfectly satisfied with their current drive, handling, steering and performance characteristics, GME has the problem, and the advantage, of having a squadron of engineers who are constantly looking for new things to do.

They have to be kept interested and excited and looking forward to their day at the drafting table. They are also supported by the GM Research Laboratories back in Detroit, where engineers and research scientists are constantly engaged in basic research into almost every discipline and technology that might bear upon the nature of a car – from alternative fuels to alternative engines, to cross currents, to the psychology of perception, and so on and so on.

But beyond such technology faddism, the engineers also work to reduce road noise, improve performance and fuel economy, increase reliability, and improve safety for both occupants and so-called 'third parties' – cyclists and pedestrians whom you might run into. And so J'89 is a catalogue of improvements and innovations including overlapping doors that won't jam shut in a crash, rear-seat headrests that stay fixed to the rear shelf when the seat folds down, improved corrosion protection, and increased use of sound-dampening materials.

All of these changes, particularly those that affect ride and handling, contribute to that old characteristic: personality.

The excitement of developing these technologies, coupled with the demands of forcing them into packages acceptable to the marketplace, produces some ambivalence on the part of vehicle engineers. How do the engineers feel about what they do? Does one model give them more pleasure than another?

Hans-Jürgen offers a wry smile. 'No,' he says, 'I hate them all the same.'

7 · PILOT AND PACKAGE

'It's no good having a car equipped like Starship Enterprise. It will be non-competitive in the market.'

Peter Negus, Manager of Product Planning

The customary way to reach Vauxhall headquarters from London is to drive up the M1 and get off at Junction 10. From there, it's a journey of no more than 3 km to the plant – along the A1083, around a roundabout, followed by a glide down a gently sloping wedge of hill. However, when I first visited the plant (and for months thereafter), Junction 10 was closed for roadworks, which meant getting off at Junction 9 and making our way along twisty B roads flanked with dense hedgerows. My colleague and driver on that first visit was unsure of the route, but we soon left the lanes behind and found ourselves in Luton centre, entrapped in a one-way system that required quick decision-making.

There were a few aggravating moments, and then, suddenly, with one bend of the road, all the confusion fell away. We found ourselves on a patch of road that my colleague recognized: the familiar round-about beckoned in the sunlight ahead. We swooped round it, shot off to the left, glided smoothly down the gentle grade and there, in the distance, lay Vauxhall Motors.

The most distinctive feature of the Vauxhall facility is the modern paint plant, completed in 1986 – boxy grey towers rising modestly into the milky sky. Apart from that, the facility looks as if it has sunken into the shallow valley that contains it. The long, low plant buildings seem to belong in sepia-toned photographs from a nostalgic coffee-table book about the industrial revolution. If Vauxhall were to give up assembling cars here, the buildings would probably be sold for conversion to luxury flats.

This is the town that used to catch cold, as John Butterfield put it, whenever Vauxhall sneezed. But the 1970s were agonizing years for Vauxhall, the 1980s were mostly nerve-wracking and the reduction (by nearly two thirds) of the work force and the rise of other local businesses mean that Luton is no longer solely a Vauxhall company town.

As of this writing, Vauxhall Motors are enjoying a period of prosperity unlike any they have enjoyed before. The company is making a profit – £263.3 million in 1989. The product line is strong and complete, with good cars from small to large. Cavaliers are selling as fast as they can be built. The Rover Group continues to slip (to about 13% of the market) and Vauxhall has moved inexorably past them to second place in sales in the UK, with about 16% of the total market. And, in November of 1989, the Cavalier became the best-selling car in the UK, selling nearly 12,000 copies, triumphantly pushing the Ford trio (Escort, Sierra and Fiesta) down one notch. Cavalier was the UK best seller again in January and February of 1990. To Vauxhall, Ford does not seem uncatchable any more. In fact, according to Director of Sales and Marketing, Peter Batchelor, Vauxhall adopted an internal slogan 'Leadership in the '90s' – a clear, but slightly guarded, declaration of war on 'Mr Ford'.

At the time of the J'89 launch, however, you could see this was a company still recovering from the difficult times it had suffered – at the hands of the marketplace, its competitors, and from its own parent company. The most obvious evidence was to be found in the long, quiet corridors lined with empty offices, in the disused buildings and empty lots, in the drab and weary look of the facility in general, and the atmosphere of the workplace. Laughter and animated conversation were in short supply. Senior managers were still bunkered at S block, a nondescript building erected in 1907. At some of the other buildings there was no reception area or receptionist at all, just unattended telephones and photocopied personnel telephone number lists taped outside locked doors.

Car manufacturing plants are not, by nature, cheerful places but there was little about the appearance of the Luton facility that would lead the visitor to believe it was a thriving, dynamic, modern, customer-orientated company.

For years after the transfer of the design and engineering activities to Rüsselsheim in the 1970s, when Vauxhall ceased to be a fully-fledged vehicle manufacturer and became an assembly and marketing operation, the company had been like a formerly obese man still wearing his old clothes: it was difficult to see how lean and fit and healthy he might be inside the flapping trousers and sagging jacket.

The problem, therefore, was primarily one of a poor image and a lack of self-confidence – and most industry people know it. Writing in *Car* magazine Daniel Ward wrote, 'Even Ford executives will privately concede that Vauxhall has a better car line-up than its own, but the Vauxhall company image is still very lacklustre.'

'We're a bit like the child that's really not too confident,' says Peter Batchelor, Executive Director of Sales and Marketing. 'We're perceived as being followers rather than leaders. And with perceptions and realities there is a long, long lag before perceptions catch up.'

Batchelor, the man most responsible for creating a new set of perceptions about the venerable Vauxhall, is another long-serving Vauxhall man, in a long-serving Vauxhall family. His father, R.H. Batchelor, joined the company in 1919, fresh out of the army, as a car tester. When his son joined Vauxhall in 1954, the father had worked his way up (through service, parts and export sales) and was serving as Export Director. Young Batchelor started as an apprentice in the components arm of General Motors, AC Delco, and qualified as a chartered engineer.

In 1959, he asked his boss in Dunstable if he could apply for a new position in Coventry, selling original equipment (that is, GM-manufactured products sold to be fitted in other makers' vehicles). The boss was sceptical but Batchelor said, 'Give me six months.' Although he found himself 'dealing with chief engineers who'd forgotten more than I ever knew,' he was nevertheless successful and 'ended up being sales director for Europe, for original equipment.'

Then, in 1980, 'right out of the blue, I was transferred across to Vauxhall' as Marketing Manager for the Service Parts operation.

'I knew nothing about motor car marketing,' Batchelor remembers, but his lack of experience didn't prevent him from being assigned greater marketing responsibilities for parts, and then being assigned to passenger car marketing in 1984. Then, 'two years later, I got chucked into this job,' as Director of Marketing for Vauxhall Motors Limited. 'I had to learn quick.'

One way Batchelor went about that was to work hard. During the preparations for the launch of the new Cavalier, Batchelor's staff found it difficult to arrive at the office earlier than he did or leave later. Batchelor is a man who wears his position of authority and influence comfortably. When under pressure, he seems to become even more deliberate and measured, rather than giving way to nerves or flares of temper.

At the time of the J'89 launch, Vauxhall's image was not much different from my own first view of its facilities: that is to say, hard to find and, once you did, not terribly impressive. It became Peter Batchelor's job to change all that, but he knew that it 'doesn't happen overnight. It takes a lot of things to change the image of a company.'

Vauxhall had not been helped through its difficult years by the fact that no one had remained in the Vauxhall Chairman's office – or that of the Marketing Director, either – long enough to become a strong representative and spokesman for the company's interests. Just as Batchelor was brought in 'out of the blue', so were many other executives.

Since 1980 there have been four Vauxhall chairmen. They appear from some other GM location or division (Opel, Holden in Australia, the US), stay two or three years to carry out a specific assignment and then are shipped out again when Detroit wants them somewhere else. As one Vauxhall marketing man put it, 'The biggest problem we have when an American executive comes over here is teaching him about the UK market. They have to take a bit of time to get with it. It really affects the whole of our marketing.' The same could apply equally to an Australian or a German executive.

Ferdinand Bieckler, a German, was charged with reducing costs, reorganizing operations and reducing employment, which he did (announcing a cut of 5,700 jobs at one memorable meeting in 1981) and then was reassigned to Rüsselsheim. Then followed Chairman John Fleming (who had been with Opel for a time) along with John Bagshaw (fresh from the US) in the top marketing job.

Fleming and Bagshaw were charged with increasing market share in the UK, an aim which was accomplished thanks primarily to the success of the 1981 Cavalier. Bagshaw was the visible one, a marketing man and an Australian: flamboyant, colourful, sometimes crude, sometimes loud, often charming. When his task was complete, Bagshaw was sent off to Germany. John Fleming left in 1986 to join Cadillac in the US, and Bagshaw returned to Vauxhall to take Fleming's place as Chairman. Then, in November 1987, Bagshaw left for Australia to work with Holden.

Paul Tosch, the current Chairman, was brought to the UK from Detroit in January 1986 to oversee the merger of the Bedford Commercial Vehicles Division with the Japanese manufacturer Isuzu, but the merger became a sale, much to the distress of Vauxhall dealers, and Tosch moved to Vauxhall as Chairman in Bagshaw's wake in 1987.

Tosch began his career with GM in 1958 as a student at General Motors Institute and progressed through various engineering positions. He was involved with the development of J'81 in the US and became Chief Engineer for the Buick-Oldsmobile-Cadillac Group product team in 1984. He is a big man – over 1 metre 80 tall – with an open, friendly manner and, it seems the heart and mind of an engineer. He is one of Detroit's 'car men' and, by most accounts, a quiet, considerate consensus builder.

But, as Albert Lee describes in his book *Call Me Roger*, the shuffling of managers and their priorities produces an understandable reaction on the part of long-term GM staff at locations around the world: they learn to say yes to the new guy but do nothing that will disturb the real programme which could be summed up as 'getting on with it'. 'American company, American bosses,' as one Opel Staffer had put it.

Perhaps if Vauxhall had enjoyed more consistent leadership over the years, the effects of its 'Europeanization' would have been ameliorated sooner. Today, the perception persists that Vauxhall is a pawn in the GM operation, an outlet for German-made, rebadged Opels – a perception that lingers from the days of the first Cavalier launch in 1975, when that is just what the new car was. But the great majority of Cavaliers sold in the UK (nearly 70%) are assembled in the UK, at Luton.

The other Vauxhall plant operating in the UK is at Ellesmere Port (across the Mersey, just south of Liverpool) where the Astra is built. At Luton, however, Vauxhall manufactures virtually none of the components that go into the cars, with the exception of the soft trim. At Ellesmere Port, there is a press line which stamps out the Astra body panels, but floor pans and body pressings for the Cavalier come from Antwerp or Rüsselsheim, the engines from Australia, Austria and South Korea.

It is, of course, standard industry practice for manufacturers to purchase a large percentage of their components from outside suppliers (although GM actually has one of the highest percentages of own-make components, at about 60% worldwide), and Vauxhall is working to acquire a greater percentage of components from UK suppliers. According to Vauxhall Chairman, Paul Tosch, 'We re-sourced £26.5 million worth of material purchases from the Continent to the UK in 1989, which helped to contain our material costs.' Also, it was announced in early 1990 that Vauxhall would produce V6 engines at the Ellesmere Port plant, many for export to the Continent, as part of the effort to correct the internal trade imbalance.

Considering that the Luton plant supplies GM Europe's second most popular car into its biggest market, its capacity is surprisingly small. At Luton, about 40 cars can be completed per hour, as opposed to about 85 per hour at Antwerp, 105 per hour in Rüsselsheim and 80 in Zaragoza, Spain.

The combination of low capacity, few home-made components – which leads to a reliance on suppliers over which Vauxhall has only minimal control – and a constantly shifting cast of characters at the top, has contributed to what was once Vauxhall's number one image problem: supply.

There just weren't enough Vauxhalls available, and dealers didn't trust that there could be. They've watched too often – all through the 1970s when they couldn't get enough of the Mark I Cavalier, in the 1980s when Carltons were in desperately short supply – as opportunities to sell cars slipped through their fingers because there were insufficient cars to sell.

With the new Cavalier, Vauxhall was determined to avoid the problems of short supply, and they would do it in two ways. First, by developing a more productive assembly operation, so that more cars would roll off the assembly line, first time, in saleable condition. Second, by staggering the introduction of models, so that they weren't trying to introduce too many variants at one time.

In the days when Vauxhall was still designing, engineering and building its own cars, there were more quality problems than there are today. Mysterious ailments could develop once the car was on the road that would mystify the local garage mechanic, and even the mechanic at the local dealership. But the Vauxhall engineers back at the plant usually knew what the problem was.

One Vauxhall engineer described the tendency of the Victor model to develop a high-pitched metallic hum when it reached a speed of about 80 kph. The only remedy for it was to open the driver's window which, for some reason, made the noise stop but was not a very satisfactory solution in cold or rainy weather.

If a customer persisted in seeking a better solution, the dealer mechanic would usually call on the factory engineers as a last resort. A factory representative would be dispatched, carrying with him a simple cure: a large glob of adhesive goo. Once at the garage, the engineer would (privately) affix the glob to the inside of the grille, and assure the customer that all was now well without going into much detail about what was wrong or how it had been fixed.

This sort of serious engineering flaw is rarer now than it used to be, thanks in part to the use of computer-aided design and engineering technologies – such as the structural analysis, flutter and vibration programs supported by the Cray supercomputer. The challenge now lies more in the interface between design, engineering and manufacturing – in getting the design off the paper and into the metal accurately, consistently and quickly. The Japanese manufacturers, in particular, have raised the standard of build quality and fit and finish for the volume car.

It is during the pilot phase that the Luton factory learns how to build the new car. The pilot programme involves checking the engineering designs that arrive from Rüsselsheim, analysing the tooling requirements and feasibility, identifying the materials needed and sources for those materials, and training the workforce in building the new car. The checking process for J'89 began in late 1987, and Vauxhall manufacturing engineers began building vehicles in a pilot area of the main plant in February 1988.

Thirty-four pilot vehicles were produced and, as part of the process, some 500 specific areas were identified for improvement – from a ripple in a door panel to the seal around the door handle. A major emphasis for J'89 was, not surprisingly, quality, the watchword of 1980s manufacture.

You've got a manufacturing plant that dates from 1907 (with additions and improvements, of course, made at various stages since then). You've got a staff of manufacturing engineers of about 150. All your product and tooling designs are coming from the central operation in Germany. You've got a workforce that has been building cars in essentially the same manner for at least seven years.

Now you've got a mandate to create cars of 'world class quality', meaning they have to be as good or better than any other car on the market, including those made by the Japanese who are working with much newer plants (such as the Nissan plant in the UK) and probably higher investment levels. How do you go about translating 'quality' into specific procedures and everyday operations?

Peter Bonner was in charge of manufacturing engineering during the pilot programme for J'89. Bonner had joined Vauxhall in 1954 and seen the company through some very difficult times. When he took over the manufacturing engineering job in 1978 he worked with a staff of 1,500 people. At launch, he had 150.

A soft-spoken man who manages to be both precise in his statements and kindly at the same time, he worked in a large office in P block, surrounded by so many empty offices and so much quiet that you felt he could be working in an abandoned building with only a secretary for company.

Theoretically, J'89 should be easier to build than its predecessor, thanks to the integrated development process, with financial and manufacturing people lobbying the designers and engineers to produce a car that is buildable. 'Styling knows the constraints,' says Bonner. 'Wayne Cherry styles something he knows can be made. Right from day one, the stylist has in mind that there are some constraints in the manufacturing area.' This is 'design for manufacture' or as Cherry often terms it, 'forgiving design'.

On the most basic level this means that the car is designed to fit together easily, but it also means that the styling should help compensate for the irregularities and limitations of mass production. For example, gaps and seals between sheet-metal segments and other components (lights, handles, windows) are extremely visible evidence of careful fitting and assembly. By making the shut lines and design lines one and the same, the J'89 designers simply reduced the number of gaps that could go wrong.

Customers notice, or at least sense, these visible details immediately. Are the gaps between sheet-metal panels narrow and of a consistent width? They notice if a round petrol-filler cover fits precisely into the hole allowed for it. They notice if the edges of bonnet or boot close evenly with the edges of the fixed panels on either side of it. They notice if two bits of rubber seal join neatly at a corner, if there is a small smear of adhesive on an interior panel, if a bit of carpet sticks up where it shouldn't. All of these details give outward clues as to the basic quality of the car. If they can't even glue the carpet down successfully, how good can the engine be, how long will the body last?

The issue for a volume manufacturer is not how to get these thousands of details right *eventually*, but how to get them right quickly and the first time. A favourite GM solution in the 1980s (with Chairman Roger Smith as a prime advocate) was the increased use of automation – the push towards the people-less or 'lights-out' factory and CIM, or computer-integrated manufacturing.

Starting up a highly automated plant is a difficult business, as Vauxhall found when they revamped the Ellesmere Port plant in

1984 to build the Astra. 'We had lots of problems. It was far too complex, far too integrated,' says Bonner. 'The cockpit module area was interlinked with the conveyor system. The minute we had a fault, it stopped the whole damned system. It seemed clever on paper, but we didn't see the possibility of a major line failure.'

So, for J'89, Vauxhall was not so eager to rush to automate the Luton plant, although the assembly operations there are relatively antiquated. Welding is accomplished manually, with lines of workers wielding heavy welding guns – none of the great, swirling robots we are accustomed to seeing in car plants.

The Ellesmere Port experience taught a lesson: 'You have to get the process right first, then automate, not the other way round. Getting all the equipment dimensionally accurate, making sure you have a sound and rigid body that conforms to specifications. Getting the ordering right, the sequence of fitting panels. Sometimes automation is done to a predetermined set of parameters and sequence. To change it means a big upheaval. But it's easy to replace a welding tool with a robot,' says Bonner.

To determine how to improve the output of a plant, Bonner and his team first had to consider what was already in place. 'The first constraint is: what have you got out there already? You break the thing up into a series of elements: you make the body, you paint the body, you trim the body, you put the mechanicals in. Now if you're going to change that significantly, you've got a massive problem – if you're going to fix a new concept in building motor cars.'

If the totally automated plant is at one end of the manufacturing scale, then the small team approach – mostly associated with Volvo – is at the other. The idea is that the new car is built at a number of stations and moved between stations on trolleys rather than on conveyors. At each station a group of workers performs a set of tasks that completes a phase of the job, such as assembling the entire cockpit module.

The worker on the conventional assembly line, by contrast, repeats the same discrete operation over and over again, such as completing a series of five or six welds. The team approach makes the work cycle longer and, according to Bonner 'is believed by some to motivate the workforce, so they don't get bored, and to lead to better quality and more flexibility in production.'

Although the team may use automated tools, it is they who are responsible for the final quality of the vehicle, and who set the pace of production. The idea of the 1990s seems to be to use automation where most appropriate and manual labour where it makes sense, depending on the current state of the plant and its volume. Bonner says, 'We've gone through periods of going away and looking for one big solution to solve all our quality problems. But we've found there is no one solution to quality, just lots of little solutions.'

Sometimes a solution for increasing quality is to be found in design and materials. A clear example is one of the most mundane: the interior lining of the roof. This used to be made of several pieces of fabric, stitched together and fitted into the car by hand. Bonner remembers: 'Sewn headlinings were one of the biggest time-consuming elements in the assembly of motor cars as far as we were concerned. There were a lot of panels, difficult shapes, quality was a problem to maintain and then it was a fairly skilled job actually to fit it up. We had two or three guys lying on their backs, doing all this fiddling around the door shuts.'

The J'89 headliner is a one-piece, moulded plastic component. 'Now you just push it in through the front window, push it up and it's there. One minute job.' Not only does the new headliner speed up the process, it also requires just one station, rather than the twenty needed for a sewn headliner.

The key manufacturing change for J'89 came in the framing line, which is the beginning of the assembly process. Here the steel pressings – the underbody, sides, front end, roof, front and rear fenders, doors, bonnet and tail-gate – are fitted on to a master tool called a jig and welded together. Because the panels are unpainted and a light, silvery-steel in colour, this phase is called body-in-white.

In Luton, the body-in-white framing line used to consist of a circular conveyor system with thirty-six framing jigs, each one adjusted by master gauges to the tolerances required for the new car. The problem with the line was that each jig could be slightly different from every other jig, which meant that no two assembled bodies were exactly alike; the exterior panels would attach slightly differently, causing inconsistencies in the width of gaps and joins of the fenders to bonnet and hood to doors.

In order to keep the jigs as close in tolerance as possible, the maintenance department had to check them every day with a set of master gauges, which was a tedious, time-consuming process. But if there was a serious problem in build quality, there was no way to trace the offending car back to the jig it was framed on.

For J'89, this entire system was replaced with three straight assembly lines, each with just one master tool each. With more workers on each line, the total output is similar to the old line but the quality is far more consistent because it's easier to keep three tools within tolerances than thirty-six. The bodies are also coded so problems can be traced back to the proper jig.

After the body-in-white, the car proceeds into the paint shop.

The closest the Luton plant comes to CIM and the people-less factory is in the paint plant. Completed in 1986 at an expense of some £90 million, it is up-to-date in terms of computer controls and worker safety.

Paint plant performance is measured by the percentage of 'first time okay' jobs. Hard though it may be to believe, the old Luton paint plant had a 40% 'first time okay' record. That means that 60% of all the jobs going through the painting cycle had to be sent back to be fixed. And, of course, only 40% of those rectifications would be correct.

'There was no end to it,' remembers Bonner. 'We had to work holidays, weekends. But we would not knowingly deliver a bad quality car to the customer.' The problem was the time and expense (including overtime pay for weekends and holidays) it took to arrive at a paint job of acceptable standard.

Theoretically, if not always in practice, every car built at Luton is built to a dealer order. It is a dizzying task to plan the assembly of hundreds of custom-made cars each day. Depending on the equipment required, each car takes a different amount of time to assemble; it takes longer to fit the higher spec cars than the standard models. The bodies can't necessarily be painted in large batches, with a hundred red cars followed by a hundred grey ones.

'Ideally, you bring all the dealer orders together, shuffle them, prioritize them, then order the line. But you may be constrained by engine availability, sun-roof availability, seat-trim-availability, a million and one constraints. It's a hell of a task.'

Much of the task is simply keeping track of which cars are which and where they are in the cycle. This is facilitated at Luton by the use of a vehicle control system called AVI (automatic vehicle identification). Each body-in-white is fitted with a small bell-shaped pod (about 25 cm in diameter) that hangs off the front end, called a transponder. It's like an electronic gene-set for the new car, containing all the information about order number, colour, trim and specifications in electronic form which can be read at stations throughout the plant.

In the paint shop control room, a central computer is linked to stations all along the line, where floor managers enter information about the cars that have been successfully completed, and any that have been sent back for fixing. The steel frame, with none of the outer skin panels attached, first proceeds through a series of dips and ovens which alternately apply undercoatings and then bake them on. It finally arrives at the heart of the operation where it will receive the surface colour – Regency Blue or Carmine Red, for example – after the doors and other panels have been attached.

Automotive paints are not something you want to take into your skin or lungs. But the surface application is still done by real people. They stand in a long, glass-enclosed booth. The cars travel along a track, having been delivered from the framing operation below, and move slowly towards a big oven at the end. Along the way, the workers apply the surface paint using spray nozzles attached to long flexible hoses.

Most of the workers wear complete protective suits, including gloves and headmasks, to protect their eyes and lungs. However, these measures are not legally required and a few of the painters, whether foolish or misguidedly macho, work unprotected in a fine cloud of spray all day long.

They move, however, with a balletic grace, manipulating the painting hose and nozzle with a series of magical moves that make it seem as if the paint emerging from the nozzle is a puppet on a single string and the painter a puppeteer who causes the paint to dance across the surface of the car.

But, as with a puppeteer, the moves the painter makes do not always seem to bear the proper relation to what the paint is doing. Because the nozzle is attached to a rigid tube about a metre long, the painter must constantly twist and turn the tool as he sprays paint into the crevices and bends of the body – inside the door frame, around the sun-roof opening. Accompanying the arm movements are a series of foot manoeuvres, allowing the worker to keep the tool the proper distance from the surface of the car.

Spraying a complete car is accomplished in the space of a couple of minutes, and it then proceeds into the oven. When he is finished, the worker presses a button and the nozzle cleans itself and loads the next colour paint required. Based on the information in the transponder, the computer determines which paint colour is delivered to the nozzle of the spraying unit. And so it is not necessary for the paint shop to run the cars in batches of colour, it can alternate colours in any sequence. This works remarkably well – the next spray emerging completely blue or green where red has just been.

Occasionally, the technology does not perform exactly as it should. There is the story of how, during the start-up of the plant, the system did not function properly. A bit of white spray was left from the previous model and, as the painter worked his way back from the nose to the rear end of the car, the nozzle only gradually delivered the expected colour – a brilliant red. The result was a car of elegantly graduated colour, with a stark white nose that lapsed into a blushing shade of pink at the passenger compartment and became a vibrant red at the tail. The car was highly prized and admired at the plant, before it was decided it should go back through the process for a respray.

The other major use of automation for J'89 was to simplify procedures that were particularly difficult or tedious for the workers – because tedium and complexity lead to mistakes. The major new piece of automated equipment was in a whole new area for fascia assembly. Rather than insert the fascia into the car and then hook up all the electrics and electronics, the fascia and all its components – called the cockpit module – would be assembled separately and then plugged into the car on the trim line.

This subassembly is accomplished by the fascia unit being mounted on a small cart called an AGV (automated guide vehicle). A number of these carts operate in the cockpit module assembly area and travel along lines installed in the floor that emit electronic control signals. These signals emanate from a central computer which governs the pace and flow of the work.

The computer communicates with the rest of the plant to determine how many cockpit modules are needed where and when. The computer operates according to instructions programmed by a Swiss company, and if anything goes wrong with the programming Vauxhall people must telephone their Swiss counterparts, who keep a twenty-four-hour vigil and will diagnose the problem and attempt to fix it from afar.

The advantages of this cockpit module assembly technique are many. The primary one is that it allows for testing of the cockpit units before they are installed in the car. With the increasing number of electronics and components in today's cars, the dashboard is a particularly vulnerable spot for such failures. Once installed, testing becomes far more difficult. By testing the units while still on the bench, faults can easily be fixed. In theory the failure rate should reach 0%.

The second major advantage is that workers are able to stand erect as they work and assemble the components with relative ease. The old method had workers squirming into the assembled and moving car bodies, reaching above their heads, trying to hook up wires and other components without enough light. If you have ever tried to change a fuse or look for a loose wire under your fascia, you know that having your arms extended over your head is perhaps the worst working position. The strain on eyes, neck and back can be not only annoying but debilitatingly painful.

At the Rüsselsheim plant, a new technique has been developed where the mostly-assembled cars are placed in a circular carriage that travels along at no more than 30 cm or so above the floor. The cars are rotated within this carriage, exposing the underbody, and workers make final connections from a standing position. To watch this line in operation is to understand the value of ergonomics (the design of machinery best to suit people): the machine contorts itself for the sake of the people, rather than the other way round.

These changes to the assembly plant, particularly the cockpit assembly area, required the workers to think about their work in new ways. Although it hardly approaches the ideal of each worker team assembling a whole car, it does call for more responsibility on the part of each worker. One person, essentially, is responsible for the assembly and testing of an entire cockpit unit.

For workers who have been accustomed to spending their entire days performing one task such as operating a spot-welding tool, for example, this is a radical difference. There are some managers at Vauxhall who believe that many workers prefer the old way; they prefer to jam on their Walkman headphones and go to work, repeating the same operation over and over again with an extraordinary economy of motion. It is not so easy to guide the large steel pieces into place, to steer the tip of the welding tool exactly into position and to make a series of welds as the car body travels slowly by. And, in fact, the training programme initiated by Peter Bonner and his team met with its share of resistance. It involved implementation of what he calls Total Quality Management, based on the quality philosophy of the American management consultant Philip Crosby and others.

The programme basically calls for the understanding of quality as an endeavour that involves everyone in the plant, involved in every part of the operation, all the time. This is essentially different from the idea of 'quality control', where a number of inspectors are employed merely to check the product as it comes off the line and send it back if it isn't right. The total quality approach asks for everyone to be responsible for his or her own work.

The world car is at least a partial reality today, with components emanating from plants and suppliers around the globe, delivered to assembly operations in various other parts of the world. For both Vauxhall and the government, this creates a serious problem, which is often exacerbated by currency imbalances and fluctuations.

The Department of Trade and Industry does not wish to see the UK car manufacturers become simply assembly operations when there is potentially a great deal of business to be had for UK suppliers and sub-assemblers. So the DTI pressures UK manufacturers to increase the percentage of components made in the UK. They may set a guideline as high as 60-80% for local content, based on wholesale cost of the components.

For a company as large as General Motors, with manufacturing plants in some thirty-four countries and as the largest producer of its own parts in the industry, to have to buy components in the UK becomes a real trial. For years, UK suppliers were not considered reliable enough to produce the quantity of parts with the required quality. But, as part of the drive for greater quality, Vauxhall now works with suppliers during the pilot programme to make sure that the quality and the specifications are right. With the new Cavalier, Peter Bonner is aiming to increase the local content by some 7%, buying such products as moulded plastic elements, pedals, lamps, locks and hinges from new UK sources.

This is a crucial issue, not just because of the government regulations, but also because of the basic criteria of what constitutes a local manufacturer and what makes a transplant. A transplant is a foreign company that has established a manufacturing operation in the UK. Because they must all adhere to the local content guidelines, it becomes unclear just who is local and who is foreign, especially when you consider that both Ford and Vauxhall are ultimately responsible to their American parents and are therefore the biggest transplants of them all.

The issue of local content and transplantation will become all the more important as the effects of the single European market take hold. In the all-important fleet market there has long been a resistance to specifying non-UK car makers. But with global sourcing in the single European market, and as new foreign competitors sell into the UK unburdened by import duties, board members will have to look hard at their purchasing policies and decide where their national loyalties end and their bottom line concerns begin.

Given this diminishing advantage as a British manufacturer and its already diminished role as an assembly operation, Vauxhall is left without much of a power base to affect product design or manufacturing strategy. And so they are in a position many companies find themselves in – as a local subsidiary reporting to a 'foreign' parent, doing battle to customize the parent company's product successfully for sale to a local market. It's called packaging.

A teacher at the Bauhaus liked to illustrate the importance of design with this supposition: if a man had to choose between two potential candidates for wives who were equal in all other qualities and assets, the man would certainly choose the one who was the better looking. (This probably holds true for women choosing husbands as well, but it is not how the teacher phrased it.)

The same idea, in slightly different form, was used by Raymond Loewy to promote his new product design business. In his book *Industrial Design* (published in 1979), Loewy, who was trained as an engineer in France, describes how he got started as an industrial designer in New York. 'I printed up a card and sent it to everyone I knew. It said, "Between two products equal in price, function and quality, the better looking will outsell the other."'

Car manufacturers, as we have seen, subscribe to this theory, although grudgingly at times. But what if the two products the consumer has to choose from are almost equally functional, well built *and* good looking – and what if there are not just two, but several? Many customers will begin to look more closely at the details and at the price of each product and to compare the competitors with greater care. That is exactly the case in the intermediate car market in Europe today: the customer's buying decision may hinge on any one of a number of features and details. So car packaging is all about combining body styles, equipment and features into a limited number of standard models and trim levels.

The process of defining the J'89 model range took almost as many years to determine as it took to design and engineer the basic car. Peter Negus is a Product Planning Manager for Vauxhall and inhabits a glassed-in cubicle in the planning area of T block. Of the five and a half years he spent labouring over J'89, he spent three living in Germany.

Negus looks to be a man more concerned with engines and trans-missions than colours and interior fabrics. But packaging is really about lobbying for local requirements and then selecting from a list of options offered by the designers and combining them in ways appropriate to the UK market.

'Starting in June of 1983 or so we began monthly planning meetings, and we had a meeting every month for five and a half years.' Some of the differences were major – the Germans, says

Negus, wanted just a notch at first, the British wanted both a hatch and a notch – but many of them centred around matters of taste. 'In the German market they tend to be a little more reserved, they don't want to overstate visually. We in the UK want all the bells and whistles.'

Basic decisions as to which body styles will be available from start of production (hatch, notch, estate, coupé, convertible) are made early in the process. But the detailing continues right up until launch with minor adjustments to interior specifications and, of course, price.

The goal is to create packages that seem to have advantages over the competition by offering a greater number of (or more appealing) standard features at a similar price, similar features at lower price, or a standard feature that no other model has. At the same time, because the number of possible combinations is virtually endless (just two body styles with five engines at six trim levels and ten paint colours could equal hundreds of models), the manufacturer cannot offer every option at every trim level or the logistics of assembly and supply would be unmanageable.

The challenge comes in determining exactly what it is the customer really wants, as opposed to what the manufacturer thinks the customer really wants, or what is easiest for the manufacturer to provide. To do this, the product planners rely on market research – both formal and informal.

The formal process involves several different types of customer research. One survey is used to check the perceived value of a whole list of features, unrelated to any specific car model. For example, the customer is asked to place a pound value on a fascia clock. If the customer rates the clock at £3, and the manufacturer knows the clock is actually worth £2 at retail, then the manufacturer knows that he is not wasting money by including an item the customer doesn't care about.

When head restraints were first offered as standard equipment, manufacturers made a lot of promotional noise about them. But Vauxhall, for one, found that people didn't really care about head restraints. The same is proving to be true about anti-lock braking systems. Customers who have never driven a car equipped with ABS place a much lower pound value on it than the typical £400-£1,000 extra it costs to have it fitted. Once they have discovered the advantages of ABS for themselves, however, their estimate of its worth is usually revised upwards.

By including a standard feature slightly ahead of its time, it is possible to get a jump on the competitors. For example, in 1983, Vauxhall decided it would be a good idea to upgrade the audio equipment in the Cavalier and made a stereo radio cassette tape player standard, at a time when standard equipment involved only a radio.

The Vauxhall move started an audio specifications skirmish that is still being fought and has earned Vauxhall a reputation as being 'good with sound'. The cassette players were so well liked, and so easy to remove, that they became a highly popular target for thieves. At one time, the hire car company Swan National was losing forty to fifty radios per week. The problem was solved with the addition of radio 'coding' – the user enters a password to make it work. And so a liability has been turned into a new feature that can be marketed as something of value.

Selected buyers of a specific new model are questioned at least four times after they make their purchase. The first contact is what's known as a 'toe dip' – a telephone conversation with about 150 people within a few days after they have bought the car. After three months, another owner survey is conducted and they are asked to rate forty elements of the car.

There is a broader survey conducted after a year of ownership, which includes issues of longer term performance and how the car meets expectations. After two to three years, there is a fourth survey to check on how the car is performing in terms of reliability, servicing and general wear and tear.

The Vauxhall product planners agree on the not-very-surprising conclusion that the British have very different tastes to the Germans and the Spaniards. 'Germany likes anything so long as it's grey, steel grey,' says Negus. The British like lighter colours and a softer touch to interior surfaces. Practical German designers view additional body panels such as skirts and spoilers as gratuitous features, whereas the British generally like them even if they know they have no real functional value. German drivers, however, may feel differently: Germany is one of the largest 'after' markets in Europe for body panel kits for DIY customization.

The key difference in the two markets, however, is the influence of the company car – or fleet – market, which accounts for about half of total car sales in Britain. In the old days of the fleet market, the 1970s and early 1980s, the fleet car was the spartan and functional one. The company fleet manager would select a make based upon price, reliability, running costs, service, and that is what the employees would drive.

Today fleets have become more flexible and there is a much higher percentage of user-choosers – employees who have the option of selecting their own car based on price guidelines and engine sizes. This has made the fleet market much more competitive.

The value of the company car and the equipment it contains has become a kind of internal leading indicator of an employee's station and recognized worth. There are the broad categories – the director's car, manager's car and salesman's car – which every manufacturer caters to. But within each category the distinctions can be sliced very fine.

Staff quickly learn the company rules of the relationship between car and salary, and it is not unusual for people to check the price of individual components (central locking, rear wipers, power steering, sun-roofs) of their fellow employees' cars to get an idea where everybody stands in the pecking order. The government, of course, plays a role in packaging, too, because the application of motor vehicle tax is linked to engine size, as is the 'benefit in kind' tax which all company car drivers must pay.

The demands of the fleet market, more than anything else, led the Vauxhall product planners to push for six trim levels for J'89 in the UK, in contrast to only four for Germany. There would be one more at the bottom of the scale, the standard model, and an additional one at the top.

At launch, the model range included twenty variants: ten saloons and ten hatchbacks, five engine options, five trim levels (standard, L, GL, CD, SRi, with the sixth, the GSi, to come later), fourteen paint colours, three interior fabrics for each trim level, fourteen factory-fitted options, three levels of audio equipment.

The planning people made two bold packaging decisions for the Cavalier line-up. They decided to offer a four-wheel-drive model with the relatively modest L-level trim specification. The idea was to bring what is seen to be 'advanced technology' within reach of more potential buyers, thereby bolstering Vauxhall's reputation as a technology leader and helping to combat the gains made by those high-technology compact competitors, BMW and Mercedes.

The second is of greater significance: the introduction of a car intended to be the top-of-the-line Cavalier, an image car dubbed the GSi 2000. The theory is that every driver wants to be driving a Ferrari or a Porsche or a Lotus, but most people cannot afford one. Also if an exceptional variant exists at the top of the range, it has a trickle-down effect on the rest of the models.

In other words, if your Cavalier L has no more distinguished relatives than the GL and the CD, it would seem to come from a pretty ordinary family. However, if it has a relation called the GSi 2000 which looks pretty much the same but has a top speed of 215 kph and features every one of the latest technological marvels, that is a different matter altogether.

Ford accomplished this halo effect in its variant of the Sierra, when it introduced an engine by Cosworth. Vauxhall now hopes to do the same with the Cavalier GSi 2000, a car which was shown to appreciative gasps at the Geneva Motor Show in 1989. Vauxhall has not had such a car in its line-up before, and they are hoping it will help improve a quantity much in need of improvement: their image.

The specification discussion goes on until the last possible moment, when everything must be fixed – about a year away from start of production. There were, for example, disagreements over the size of the spoiler for the sporty SRi version – the British wanted a big spoiler, the Germans didn't want one at all, so Vauxhall compromised on a small one that, according to Peter Negus, 'looks like a compromise'.

There was a great deal of toing and froing about something called 'wheel-trim strategy'. Although wheel-trims appear to be designed for some functional effect such as cooling or aerodynamic efficiency, these are not the primary considerations. Trim level differentiation and vehicle 'personality' are. How many wheel-trims would there be? Which designs?

All the while, the product people were watching the competition. The new VW Passat was launched in the spring before the launch of J'89. In looking it over, the Vauxhall packagers felt that there were some elements in the Passat interior that would up the expectations for the competitive J'89 models and so they quickly made adjustments.

Knowing that Ford would probably improve the specification for its Sierra models as a way of combating the new Cavalier, Vauxhall took a bold move and made the sun-roof standard on the L model. After the decision had been made, they were pleased to learn that Ford had indeed upped their specification by adding a sun-roof as standard to the LX Sierra, a trim level higher than the L. So Vauxhall scored a small coup.

Of course, these moves and counter-moves cannot be made at the last minute, and sometimes they cannot successfully be made at all. The sun-roof decision, for example, put a heavy demand on sun-roof suppliers. By specifying sun-roofs for the L model, Vauxhall had increased their requirement from about 3,000 to about 60,000. The supplier could not deliver, Vauxhall had to look elsewhere, and this eventually led to delays in production.

If the industry's fear of leaking new model information is bad during the design phase, it intensifies into paranoia during this packaging phase. There is real harm if the basic shape of the new car is scooped by the press early on, because it can affect sales of the preceding model – who wants to buy the old one when a new one is just around the corner? And if a competitor can get hold of information about the specifications of the new models that is very serious indeed, because competitors can sometimes react by matching specification in their own cars.

Does General Motors employ professional spies? How does Vauxhall gather inside information about what the opposition is doing and will probably be doing? No one will admit that they use professional information gatherers, or spies, and the major sources of information are the ones you might expect.

The most consistent source is the one everybody uses: the press. Designers and managers read the motor trade press faithfully. From the popular UK magazines, such as *What Car* and *Auto Car and Motor* and *Car* and *Performance Car*, they gather information from interviews, articles based on press releases, and photographs.

The most important information is not about numbers, since sales and production figures can be found in a variety of industry sources, including the Society of Motor Manufacturers and Traders. The important questions are: What does the new model look like? When will it be launched? Who is in and who is out in the management structure? What about manufacturing facilities – which are being opened, which closed? Who is forming joint ventures with whom?

The quintessential industry story is the new model scoop – an article about some forthcoming model before information or photographs have been officially released. But it really has very little competitive effect. Most companies know when a competitive model is scheduled to emerge – and news starts appearing in the trade press about a year beforehand. But the scoops are annoying because they show that information is getting out of your organization that is not authorized. A story about J'89 appeared in a German auto magazine some months before official press coverage was allowed. The theory was that someone inside the Opel organization talked.

These preview articles are always accompanied by at least one photograph of the new model. It is usually shot with a long lens and appears to have been snapped quickly. Often there are two or three men standing around the car, usually looking with annoyed expressions towards the camera as if to say, 'Oh dear, we've been spotted.'

Despite all the secrecy surrounding the development of a new model, a car is a relatively large object and difficult to conceal. When the new model is being tested, it is usually transported from a plant facility like Rüsselsheim to a test facility such as Dudenhofen, or from Luton to Millbrook. If a photographer is clever and reasonably patient, he will eventually detect cars emerging from the manufacturer's gates.

Often the cars will be photographed during the road testing. The American South-west is a favourite spot. Again, in General Motors' case, there is a large test facility in Arizona, where the cars will eventually appear. When testing the new Carlton, Hans-Jürgen Pache, the Opel engineer, met up with a team from BMW who were testing their new 7 series. The launch dates for the new cars were similar and each team could tell just by looking how far along the other one was. Nevertheless, no changes were made to the Carlton based on what was seen.

Photographers have also been known to stick their lenses through the bushes skirting the well-known test tracks. And there is always the possibility that some of these photographs are staged, with manufacturers letting the press know that such-and-such a car will be on such-and-such a road on such-and-such a day.

The manufacturer has no control over these stolen images, which don't always present the car in the most attractive situation or from the best angle. Every car has its best side, and car manufacturers, knowing this, ensure that photography minimizes the least attractive views.

Another major source of information is the suppliers. If you are manufacturer A who goes to your sun-roof supplier and says, 'We need to up our order by 25%,' and the supplier says, 'Sorry, I can't accommodate you until a later date,' you ask why. He says, 'I can't say, but I've just got a big order in for sun-roofs from manufacturer B, which I'm not sure I can fill.' You now take your supplier out for lunch and eventually you discover that manufacturer B is planning to install sun-roofs on every L model. Or you have a pretty good idea who else your supplier sells to, and you make the necessary connections and draw the proper conclusions.

This is perhaps the most valuable source of information because it most directly relates to that critical secret: specification. Radios, tape players, central locking mechanisms, rear wipers, sun-roofs, vanity mirrors, and dozens of other such items all come from known sub-contractors.

Finally, there is a good deal of direct contact among manufacturers. With so many joint ventures taking place and so many links between companies, a certain amount of information is spilled or leaked that wasn't intended.

Spilling information in the proper way at the proper time is what the launch events are all about.

8 · LAUNCH

'What we had to do, in essence, was make the Cavalier famous.'

Terry Edwards, Media Planner, Lowe Howard-Spink

I had my first taste of the automotive launch business in the autumn of 1986. 'Launch' is a term that encompasses all the activities involved in introducing a new car, or any new product, to the marketplace. A launch programme usually involves advertising, public relations and internal promotions (to a manufacturer's own employees or dealers).

In 1986, for example, Vauxhall was preparing to launch the newly redesigned Senator, the top-of-the-range car. Part of that launch would be a series of meetings of members of the Vauxhall dealer organization, the purpose of which would be to inform them about the new car and get them excited about it as well. At the time, I was working with a London company, Spectrum Communications Ltd, who were to be producers of the forthcoming launch event. I would be writing the media scripts and speeches for it, including the opening remarks for Managing Director John Bagshaw.

I asked a member of the Vauxhall marketing communications staff if he could set up a meeting with Bagshaw to discuss his remarks. 'Oh no,' I was told, 'you write an outline first and we submit it to him for his comments.' But I had no idea what he wanted to talk about, or what his speaking style might be. Finally a meeting was agreed, but not a simple meeting between the two of us; four of the Vauxhall account team from Spectrum would be present, as well as three members of the Vauxhall marketing communications staff.

The Spectrum team arrived early, and we were led up the mellow stairs of the administration building and into the executive conference room, with its old mahogany panelling, hearth and large mahogany conference table. We arrayed ourselves on one side of the table, the Vauxhall staff on the other side. A few minutes later, John Bagshaw breezed in.

My first impression was of an Ebeneezer Scrooge character, slim and angular, with a hooked nose, sharp eyes and a crotchety manner. He began the meeting with a peremptory but not unpleasant 'all right'. He listened with a non-committal lack of comment as his staff explained the basic plans for the Senator launch. When it came to the critical issue Bagshaw's eyes took on a new glitter.

It was suggested that Bagshaw should attend the series of dealer meetings personally and make a few opening remarks at each of them. Bagshaw cut abruptly into the flow. 'Why the fuck should I?' he asked in his harsh Australian accent.

Everybody winced. 'I'm not saying I won't, but why should I?' continued Bagshaw, perhaps trying to ease the shock he had caused. 'Well, John,' explained one of the Vauxhall team after a pause, 'this *is* the top-of-the-range, prestige car, and you are the Managing Director.' Bagshaw pondered for a half a second. 'Well, we'll have a look at the diary,' he said, 'I know I have a problem with that first date.'

It was finally agreed that he would record his remarks on videotape, in case he couldn't make one or two of the dates. He proceeded to mention a few points he might wish to make, including 'something about the labour situation in Spain', and a few weeks later he approved the script draft with a few minor changes. But when it came to the launch event itself Bagshaw appeared at none of them, and the audiences had to make do with his video persona. He had probably made up his mind in that half-second of thought.

The launch period marks a tense time in the development of the new car – the end of the development process and the beginning of the car's life as a real product. This final phase bears a relationship to the earliest design phase in that it is highly emotionally charged.

In the initial phases, the designers, aerodynamicists and engineers are struggling to define an essence and identity for the car-to-be. It is a period of possibility, expectation, eagerness. In the final stages, the goal is to make the rest of the world understand about this new product, to tell them why it is good and why it is important.

Designers and engineers and manufacturing and finance people all have their worries and concerns throughout the long development process, but the people at the launch end may be the most jittery. Not only is the whole thing coming to a head, it is doing so in a highly visible and public way.

John Butterfield was Marketing Communications Manager during the run-up to the J'89 launch period and, as such, presided over the development and implementation of what became the biggest car launch in UK history.

Butterfield joined Vauxhall in 1955 as a graduate trainee and progressed through a number of positions, including Parts and Accessories Representation, District Sales Manager for the West Country and Zone Manager for Scotland and the North of England. In 1975, he came to Luton as Marketing Manager, then General Sales Manager and arrived in his post as Marketing Communications Manager in 1985. And here he was, responsible for the million details involved in the production of advertising, public relations and internal communications events. His solution to controlling the creative chaos around him seemed to involve working longer and longer hours and presiding over more and more lengthy and detailed meetings, all the while maintaining a gentlemanly, almost courtly, manner.

'The launch of the new Cavalier will be the most important car launch in our history,' said Butterfield. And perhaps it was: J'89 was actually supposed to be J'88 and was therefore already a year late to market. Cavalier was Vauxhall's best-selling car, but its sales had begun to drop seriously in 1986 and this was directly affecting Vauxhall's total market share. It was hard to imagine that Vauxhall could or would be allowed to survive another grim period like the one from which it had so recently emerged. So the launch of the new Cavalier was eagerly anticipated by Vauxhall.

A launch is all about creating awareness and generating enthusiasm for the new car, and it must be done in different ways for different audiences, the primary ones being the Vauxhall dealers, the trade and national press, and the great and general public of potential new car buyers. A highly visible and memorable launch can have a tremendous positive impact on a new car's success.

The launch of the new Cavalier was to come just a year after one of the most memorable launches of recent years, for the new Peugeot 405, a direct competitor in the intermediate market. Not only was it a big launch in terms of money spent and media used, it employed a dramatic and controversial creative approach that attracted a great deal of attention. 'We certainly had a very keen eye on what Peugeot did to launch the 405, because we see the 405 as a very serious competitor,' recalls Butterfield. The launch of the 405 helped create for Peugeot a worrying (to Vauxhall) rise in UK market share.

Of course, the success of a launch also depends heavily on factors that have nothing to do with advertising and promotion. Perhaps the most critical and nerve-wracking question is: will there be any cars available? Vauxhall dealers recalled the miserable days of the late 1970s when the company could not deliver enough cars to meet demand. 'We consistently failed to produce the scheduled run, which led to declining market share right through the back end of the '70s,' says Butterfield.

There is nothing worse for a dealer than trying to sell cars that don't exist. It's one thing to wait two or three years for a Morgan, but no one wants to wait very long for a Vauxhall. That is why the pilot programme is so important. It is during this period of pre-production build that Vauxhall managers (and, indirectly, the dealers) get an idea of how well the new car is going together, and how quickly it can be built.

Vauxhall marketing set a target of 7,000 production cars in the dealerships by public launch day, 14 October 1988. On that day the new Cavalier would officially be offered for sale at dealer showrooms around the country.

With so much riding on the presentation of a single new product, the hyperbole tends to escalate during the year it takes to develop the launch programme. Listening to it, you could believe that the entire world was waiting for the arrival of the new Cavalier, that no other product had ever been of such great import and that drivers everywhere were postponing their car-purchasing decisions to be able to have a look at the new model. And, of course, that is just what Vauxhall wanted the world to believe.

If your dealers aren't enthusiastic about the new car, so the reasoning goes, they won't promote it to their customers with enthusiasm. If customers perceive that dealers are ho-hum on the product, they will be too. In a market where there are many good cars to choose from, the idea is to find ways to add value to yours – to make it seem better, appear to have something the others don't. Some of that perception of added value will be based on illusion, some of it based on reality. In order to get the dealers to understand the reality of the new car and to buy into the *idea* of it as well, the motor industry has developed a phenomenon known as the dealer launch event.

The dealer launch may take any number of forms, but two ingredients are absolutely essential. One, you must see the car for the first time 'in the metal'. Two, you must hear from the senior managers about why this car is so good. Oh yes, and third, you should get a decent meal and some entertainment into the bargain.

There are about 620 Vauxhall dealers throughout the UK, a large percentage of them in the North, and you only have to drive through the countryside to see that the dealerships are inconsistent in terms of quality and appearance. There are still some signs lingering from the old days of Vauxhall/Opel, with the gaudy, multi-coloured tri-logo – Vauxhall, Opel and GM. There are some big, bright, obviously well-managed operations and there are some shabby little ones that aren't much more than a local garage.

Vauxhall dealers have been through hard times along with the company. Their numbers were drastically reduced in the restructuring days of the mid-1970s. They suffered through years of undersupply until the end of the 1970s. Then, just as Vauxhall was able to supply more cars, the worldwide recession hit, in 1980. So many cars became available that Vauxhall was parking them in fields and could scarcely give them away.

There followed the rationalization of the Vauxhall and Opel dealership in the early 1980s, with some dealers refusing to move from the prestige Opel make to the more downmarket Vauxhall brand and leaving the fold. There were years of the company losing money. Years of short supply. Years of working with a company that was

dominated by Germans and Americans. The brightest spot had
been the Cavalier. Considering all of this, it was not surprising that
Vauxhall dealers were sceptical. But, at the end of 1988, things were
looking better. Vauxhall was in the black. And the new Cavalier was
on the horizon.

John Butterfield attended his first Vauxhall launch event in 1957. It
was for the Vauxhall Victor and it was, in his memory, an extraordinary
happening, featuring show business star Arthur Askey, supported by a
contingent of the Coldstream Guards. It impressed him, as it would
most young men, and perhaps remains a personal benchmark for
what such events ought to be.

Over the years, the revealing of new cars to specialized audiences
has evolved into a minor art form. Of course there have been motor
shows and fairs since the turn of the century (there were five motor
shows in London in 1902), which are basically exhibitions of a number
of new cars arrayed for all to see. The simple act of placing a car on
display does not achieve the necessary effect: the manufacturer can't
explain it, can't add value to it. The car, which should be a dynamic
product, just sits there. Even taking a car for a test drive, before
you've heard the story, won't do the trick. It takes an event to bring
the car alive.

General Motors have been in the business of presenting their new
designs to the public for years. The Futurama pavilion at the New
York World Fair of 1939 was the most elaborate GM presentation,
featuring displays, exhibits and a ride above a scale model of the 'landscape of tomorrow' which, in this case, was deemed to be 1960.

It was this presentation that inspired the travelling Motoramas,
one of which, as we have seen, eventually captured Wayne Cherry's
imagination. The basic ingredients of these public presentations were
fantasy, technology, futurism, engineering and glamour.

In developing initial concepts for the J'89 dealer event, this
tradition of extravagant public presentations, World Fairs and
Disney theme parks kept intruding itself. Spectrum Communications was charged with developing the approach to the event,
which involved producing whatever films, videos, slide shows or
live presentations might be required, and staging the entire event
as well.

The initial concept was to create an hour-long ride – similar in nature to that of a Disney ride – that would highlight all the key phases of the development process, illustrating them with props, exhibits, media and live action. A greenfield site, or huge 'black box' structure, was deemed necessary for the project and, after it became clear that film producer Albert 'Cubby' Broccoli might need his sound stage at Pinewood for the forthcoming production of his new James Bond film, a new venue was identified – an aircraft hangar at the Northweald airfield in Essex.

Spectrum worked with a talented independent designer, John Furneaux of the London firm Furneaux-Stewart, to develop a new look for the structure. Whether consciously or not, his solution echoed that of the 1939 World Fair. The central structures at that event had been a soaring 200-metre high pyramidal obelisk called the Trylon and an adjacent 60-metre diameter sphere called the Perisphere.

Furneaux's initial design for the J'89 event called for three large temporary structures attached to the Northweald hangar – a pyramid, a sphere and a cube. Although the Vauxhall marketing communications staff were initially intrigued, practical considerations – notably the expense – eventually prevailed. The dealer presentations would be held instead at the Royal Lancaster Hotel in the Bayswater Road, London.

It was to be a full week of presentations, beginning on Monday 24 August and continuing until the Friday. Dealers arrived at the Royal Lancaster by coach and chauffeured cars (Carltons and Senators, of course) and proceeded into the foyer for coffee and biscuits, and then into the main ballroom.

Here they found that the dowdy Nine Kings Suite had been transformed into a private theatre, complete with elaborate projection equipment (dozens of slide projectors and three 35 mm motion picture projectors) trained on three large screens. There was a central turntable, raked seating with plush new red seats purchased especially for the occasion, and two mysterious, shimmery mirror-surfaced side walls.

A reasonably shiny, black 1978 Vauxhall Cavalier GL in mint condition was parked peacefully on stage. While the dealers were

waiting for the presentation to begin, the screens filled with nostalgic images of the thirteen-year life of the Cavalier, including old
television advertisements. The slides and films alternated with live
entertainment: three young male dancers bopped out and performed
a stylized dance rendition of a car-polishing routine.

The presentation was structured (following the original plan) to
give the audience a feel for the various phases of development of
J'89, including the marketing background, design process, aero
development, engineering, packaging and launch planning for the new
car. In order to add as much credibility as possible, it was decided that
Vauxhall staff – rather than professional presenters – would make the
presentations, backed up with lots of media, props and the occasional
appearance of singers and dancers for light relief.

For the first two days of the presentations, at least, the senior
managers dutifully played their parts. Peter Batchelor, Director of
Sales and Marketing, acted as host. He and Chairman Paul Tosch,
along with John Butterfield and Ian Coomber, the fleet sales manager,
performed well. But it was Wayne Cherry, who had been lured over
from Germany to appear, who proved to be the star of the show.
Unlike the other managers who relied on the autocue monitors to
help deliver their speeches, Cherry had memorized his remarks.

As Cherry talked about design – 'Each surface element makes
a flowing transition into the next' – he swept his hands over the
lines of the full-sized fibre-glass model on stage. He got down on
his knees to explain the aerodynamic contribution of the lip at the
front end of the new Cavalier. He turned upstage and nodded at
the actors who represented clay modellers, scraping silently away at
a fifth-scale J'89. He smiled. He seemed to love the car and believe
what he was saying. He was, in short, a fine performer.

Next, John Butterfield spent nearly fifteen minutes describing to
the dealers what Vauxhall would do for the public launch as well as
what would be expected of them in return. 'Check that your customer
mailing lists are ready,' said Butterfield. 'Be sure you have enough
sales people, and that they are properly trained. You'll be pleased to
learn that your service colleagues will need only two additional Class
1 blanket tools.' Lunchtime was approaching, and there was a slight
shifting of bums in the audience.

Paul Tosch made a few closing remarks, his soft American accent standing out sharply in contrast to his British colleagues.

Then came the key moment, known in the presentations trade as 'the reveal'. This is the electrifying (or sometimes stultifying) moment when the new car is finally revealed to the audience. Usually this comes quite early in the presentation so that the audience can have a good look at the car while it is being discussed. For J'89, the decision was made to withhold the reveal until the very end of the presentation. The audience had caught glimpses of the car in the films and slides and had seen its shape in clay and fibre-glass models, but it was only at the end of nearly eighty minutes of visual stimulation and verbal encouragement that J'89 came fully out of hiding. There was a blast of recorded music. Two singers – one male, one female – perched on balconies on either side of the screen began to extol the new Cavalier as 'a step beyond'. The two mirrored side walls turned transparent, one car revealed behind each. The cars rose slowly, on concealed hydraulic lifts, surrounded by bursts of dry ice. Two more Cavaliers smoothly emerged from the wings and drove towards centre stage. A fifth came round on the central turntable. The troupe of dancers danced with the cars, gesticulating towards them. The music climaxed. The song climaxed. The dancers froze. And, sitting placidly at the centre of all this attention – the frantic lights, drifting smoke and firm-thighed dancers – was 1800 kg of metal and plastic, rubber and glass. The audience cheered.

Upstairs, the car park of the Royal Lancaster had been transformed into a showroom and bar, where the audience could have a drink and take a closer look at the new models. Just before the audience trooped in from the first presentation, Wayne Cherry was upstairs looking at the cars. He was not happy: the wheel-trims were wrong. After all those years of design, discussion, packaging, negotiation – the right wheel-covers were on the wrong cars.

It didn't seem to matter to the audience. After a drink or two, the dealers proceeded into the foyer (which had been reset with round tables during the presentation) for dinner and a few after-dinner jokes and songs by the venerable entertainer, Bruce Forsyth.

August was the month to hear about the car, September was the month to drive it. During three weeks in September, Vauxhall invited over 8,000 dealers, fleet operators, press people and other guests to a series of events known as 'ride and drives' at the Millbrook proving ground.

Two brightly striped tents were set up adjacent to the steering pad (a huge circular concrete area for steering tests), one for presentations, the other as a holding area for waiting drivers. Parked on the pad itself were seventy-five brand new Vauxhall Cavaliers, in six different models.

Guests were greeted at the entrance to the facility by one of several young women who were acting as event hostesses. You were instructed to follow a pace car (with a large sign affixed to the rear end proclaiming 'FOLLOW ME') to a car parking area, where you left your car and boarded a mini-bus to the steering pad. Here, eager dealers and press disembarked.

Many chose to ignore the Vauxhall presentation (hadn't they heard everything about the car they needed to, and more?) and went straight to the main tent. Here, tagged ignition keys hung from a large board. It was only necessary to take the keys of the car you wanted to drive, report to one of several hostesses who sat behind a low, skirted table, and off you went.

Driving instructions had been given during the presentation: no driving faster than 90 kph on the access roads or 160 kph in the high speed bowl, spend no more than an hour in any one car. Waiting lists quickly developed for the most popular models – the four-wheel-drive, the CD and the SRi. And then it was boys' and girls' day out. Dozens of men and a few women were free to pick from any car they chose (so long as it was a Cavalier) and range freely over kilometres of track, acting like boy racers or long-distance eventers.

Unlike the ride-and-drive sessions for the Senator a year earlier, during which there had been a fatal accident, the Cavalier sessions went off with no serious problems. According to one of the hostesses, Melanie MacDonald, who spent nearly a month tending to the wants and needs of the guests (occasionally rescuing one from a car that had run out of petrol) there were only two mishaps. First, the tents were nearly blown over by high winds. And, second, a hare – which had chosen to cross the road at an inopportune moment – was run over.

From mid-September, the British motoring press were invited to evaluate the car in a slightly more palmy setting, the twisting country roads near Cannes in the South of France. It was the results of these tests that were reported in newspaper articles in early October. As the *Financial Times* reported, 'The coast road from Mandelieu to St Raphael is pretty rough in places and has lots of tight bends. The N7 back to Mandelieu goes through the hills and is a bit smoother, but has the kind of curves that test any car's suspension.'

Meanwhile, dealers were urged to invite members of their local press to one of two dealer 'driveaway days'. Seven hundred production cars, all to dealer order, had been shipped to Millbrook ready for delivery. On the appointed day, 28 September, the cars were parked on the 1.5 km straightaway and dealers drove the new Cavaliers off the grounds in a gleaming procession that led from the straightaway to the front entrance. According to Peter Batchelor, 'It was very, very impressive. For the dealer, the event was a little bit symbolic. It said, we've got the confidence to say there will be about a thousand cars built and ready to drive away by September the 28th.' It was also an effective public relations event, because most of the dealers brought along a local journalist, who, for the most part, was the one behind the wheel as the car left Millbrook. The driveaway also reminded Vauxhall managers of just how far they had come since the launch of the 1981 Cavalier: in that year they had driven just a hundred cars away from the Luton plant.

The first press announcements that a new Cavalier was truly on its way had appeared in late August, and first press reports based on the driving sessions were published on 5 October. The news was very good. Excitement was growing. Public launch day was not far away.

'We set the agency the task of bettering the 405 launch,' recalls John Butterfield, and the agency he was referring to was Lowe Howard-Spink (LHS). This well-known London advertising company, whose clients include Lloyds Bank, Hamlet cigars, Bells whisky and many others, had been Vauxhall's agency 'since God was a boy', as one Vauxhall staffer put it.

Whether or not they bettered the Peugeot 405 launch campaign is difficult, if not impossible, to quantify. But they created the most expensive new car launch in British history, spending in the neighbourhood of £10 million on advertising alone. That helped make Vauxhall the biggest advertising spender of any UK car manufacturer in 1988 – spending £31 million, in comparison to £28 million spent by Rover and £27 million spent by Ford in the same year.

Terry Edwards, a media planner at LHS who worked on the Cavalier campaign, described their mission. 'There are over 200 products advertised in the UK in any one week, of all kinds. So the public weren't sitting on their bottoms saying, "Oh, there's going to be a Cavalier launch soon." What we had to do was make the Cavalier famous. And we had to make it famous very quickly.'

The agency team began work early in 1988, by travelling to Germany to drive J'89 prototypes at Dudenhofen. They interviewed the designers and engineers. They reviewed Vauxhall's past sales results and the findings of the two J'89 clinics, they conducted six discussion sessions with groups of drivers of the current Cavalier and drivers of competitive cars, and they talked with some twenty-five fleet car buyers. The goal of this early research was to understand how the public (including the business public) felt about the current Cavalier and what they expected from the new one.

The team found, not surprisingly, that people generally held the current Cavalier in high regard but felt that it was simply getting old. Many people felt the Cavalier name was still stronger than the Vauxhall name. They expected the new car to carry on from the old, but to be better, particularly in terms of specification.

Fleet buyers wanted the car to 'make sense' – meaning a practical, economical, serviceable car for companies to run – as well as keep their drivers happy: in other words, to have enough of the luxuries and amenities that fleet drivers have come to know and love. In general, people were looking forward to the coming of the new Cavalier (if not sitting in rapt anticipation) and particularly interested in some of its technical attributes, including the four-wheel-drive system.

Based on the findings of this research, the LHS team developed their creative approach. According to Ken Hoggins and Chris O'Shea, joint creative directors for the Cavalier campaign, this meant 'simplifying all that information into one or two thoughts, to the barest elements really. To "this car is fast", or "it has four-wheel-drive" or it's "very comfortable". We did a lot of work in the early days to get down to one memorable thing.'

Three 'core messages' were developed. These were not theme lines or slogans, but candidates for that simplified, underlying memorable 'thing' the team needed as a basis for their work. Core message number one was that 'The new Cavalier offers the latest in car technology.' Core message number two stated, 'The New Cavalier offers the latest in four-wheel-drive technology.' And number three stated simply 'The all-new Cavalier is here.'

Three different creative approaches were developed, based on these core messages, and tried out at another round of group discussions with new car choosers and drivers. These were conducted by an independent research firm, and held in private homes. The principal researcher would journey to a city or town in the target market area and recruit candidates off the street. They were told that a car manufacturer was planning to introduce a new model and wanted to try out some of the advertising lines.

Out of curiosity, John Butterfield attended a 'fascinating' session in Leicester which involved eight men and women who convened at the house of a ninth volunteer. After being served a drink, the group were treated to a 'warm-up', which included discussion of what the advertising was attempting to accomplish. They were then shown mock-ups of the key advertising materials, starting with the proposed posters. The theme line that garnered the most positive reaction at these sessions was the one that was finally adopted: 'The Future. Now.' It embodied, really, all three core messages: that an advanced technology car (which, today, virtually implies four-wheel-drive) was here, now.

The Lowe Howard-Spink team realized that what they should be doing was more than just advertising a car. According to O'Shea, they 'became aware as time went by that we were not just selling a new car, we were actually making it into an event. For a certain period, the advertising had to be bigger than the car itself.' It also had, in some ways, to better the recent Peugeot campaign.

'The big thing about the Peugeot 405 launch was that their

television advertising was extremely good. And the recall on that was very strong,' says Butterfield. The launch of the Peugeot 405 had centred around the theme line 'Takes Your Breath Away' from a popular song, and featured the car ripping along a country road at dusk, the road skirting along the verge of a cane field on fire. The image of the burning field and a car racing alongside it was filled with a sense of danger and mystery. Why was this field burning? Who would be racing alongside a burning field anyway? Did this person start the fire? What is going on?

The ad caused a mild furore in the ad community; a perfectly good cane field seemed to have been wantonly set on fire in the cause of moving more automotive metal. It turned out that burning cane fields in the Bahamas is standard procedure, one that the creative director had witnessed and harnessed for his client. Whether or not the ad sold more cars or just made more noise is hard to determine. As Peter Batchelor puts it, 'Advertising is something you know you have to do. Although it is very difficult to measure its results.'

Despite its novel backdrop, the Peugeot ad was quite traditional in that it featured a picture of a car moving fast, accompanied by effective music. And, although the backdrop was novel, it conformed to the values that car ads have been pushing for years: danger, speed, mystery, excitement.

Because the Peugeot ad had had such an impact on the public, and the centrepiece of the new Cavalier campaign was also to be a television commercial, the ad agency, striving for even greater impact, settled on the production of a ninety-second commercial. Most commercials run thirty or sixty seconds, with many running fifteen seconds or less. Television commercials are extremely expensive for advertisers: they are expensive to produce (Vauxhall spent about £460,000) and to purchase air time is also expensive (Vauxhall spent about £4.3 million). Although discussion continues in the advertising world as to whether or not TV is the most effective medium in terms of getting results, there is no doubt that TV is the most prestigious and visible medium of all.

The best effect of television advertising is not in the delivery of information, but in the delivery of emotional impact. You use it to achieve an emotional reaction that will then, theoretically, cause the viewer to look further into the product. In the everyday clutter of advertising, the role of the TV ad is to grab your audience's attention, first, and then to create a positive impression with a few emotional overtones that bear upon the general marketing objectives you have set for yourself. The rationale seems to be that the longer you hold the attention of the audience – with ninety rather than thirty seconds – the greater impact you will have.

So, the creative work began with the development of the television commercial and all the other materials – radio, press and 'outdoor', or posters – would flow from the television treatment. To bring the theme line to life, Lowe Howard-Spink developed a complicated dramatic concept. They decided that the commercial would take the form of an episode of an imaginary television programme, circa 1958, called 'Step into the Future'.

The subject of the commercial-cum-programme would be the 'motor car of tomorrow' (the tomorrow of 1958 being defined, in 1988, as the year 2000) which would actually comprise features to be found in the new Cavalier. These would include 'scientific streamlining' and 'non-locking brakes', all part of 'a car that will think for itself'. And then we would be treated to a view of the Cavalier itself – the car of the future, as it were, realized a decade before its time. The desired impression was that the new Cavalier was an advanced automobile, delivering technology only dreamed of thirty years ago.

The original concept for the ad was to focus on the 'Step into the Future' television programme and reveal the car only at the very end of the commercial. In this way, the concept flirted with the most daring of all advertising approaches: not to show the product at all, or, at least, not to feature it. Rather, feature an *idea* about the product or a benefit of the product. The rationale for doing this is that, in a market filled with good cars, it is not the car itself that people buy, but the image.

In fact, a year after the new Cavalier was introduced, the new Nissan Infiniti luxury car was introduced in the United States with an extreme variant of this approach. In a teaser campaign that continued for so long that the tickle turned into torture, the car did not appear *at all* in either television or print ads.

Rather, the ads featured placid images that were supposed to embody or symbolize the approach the Japanese company had taken to building the car. In one of the print ads, a row of russet haystacks in late afternoon light was related to the timelessness of the new car. A zigzag of fences was linked to the barriers created between car and driver in conventional motor cars. Waves swirling around a rock at the seashore related to 'the natural patterns to driving'. The television commercial was filled with lulling natural images, with a raspy voice-over narration that was startlingly reminiscent of the Chrysler Airflow copy from 1934 which cited the natural inspirations for the new car's shape.

Although the Vauxhall campaign did prominently feature the car itself, it took its time to do so. The television commercial began with the set-up of the 'Step into the Future' programme, before getting into the details of the car itself. The original concept called for the new car to be revealed only at the very end of the ad, but, after much toing and froing, it was agreed to have quick cutaways of the new motor throughout.

This is a minor debate, but certainly one of the most enduring in the world of advertising. Many clients believe that the biggest impact for a product is generated by seeing it right away and as often as possible.

Their argument is, I'm spending a lot of money to promote my product, not – in this case – a fifties-style television show. I want to see the product big and bold and often. The counter-argument is that showing the product at exactly the best moment, and not before, produces the greatest impact of all – and that moment is the climax of the story you have created. In this case, the client prevailed and the ad had it both ways.

Advertising agencies are not film production companies, and they do not actually do the nitty-gritty work of making what is known as 'the film'. There is an in-house producer and copywriters, but the director and the production crew are all hired in. The top director at the time, if you had enough money to spend (about £7,500 per day), was Ridley Scott. Scott is a commercial director who made the big leap to theatrical direction with such movies as *The Duellists*, *Alien* and *Blade Runner* as well as blockbuster commercials like the Apple *1984* commercial, which seemed to pit Apple against IBM in a futuristic battle between good and evil. Although Scott agreed to direct the commercials, his schedule changed and he had to withdraw, so the agency selected Hugh Johnson. Johnson is a well-known commercial director and had, in fact, shot the Peugeot 405 ads. He was also substantially cheaper, at about £2,500 per day.

The commercial was to be shot as a live-action film, as opposed to animation. That meant casting actors, building a realistic TV programme set (at Shepperton studios) and, most intriguingly, creating a real 'car of the future'. This sleek vision of the automotive tomorrow was built as a full-scale (though non-functioning) model by Mike Beard and his Warwick-based company, 3T, model makers for films and television. The car, completed in five weeks, was a long, silver-skinned, bubble-topped job with a front end reminiscent of a jet aircraft and a ridge running longitudinally along the boot – tail fins sprouting out of it – that came to an end in a fixture that might be an exhaust fan or an afterburner. It actually shared a number of family traits with a series of experimental cars called The Firebirds, built by General Motors in the US in the 1950s, which also had bubble tops and tail fins in various configurations.

The commercial opens with a young 1950s lad, alone in his room, watching the television show 'Step into the Future'. A stentorian presenter, played by actor Ian Price, previews the car of the future. The lad shoves his horn-rimmed spectacles up his nose, the better to get a look at all the nice features that the new Cavalier will obviously have. Intercut with this little story are the cutaway images of the new Cavalier dashing along an assortment of moody roads.

The commercial ends by cutting to 'the future' – that is, now – and we rediscover the young boy, who has become a perfect A1 City type and wants a high technology compact car all his own. We know it is the same young boy – become a man – because he shoves his spectacles up his nose in the same way he did as a boy watching television. Reflected in these glasses: the new Cavalier.

The man, who is living to see the future come to life, jumps in the new Cavalier and drives away. The spot carries a strong emotional impact, which has to do with growing up, aging, dreams coming true, being a grown-up, getting what you want, remembering childhood.

Of course, it has very little to do with the new Cavalier, which is no greater an embodiment of the car of the future than many other cars in its class. But the point is made that the Cavalier is no slouch in the technology department, that it is up to date, that it is new, and that people (at least the young man on the screen) are eager to have it. In short, it gets the core messages across.

The television commercial, no matter how long it was or how often it aired, however, would not be enough to create the Cavalier 'event' that Vauxhall and Lowe Howard-Spink were after. The 'Future' concept would have to be everywhere in order to make Cavalier famous. So, LHS developed a campaign that would begin over a month before public launch day, and utilize *all* the major advertising media – including posters, trade and national press, and radio as well as television.

Rather than rolling out the campaign in a leisurely fashion and running it for months, it was decided to concentrate all the advertising in a short period of time, with most of the activity taking place in a four-to-six-week period. Each medium would be used for its best effect. Television, radio and outdoor advertising – which are most effective in creating impact and image – would be used to announce that car had indeed arrived and do so in a memorable fashion. The national press ads, as Terry Edwards put it, would 'actually tell them about the car, give them more detail of what the car offered'.

In the press, the ad was designed as a 'Step into the Future' 1958 Annual 'from the popular TV series', an eight-page, full-colour, gate-fold booklet that featured fifties-style illustrations of the car of the future, as well as a centrefold spread with a photograph of the new car itself and a good deal of copy describing its features.

The campaign kicked off in early September. To build suspense for the launch and for the debut of the commercial itself – and to contribute to the launch as 'event' – the campaign began with a full-page, national press 'teaser' ad. It showed a glowing tent pitched outside a Vauxhall showroom at night with the headlines, 'There's an easier way to test drive the new Cavalier'. The copy urged the reader to return a coupon. The replies were processed by a response house who in turn funnelled them to the local dealer closest to the respondent who used them to develop a list of prospects.

These people would be invited to launch parties and test-driving sessions.

The tease for the launch advertising itself began in early October, when posters went up on 220 outdoor sites around the country. Many of these were the largest standard posters available, known as ninety-six sheets. In a few locations, such as, appropriately, Vauxhall Bridge, extra-large 144 sheet posters appeared. The crisp, black-and-white poster showed a happy, space-age family (mum, dad, brother and sister clad in shiny jumpsuits) admiring the sleek, bubble-topped car displayed on a turntable. 'STEP INTO THE FUTURE' urged the headline, and, in smaller type below, 'ITV, Thursday, October 13th, 10.15 PM.' Was this an ad for a new television programme? A new car? Similarly teasing ten-second television commercials, as well as radio ads, were aired early in the week before launch.

On the morning of the day before launch, all the posters were 're-posted'. A red banner appeared in the corner with the single word: 'TONIGHT'. That night, the blockbuster television commercial broke as promised, during the ITV programme, and the television campaign continued throughout November. Late at night on 13 October, the 220 posters were all re-posted yet again, the new batch bearing a huge photo of the new Cavalier itself with the bold strapline, 'THE FUTURE. NOW'. The new Cavalier was now, officially, revealed.

The car was on display at mainline railway stations, at motorway service stations. 'Ad vans' – posters mounted on travelling vans – cruised around London, paraded past the Houses of Parliament and were parked at a Ford administrative car park, 'just to get up people's noses,' says Terry Edwards. Over the weekend, the press campaign hit with the eight-page, gate-fold booklet. Everything led up to the Motor Show, which began in the middle of that week in Birmingham, where the Cavalier would be the focus of the Vauxhall stand.

It was indeed difficult to miss the new Cavalier during its launch week. There was little doubt that an event was taking place. Just how many people saw the TV commercials, the posters, the ad vans, heard the radio spots? According to one account executive at LHS, some 82% of the target audience of ABC 1 men had an average 'opportunity to see' the press campaign of 3.4 times. Whether they actually did see it, and whether they took note of it, is another matter. The television campaign reached over 90% of all adults in the country, eight or nine times. 'They were very aware of it,' says Edwards. 'In terms of millions of people, how many people? A *lot*.'

The campaign was also recognized in advertising circles. The magazine *Marketing Week* runs a feature called Adwatch each week, a regular survey of 'image awareness'. The new Cavalier went from 0% awareness to about 70% in just five days. *Marketing Week* wrote that the 'big budget launch scores 65% awareness and will set the standard for car launch activity in the coming years.'

Qualitatively, the campaign was well-executed and created the desired event 'atmosphere'. The 'Step into the Future' theme had the advantage of being appealingly tongue-in cheek while presenting the opportunity for unusual visuals and fifties-style graphics. A possible disadvantage, however, was its complexity and inaccessibility; at first glance you couldn't immediately tell that the advertising was about a new car, much less the new Cavalier. You would have to be intrigued enough by the opening of the television commercial or the cover of the 'Step into the Future' booklet, inserted into your newspaper supplement, to want to learn what it was all about. If the approach worked, it was likely to prove more memorable than a straightforward approach. If not, you might miss it altogether.

Whether the idea is believable or not, it fits the motor industry. The idea of the 'car of the future' is a persistent one – a model that will ultimately define the modern car and incorporate all the latest technology. Of course, no such car has ever existed, nor is it likely to exist, the car being an evolutionary product that gradually incorporates new ideas and new technologies as they become available and producible. But the 'car of the future' idea remains an extremely appealing one.

Now it was the dealers' turn. Vauxhall had done their bit, having treated the dealers to the formal presentations at the Royal Lancaster in London, let them loose on the high speed bowl at Millbrook and delivered an extensive advertising campaign. In addition, Vauxhall supplied the dealers with plenty of free materials (including, for example, a Launch Planning Guide, window-trim, literature) and made available plenty of other items the dealers could buy (pennants, giveaways, point of sale display units, livery for demonstrator cars, mobiles, car toppers, a video, even a new Cavalier franking block and specially bottled champagne).

What Vauxhall wanted every dealer to do now was to throw a big party on launch night eve and invite as many prospects as could fit in the showroom. All of the national attention and excitement would be wasted if the local dealer didn't care about the new car.

The relationship between Vauxhall dealers and Vauxhall Motors Ltd is a complex one. Dealerships are franchises, and the manufacturer has the right to revoke a franchise if it feels proper standards or business procedures are not being observed. The manufacturer is also the sole source for the dealer's product; there are no sources of supply for Vauxhall cars other than Vauxhall, except for those trade-offs a dealer can do with other dealers.

In addition, most Vauxhall dealers sell no cars other than Vauxhall cars. So, from one point of view, it would seem that the manufacturer is in the dominant position and holds most of the cards. At the same time, the manufacturer is completely dependent on the dealers for revenue. With no direct sales force, Vauxhall has a limited set of tools with which to influence the dealers, and therefore, sales. They can use persuasion, they can use threats. They can offer incentives and factory rebates, financing schemes, special promotions. But all of it is indirect, all of it must be executed by the network of dealers and their staffs, over whom Vauxhall does not have ultimate control.

The relationship is made more complicated by the fact that Vauxhall (at the time of J'89 launch) was number three in the market and did not have a particularly good track record with dealers. When a Vauxhall dealer takes delivery of a new car, he does not pay for it. He lodges a percentage of the wholesale price with the manufacturer as a kind of deposit.

As a general rule, the dealer pays the manufacturer the full amount when he himself sells the car. If the car is not sold within six months, theoretically the dealer can choose one of two courses of action. He can return the car to the factory, or he can pay for it himself. In practice, dealers do not return cars to the manufacturer. But if they have to buy the cars themselves they may have to seek bank financing, and then the cost of credit is added to all the other costs of doing business.

Manufacturers do not like to keep cars at the factory either. If they have overcapacity they will go to great lengths to push the cars on to the dealers, primarily by reducing the purchase price to them.

One manager at a large dealership remembers the days of the early 1980s when the long drought of undersupply during the 1970s turned into the oversupply glut of 1980. 'In crude terms, they buggered the market completely for a while. It was distress marketing – anything to get rid of the motor car.'

The most visible evidence of the oversupply of cars was the rows and rows of shiny new Cavaliers (the Mark I model) parked patiently in fields and pastures because there was no room for them anywhere else, particularly on the dealers' forecourts. Given the way cars are constantly changing in specification, six months sitting and waiting for a sale can make the new model seem dated.

'Vauxhall realized that dealers were fed up with buying a car that had been in a field for six months,' said this manager. 'You can't keep it quiet. Some guy goes past an airfield with 500 cars in it. He gets wind of it, cars are being stockpiled. He starts asking. "When was this car actually built?" He wants the latest specification. But the cars in the field haven't got electric mirrors or sun-roofs, they've got birds' nests in the back seat. It gets embarrassing.'

That's bad enough, but undersupply is perhaps even worse. Customers tend not to mind waiting a few weeks for their new car, but a wait of more than two months for a Cavalier and you begin to wonder if the whole thing is worth it. And if you lose the sale of a car to a customer because he doesn't want to wait, it is not like losing the sale of a packet of razor blades – you've lost that person for years, and possibly forever.

'The healthier situation is when there's a little shortage, a reasonable lead time,' says the manager. That is why the Luton factory struggled so mightily to have enough cars on hand for the launch: the dealers just didn't have faith that they could deliver.

Fortunately, the dealers reacted well to the launch presentation at the Royal Lancaster. They enjoyed the ride-and-drive sessions. They seemed to believe the new Cavalier was just about right – it was going to be the car they needed – and they heard reassuring words about availability. After seeing an event like the one staged at

the Royal Lancaster, which cost well over £1 million and was nearly
a year in the planning, the dealers began having visions of staging
their own extravaganzas on their own premises.

Jack Newlands is the dealer-principal at Marlboro Motors, one of
two Vauxhall dealerships in St Albans, about 30 km north of London.
After nearly twenty years working with Ford, during which time he
worked his way up from cleaning cars to become a dealer-principal,
Newlands left Ford to join the Vauxhall dealership owned by his wife's
parents. The dealership was small when he first joined them, selling
250 to 300 new cars and 100 used cars per year. After six years, with
Newlands and his wife injecting new energy and commitment into
the business, Marlboro Motors now sells 2,000 new cars and 600
used cars per year.

Newlands is a bundle of entrepreneurial enthusiasm and he is justly
proud of his operations, which include computer system, executive
offices ('This is my wife's office, which is why the colour scheme is
what it is'), car wash, service area, hire department, spares operation
and showroom complete with kiddy corner ('We do find we lose toys
from time to time, but if they're spending £7,000, what's a toy, do you
follow me?') You also get the distinct impression that, beneath his
jovial manner, there is a high-powered corporate executive struggling
to get out.

The launch party held at Marlboro Motors was a huge success.
'It was a lot of work. We obviously sent off all the invites three
weeks before, but we didn't actually start to do all the build-up of
the workshops and all of the hard work till at least twenty-four hours
before.' The plan called for guests to enter the showroom, although
there would be no new car there for them to see – yet.

The guests – about 600 in all – were treated to drinks and
light refreshments. As Newlands recalls the night, he points at
a nearby colleague. 'Derek organized all the food, right? I must
admit the food seemed to go very quick on that night, didn't it,
Derek? I thought we'd ordered enough drink, there was so much
drink, I looked and I thought, bloody hell, what we going to do
with all that drink? We didn't have one drop of drink left. You
know, Derek did lose a little bit of hair, but the response was
terrific.'

Newlands snaps a video of the event into his video player. Some murky images begin to appear, the video has obviously been taken on a home system, perhaps by a member of the Newlands family. There are many shots of people mingling in the dim light of the converted workshop.

'We invited the police too,' said Newlands. 'That way they felt a part of things, if you know what I mean.' The highlight of the tape, of course, and the event, was the 'reveal' of the new car. It began with a procession by the St Albans Junior Children's Band and was followed by a show of laser light, albeit from small lasers, that traced madly around the room in garish colours and spelled out the words, 'Marlboro Motors bring you the Future Now in the New Cavalier.'

And then, with a great burst of music, girls in tight-fitting costumes waved the new Cavalier out from its hiding place in a cloud of artificial smoke. Although no one could tell because Newlands had so success-fully decorated the garage, the new Cavalier was actually descending along a ramp that led to the painting area of the workshop.

There was applause. People thronged forward to have a look. Whether they could form an accurate impression of the car – after guzzling all that drink, half-blinded by laser light and trying to keep one eye on the retreating showgirls – is immaterial. This was an event. Newlands' video ends with a summary title: 'Now You Seen the Car of the Future.'

'I think we did very good out of the Cavalier launch,' says Newlands. 'It was a really successful night, we got people coming back.' He sold over a hundred Cavaliers within the first few months and 'I reckon we've got two or three in stock at the moment, and we could sell them today.'

But, generally, Newlands is enthusiastic about the new Cavalier, as are the other dealers around the country, and it showed in the scope of the launch party. 'Everybody did the same thing,' says John Butterfield, 'so we certainly got dealers to move, and that was the whole idea at the Royal Lanc, not only to tell them about the car, but to light their enthusiasm to go out there and promote the car really strongly, and they did. Oxford had 2,000-plus people. I went up to Aberdeen and there were nearly a thousand at a little village fourteen miles from Aberdeen. A dealer in Newbury got David Hamilton, the disc jockey, and a Liverpool dealer got a country band in and filled the cricket club and it went on for hours.'

Despite all this activity, it is well known that there is dead wood in the Vauxhall dealer organization, and that Vauxhall sometimes is not the hard-nosed organization that Ford can be. 'You find that Vauxhalls are more gentlemen than Fords,' says Newlands. 'They don't put the pressure on dealers the same way that Ford do. Fords, if they tell the dealers to get off their asses and do something, they mean it, right? If Vauxhall, they want something, they go about it in a much more gentlemanly way. I'm very straight talking – I think they should turn around and say what the bloody hell do you guys think you're doing.' Some of the Vauxhall dealers, according to Newlands, should lose their franchises because 'they're just not professional.'

Newlands talks about service and how important it is. People are scared when they buy a new car. They're facing a big investment. You have to treat them right, look after them. He has the opportunity to demonstrate what this means.

I have been driving one of the Vauxhall fleet for the past several days, a Carlton CD. Unfortunately there has been some disagreement between me, the electrical system and the radio. And the radio, which is coded to prevent use if removed from the car, has decided I am a burglar. It refuses to work, and I don't have the code. It is the weekend, so I can't call Luton and ask for the code. 'We'll have a look at it,' says Newlands, 'where is it?' 'It's just up the road,' I say, 'I'll go and get it.' 'Give me the keys,' says Newlands, 'we'll send one of our lads.'

Within half an hour, unable to break the code, they have installed a brand new radio/tape player, washed and polished the car, and I am on my way.

Launch day was just the starting date for a flurry of activity around the country. New Cavaliers were displayed at each of ten airports, eight mainline railway stations, and thirty-eight of the busiest motorway service areas. Each location was attended by a 'personality girl' – a young woman chosen (with great care and attention by the marketing communications staff) for both attractive appearance and ability to talk with some enthusiasm about the car, after suitable training. And it all led up to the opening of the Motor Show, held at the National Exhibition Centre in Birmingham every other year.

There are several major motor shows throughout the world, including ones at Birmingham, Detroit, Frankfurt, Turin, Paris, Geneva and Tokyo. Motor shows are where new cars are revealed and where so-called concept cars are displayed. They are a combination of the simple exhibition (real cars on display), demonstration (personality girls), new car showroom (company reps on hand for talk, but not deal-making), image-making (presentations of various types) and, according to one automotive writer, 'nothing less than open warfare'.

Industry insiders come to see what's happening. Designers have a look at the concept cars to get a clue as to what might be coming next from competitors. The general public comes in to gawk and decide which model to buy. The press writes it all up.

Following its public launch début the week before, J'89 was positioned as the star of the Motor Show. Just exactly how a car becomes the star of a show is hard to say; perhaps if you proclaim it loudly enough, it is. Vauxhall certainly took a lot of space: at 1650 square metres theirs was the largest stand at the show. Thirty-eight new Vauxhalls were displayed, many of them on the four turntables, two of which were devoted to new Cavaliers. A video-wall – which was the current presentation technology of choice – consisting of fifty video monitors in a grid above one of the rotating cars, extolled the virtues of the car.

Stand design is a specialized category of the corporate communications industry. And, although the Vauxhall stand was large, it was not necessarily the most electrifying. The automotive design leaders tend to lead the way in all aspects of design and this is true of motor show stand design. Porsche showed its models in rotating platforms that tilted at an alarming angle, with the conference area tucked mysteriously away inside this wall of cars. Volvo had embedded a series of front ends into a waterfall. Ford, with another massive space, opted for a clean design with painted canvas banners.

At the Vauxhall stand, there were the inevitable attractive young women draped around the car, answering questions and directing customers to the right Vauxhall people to talk with. Bill Mouland, writing in *Today* tut-tutted about the employment of young women as car salespeople. In his article of 22 October 1988 headlined 'Nice car, shame about the bimbo', Mouland wrote that Vauxhall 'was using girls in split sheaths of silver to draw attention to its new Cavalier. It was a toss-up who had the most curves.' Mouland quoted Ken Moyes, then a public relations manager for Vauxhall, who rebutted the popular view of the motor show girls, saying, 'Our girls are not just glamour girls. They know the cars. They have been on a course. They are experts on the cars and are not just there for show.'

Also on hand was the 'car of the future' that had starred in the television commercial, drawing more attention than perhaps Vauxhall would have liked. As Peter Batchelor relates, 'The interest in that car was phenomenal. We left it on the stand for the whole ten days. I wondered whether it was working for or against us. Kids were saying, "Hey, Dad, there's the car that's in the advert. We must look at that tonight."'

The Motor Show was well-covered on television. The BBC and ITV had special reports from Birmingham, and featured reviews of the new Cavalier. Mike Scott of ITV's *The Time, The Place* programme which was broadcast on 19 October, interviewed Wayne Cherry who, once again, proved his abilities as a spokesman and performer. 'Does the cosmetic part of your job worry you at all? Do you ever say to yourself, goddamn it, this is superficial? Or do you actually say no, this is deeply important?'

Cherry looked at Scott with bewilderment, but answered with characteristic seriousness and affability. 'Not at all,' he said. 'The car is a blend of aesthetics and function.' And he went on to describe the key features of his latest achievement.

By the end of November, with the Motor Show over and the launch phase of the advertising campaign and the special events all completed, Vauxhall had spent some £12 million. Now there were two questions remaining. One: how will the public respond to the new car? Two: can we build enough new Cavaliers to meet demand, if the response is as good as we hope it will be?

9 · J'89

'The minute people saw the car and sat in the car, they said,
"That's just right."'

Peter Batchelor, Executive Director, Sales and Marketing, Vauxhall Motors Ltd

Judging by the reactions to the car in the press, the new Cavalier was both an immediate and a longer-term success. The initial announcements came out at the end of August, with evaluations and more in-depth reports appearing from the first week of October, primarily based on the press drives held in the south of France.

Most writers had some reservations, of course, but the reports were basically solid; there was no suggestion that the new car was a travesty of the old or had some lurking, devastating weakness.

The *Financial Times* reported that 'even on a paper assessment [the Cavalier] was obviously going to offer stern competition to class rivals like the Ford Sierra, Rover Montego and Peugeot 405. Having driven it, I can now say that the Cavalier is ahead of the pack.' In the *Daily Telegraph*, John Langley wrote, 'In most respects, it is significantly better: quieter, roomier and more comfortable. I am glad to report it is still fun to drive.'

The *Daily Express* writer was enthusiastic: 'I have seldom stepped into a new car and felt more at home.' In the *Mail on Sunday*, Frank Page said 'The new Cavalier is not radically different in any single feature, but a number of improvements in refinement have produced a very attractive car.' From *The Times*: 'The Cavalier is an object lesson in marketing strategy, with graceful, rounded styling. It is still recognizably a Cavalier, not radical and unfamiliar like the Sierra when it replaced the Cortina . . .'

The motoring magazines looked at the car even more closely. The
5 October issue of *Autocar and Motor* described the results of an
evaluation of the principal competitors – the new Cavalier SRi (the
sporty model), Sierra 2.0i Ghia and the Peugeot 405 SRi – and
reported that 'the new Cavalier is exactly what Vauxhall needs in the
UK. Sleeker, faster and more comfortable, it also offers driver appeal
like no Cavalier before it. Combined with an extremely competent
chassis, the package is good enough to put the Cavalier back on top.'
The magazine's verdict, however, went in favour of the Peugeot 405,
primarily for its 'blend of grip, handling and ride comfort'.

The new Cavalier was also mentioned everywhere in the regional
press – proving the success of the driveaway days at Millbrook, when
each dealer who intended to pick up a new car had been urged to
bring along a local press representative. As a result, the country was
blanketed with coverage.

The reports in the hundreds of local and regional dailies and
weeklies tended to be a mix of the local angle (often an interview
with the nearest Vauxhall dealer), personal reaction of the writer to
the driving at Millbrook, and information revised (and sometimes
used verbatim) from the voluminous press releases.

Headlines, when they weren't straightforward, were often breath-
less and sometimes shamelessly partisan. 'Vivacious Vauxhall!' crowed
the *Bolton Evening News* in bold type. 'Cavalier Reborn!' effused the
Lancashire Evening Telegraph. Everywhere, plays were made on the
Cavalier name. This was the laughing Cavalier, the dashing Cavalier,
the bold Cavalier, the gallant Cavalier, the classy Cavalier, the gay
Cavalier, the swaggering Cavalier, an uninspired 'Significant Cavalier'
and there was lots about the 'Cavalier attitude'.

There were many ominous headlines about the car marketing warfare to come. 'Watch out, Sierra: it's the new-look Vauxhall Cavalier!'
warned the *Great Yarmouth Mercury*. It's a 'Sierra Stomper!' according to the *Aberdeen Evening Express*. The *Liverpool Echo* reported that
'Cavaliers Storm the Fleet.' 'Cavalier Comeback?' asked the *Runcorn
World*. And 'Cavalier Plans Carve-Up' announced the *Eastern Evening
News*. The new Cavalier is the beefiest, the hottest, it is super-smooth,
it has 'rare quality', and, in the words of the *Borehamwood and Radlett
Advertiser*, it is 'Fast, Furious and Affordable'.

Most of the reports beneath the headlines were glowing; some were thoughtful and incisive. There was also plenty of inaccuracy and fuzziness. The new Cavalier shape 'was developed in a wind tunnel', stated the *Wells Journal* of 13 October. The *Epsom and Ewell Herald* reversed the Cavalier-Sierra leapfrog, stating that 'when the current outgoing [Cavalier] model hit the market at the end of 1982, families and fleets were just beginning to decide that they didn't like the "jelly mould" Sierra shape after all.'

The *Kettering Evening Telegraph* showed a thorough lack of understanding of the new car development process when it revealed that 'when Vauxhall launched the "new" Cavalier seven years ago, it was desperate to keep a secret . . . a new body was already taking shape. If the news had leaked out it could have seriously damaged sales of what became one of the best-selling cars in Britain.'

But it was all good news for Vauxhall. There was virtually no escaping the fact that the big contender for sales in the fleet market had arrived on the scene.

In most reviews of the car, the writers began with an assessment of the exterior styling, usually followed by the interior styling and then on to the driving characteristics. Opinions about the exterior were quite consistent, and in describing it writers often referred to the old rivalry of the 1981-2 Sierra-Cavalier battle.

Judith Jackson wrote in the *Guardian*: 'When Cavalier and Sierra were launched six years ago, the Sierra shape invoked cries of "pudding basin". Today, of course, it looks in tune with the times. If you stand one next to the new Cavalier, you will notice similarities – the third window on the side of the saloon and the high tail.' In the *Mail on Sunday*, Frank Page wrote: 'The wind-cheating body, rounded body shape is easy on the eye – with near-flush glazing, a smooth front end, concealed wipers and faired-in mirrors. The tail is high and tapered to help the air flow.'

John Langley referred to the car as 'curvaceous'. The *Sunday Times* said 'well-proportioned and fashionable'. David Vivian in *Motor Magazine* called it 'smooth, glassy, almost Audi-esque'. Clean, tidy, neat, sleek, smooth, curvy, rounded were the operative words. There were a few more evocative descriptions. Roger Bell, motoring writer for *Country Life*, said that 'the new Cavalier has much in common with the cousin Carlton, not to mention a Flo-Jo leotard'. John Langley referred to 'the bland, roly-poly styling'. *Autocar and Motor* called it 'almost bulbous'. And, although *Today* chose the new Cavalier as one of the top five cars for men, the newspaper judged that 'styling is so dull few women would be interested'.

Richard Bremner, writing in *Car* magazine, summed it up by saying, 'If you wanted to show a man fresh to the world of motoring the current state of development of the average car, you'd do well to show him the new Cavalier. It has all that is fresh and fashionable, without leaning too far towards the flip and futuristic.'

The new Cavalier is so well-refined, unassuming and dominated by its aerodynamic intentions that it is not an easy shape to perceive at first sight. With some cars, that quarter-second glance offers an unmistakable characteristic or two. Some of these are distinctive primarily because they have been established over time, like the grilles and bonnet ornaments that we have come to associate with Jaguar, Rolls-Royce, Mercedes and BMW.

It has become a common complaint, however, that new cars are looking more and more alike, with differences only to be found in the minor details. This is true, but really only within narrow segments. Jonathan Glancey, writing in *The Independent*, put it well: 'Pick up your Dictionary of Design Cliché. Turn to the page on cars and under "A" in the listing you will find the hoary old adage: "All modern cars look the same." In a world where Jaguars, Citröens, Skodas and Porsches are still manufactured, this is clearly a lie. If the entry is to be believed, then it should read: "All modern fleet cars look the same." Study the side views of the new Peugeot 405, the Volkswagen Passat and Vauxhall Cavalier. At a glance, can you really spot the difference?'

The real distinction of the J'89 exterior is its flowing smoothness. It is designed so that almost nothing sticks out physically, and one result is that almost nothing sticks out visually either. Because all the surfaces are curved and blend smoothly into their neighbours, the eye has few definite starting and stopping places. It's hard to judge where the corners are.

It's much easier to look at a car with sharper, straighter lines, because of its clarity of outline. You can tell exactly where the fender meets the bonnet. But with J'89, the fender doesn't really meet the bonnet at all. The individual sheet-metal sections do not serve to define elements of the shape, they act as wrapping for the entire form.

The smoothness of the form also makes it appear very different from different angles. In side view, the car looks flat and rather lean. It is this view that tells the least about the car, and as a result makes it look the most like its closest competitors. But from other angles, the new Cavalier has more distinctive looks.

From a rear three-quarter view, at about standing height, both the hatchback and the saloon look sleek and well-balanced. The rear view from ground level, however, makes the roundness of the bonnet look bulbous. A three-quarter front view, from standing height, presents the car at its best. The car foreshortens itself. The front end reminds one of a streamlined sea creature, blunt and smooth, like a dolphin without its beak or a small whale. The reflection line curves gently upward from nose to tail, making it look positive and purposeful. And the rear fender and boot line round off into a jutting hip that looks taut and well-finished.

Of course, other writers disagree. *Motor Magazine* states flatly that the 'smooth new styling is more successful from the rear than from the front'. The car perhaps looks best from a perspective most people seldom see – almost directly above. In the plan view, you can see how the sides bow slightly out. The wheels disappear. The greenhouse forms an elegant rectangle, set against the second, longer rectangle of the sheet-metal body.

When you see the car close-up and 'in the metal' rather than in photographs or at speed on the motorway, you can almost feel how slippery it is. There is a sheerness about the lines that can produce a kind of vertigo in the sensitive beholder, creating a feeling akin to the one you feel on top of very tall buildings: smooth, dropping surfaces offering nothing to cling to. There is something about the notion of a pure uninterrupted stream of air gliding along a slippery surface that can cause the palms to tingle and the tongue to develop a metallic taste.

In short, the new Cavalier, like any car, like many forms, is dynamic and protean. It looks different from every angle and height, in different lighting conditions, at different speeds, in different colours.

One fleet operator complained that too many of the J'81 colours were carried over to the new model and that some of them were not appropriate. The dark colours, in particular, seem to make the shape more difficult to perceive. But the lightest shades – light silver and white – don't do the shape justice either. Medium tones for the intermediate car.

The critics are less in agreement about the relationship of the new car to its predecessor. Does it carry on the 'Cavalier character' or is the old model simply abandoned? *The Times* felt that 'while it is a new car it is not a world apart from its predecessor'. *What Car* magazine agreed, saying, 'Cavalier is a great car. It's close enough in character to the model it replaces to satisfy any devotee of the marque, yet different enough where it matters to appeal to the more fashion-conscious.'

The *Autocar and Motor* of 26 October disagreed. 'It's hard to judge where the styling influences lie; the car does not bear a strong resemblance to any other Vauxhall and is not as positively penned as the Audi 80. Links with the previous model have been cleanly severed.'

There are fewer links between J'89 and J'81 than there are to the other members of the current Vauxhall family. Sue Baker of the *Observer*, for example, agreed: 'The styling is certainly strongly "family", echoing the lines of its larger brethren, the Carlton and Senator.' The *Daily Telegraph* found the shape 'redolent of the Senator'. *Motor* magazine saw the resemblance in some specifics: 'The nose treatment borrows elements of Astra and the tail-light clusters are reminiscent of a Carlton's.' *Motor* also found that the new Cavalier was 'more of a scaled-down Carlton than a pumped-up Astra'.

This 'familyness' is really a phenomenon of the 1980s for General Motors in Europe – the Astra, Carlton, Senator and Cavalier all having been restyled since the turn of the decade – and the resemblance is most strongly concentrated at the front end. Except for the Nova, the cars share that beakless dolphin, smoothly drooping nose, culminating in a wedge-shaped grille. The sides are also similarly outward-bowed, and the rear door shuts are gently curved, as opposed to the sharper lines of J'89's principal competitors.

Family resemblance is also a function of a thousand items – hardware, colours, trim – not to mention the clue you get from the griffin badge on the nose. This family resemblance is undeniably important. It makes the GME look a real presence on the roads, and the more people see a look the more they get used to it. The more they get used to it, the more they accept it and the more they are willing to buy it. Even the radical Sierra shape became acceptable through the sheer force of seeing it often enough, and living with it.

Of course, the character of a car is more than the bends in the sheet metal. You spend most of your time with your car inside it, and most of that time is spent driving. The J'89 interior is perhaps the greatest improvement of all over the old car. The J'81 interior seemed a cramped, dark cabin with a wall of plastic facing you, crammed with ill-fitting dials and gawky stalks.

The new interior is light, airy, comfortable. If you know what an H-point is, you can feel that it is higher in this car, and it feels better. The moulded liner overhead looks neat and adds quiet. The slim pillars (thanks to the Cray and its mulling over of those 120 body shells) obstruct vision very little, and admit more light. The C pillar, in particular, does not present you with a dangerous obstruction, a blind spot within which onrushing lorries can conceal themselves.

The binnacle, which shelters the instrument panel, is gently curved. The analogue gauges are easy to read, pleasantly backlit. All the levers and buttons seem to work effortlessly. The comments of the *Independent*'s Richard Bremner would delight the designers: 'Slim pillars and plenty of glass convey an airy feel, the dashboard no longer resembles a cliff overhanging your knees and you do not sit so close to the floor that you must crane to see out.' The *Evening Standard* agreed: 'Soft user-friendly contours dominate the fascia, and work areas are lightly framed – the Sierra looks desperately heavy by comparison.' Most writers also took note of the little details that have come to be weapons in the interior specifications battles. Judith Jackson was enthusiastic: 'Natty little rubber mats line the various niches in the fascia and stop things slithering around.'

Although the interior is greatly improved, rear seat accommodation still falls short. The in-depth report in *Autocar and Motor* said, 'Starting with a clean sheet, GM's designers had the opportunity to create a car with class-leading space utilization and adequate space for five adults. And they almost succeeded. It is only the rear seat accommodation that fails to come up to expectations. With the driver's seat set for a fairly tall driver, rear knee room is marginal. To make matters worse, head room is poor and shoulder room for three rear passengers is very restricted.'

Considering that this started out as a top priority and that the designers succeeded so well in achieving their other objectives, it is tempting to believe that GME doesn't really care about the back seat. As *The Times* of 7 October put it: 'Improved access to the rear seats promises much but the leg and head room are disappointing. Vauxhall argues that company car drivers, who will account for 70% of Cavalier owners, spend most of their time in the car alone, so rear accommodation is not a priority.'

Much of what could have been rear accommodation space is actually consumed by the boot, which is truly capacious. Lift the lid and it soars to a position almost ninety degrees to the horizontal. The opening dips all the way down to bumper level (which is still higher than the boot floor level, however), and all is neatly carpeted. The spare tyre is hidden away. It is all so tidy and cleanly organized that it seems a shame to chuck anything but neatly wrapped Christmas gifts into it.

And (once again, thanks to the Cray) the fold-down rear seat and centre load-through allow you to drive off with whatever long skinny things (skis, rakes, carpets, ornamental bushes) you might need. Even the structural sheet metal that is exposed when the boot lid is lifted is nicely finished.

In addition to the repositioned H-point,the new pedal positions did not go unnoticed. 'Full marks to the engineers who created the driving position,' wrote *Autocar and Motor*. 'The relationship of seat to wheel and pedals is excellent . . . The pedals are worthy of special note, for this is the first new Vauxhall with ideal spacing and height-matched brake and accelerator for easy heel and toe.'

Standard equipment was judged to be beyond the expected, with deadlock central locking, six-speaker audio and sun-roofs standard in all models save the bottom-rung Standard.

Most satisfying to Peter Bonner and the manufacturing team at Luton, the build quality was singled out for high marks. 'Panel fit and finish is good considering the number of complex curves that make up the Cavalier's shape,' reported *Autocar and Motor*. 'Shut lines are uniformly crisp and the light blue paint of the test car was smooth and blemish-free. The interior is equally tasteful . . . fit and finish is of a high order.' The *Independent* said, 'It is a solid, taut car that gives the impression of being competently screwed together.'

I picked up the German-market version of the Cavalier – an Opel Vectra – in the top-of-the-line CD specification, at the special Opel car park across the tracks from the main gate in Rüsselsheim. Dark grey paint. Understated grey fabric covering for the seats. 2.0i litre engine. Ignition on, and a small light on the fascia informs you that you have ABS, the anti-lock braking system.

I waved sedately to the guard, turned right into the street, and headed for the E1 autobahn that would take me to Montreux, some 400 km south at the eastern end of Lake Geneva. On autobahns and through back roads, the new Cavalier proved to be a pleasant car to drive – as did all the models I drove (including a 1.6L, 1.6GL, the 2.0i CD and SRi). Responsive, sure-footed, stable, well-mannered. The controls are so logically placed and easy to use, that they seem completely familiar from first use. The car is light inside. The detailing is modern and attractive. The cabin is quiet, there is very little wind noise. The sun-roof, central locking and good radio make living with the car effortless and appealing.

The dominant impression is that this car has been thoroughly thought through: it is totally designed, down to the mats lining the oddment trays. Everything is where it is for a good reason, not merely because it just ended up there. The needs of the user have been placed above the obsessions of the designer or the limitations of the manufacturer. Which is not to say there aren't a few quirks. When driving on the motorway at speed and changing lanes, for example, the little swish-swish-swish-swish of tyre noise as the car crosses the raised reflective lines that mark the lanes is particularly pronounced.

This may be because road and wind noise, in general, are very low and the tyre noise stands out against the relative quiet.

The most striking evidence of the aerodynamic quality of J'89 is the way rainwater behaves on its surface. Rather than being channelled around windows and surfaces by drip rails and mouldings, the water is free to swirl wherever it likes. Back up from a parked position, and the rainwater comes coursing forward and across the front windscreen in a sheet. Open the door and, although most of the water collects in the concealed drip channel, there are a few unwanted drips off the top edge of the door.

Drive for some distance through a smoggy city or dirty countryside where there is also rain, and you produce visible evidence of stream-lines on the car. Water and dirt dry along the surface in patterns of lines that are reminiscent of a wind tunnel method of showing streamlines using oil paint on the car's surface.

In comparison to its British competitors – the Sierra and the Montego – the new Cavalier seems superior in ride and handling. To most observers, the car earned high marks in these areas, but not stunning ones. Many felt the Peugeot 405 outshone all its rivals in the intermediate category.

After the Cavalier test drive in southern France, the *Financial Times* writer said: 'The first thing I noticed was the ride quality.' He was particularly impressed by the behaviour of the four-wheel-drive variant: 'The 4WD was the best of the lot. It felt perfectly balanced on fast corners, accelerated vividly on loose surfaces without spinning its 60-series tyres, and ran arrow straight on the autoroute.'

John Langley of the *Daily Telegraph* wrote, 'Although the car feels softer and quieter, it still handles well. It is a practical all-rounder with the added bonus of being enjoyable to drive.' The London *Evening Standard* noted that 'the smooth and supple ride, with impressively little road noise, faltered over lumpy roads taken at low speeds.'

Richard Bremner tested a 2.0iL model 'that will outsprint a Golf GTi, but does not sound as if it will get a hernia doing it.' *Autocar and Motor* found the Cavalier lacking in comparison to the 405. 'Of the three, the third being the Sierra, it is the 405 which puts power down most effectively. Over tight and bumpy roads there is no torque-steer and little wheel-fight. Over the same roads the Cavalier spins power away through its inside front wheel, while the Sierra does the same with its inside rear wheel.'

Roger Bell, writing in *Country Life*, liked the Cavalier ride, but found that the 'exceptionally low wind whoosh (another by-product of good streamlining) throws into prominence a hard, thrummy engine noise that is more intrusive in the lower-geared cars than in the long-legged ones.'

He found the four-wheel-drive to be a winner. 'On wet roads, I found it impossible even to chirp the tyres, let alone to spin the wheels under brutal first-gear starts. Under hard acceleration, there is no unruly steering tug or weave, a weakness among many front-wheel-drive cars from which the SRi suffers mildly.'

In its April 1989 issue, *What Car?* magazine named the Cavalier 2.0iGL its best of class for family hatchbacks, citing its good performance, 'wonderfully tight handling, a neat interior and high levels of equipment', as well as its clever pricing – some £800 less than the equivalent Sierra.

Many of these distinctions (apart from pricing) are ones that the average motorist will not notice. The motoring writer's job is to push the new car to its limit, to see where it will cave in. When cruising along the motorway at legal speeds and purring gently along A roads, the owner of the new Cavalier will wonder what this minor torque-steer or wheel-spin is all about. Issues of fuel economy, reliability, ease of maintenance will be much more important. And, in these areas, too, Vauxhall has claimed to make many improvements – although it is only over time that the claims can really be proved.

Not everything about the new Cavalier could be considered a success. It failed to win the Car of the Year (COTY) award presented by a panel of European motoring writers and considered to be the major European automotive prize. J'89 lost out to the Fiat Tipo, an ingenious and quirky-looking little car designed for Fiat by the Italian firm called IDEA.

The new Cavalier, however, did win some nineteen other awards, including the Top Car of the Year 1989 award from the Guild of UK Motoring Writers, with the highest margin of victory ever. However, in a year when no direct competitors were in the running the win meant rather less glory than it might otherwise have had. The car was named 'Auto der Vernunft' (most sensible or commonsense car) for 1989 by the German magazine MOT. It won the Gold Medal in the International Coachwork Competition '88, sponsored by the Carriage and Automobile Manufacturers of Great Britain. It was Import Car of the Year '89 in Spain, Car of the Year '89 in Belgium and Most Remarkable New Car in Finland, awarded in 1988. There was the Japan 1989 Good Design Award for Outstanding Foreign Product for the Vectra CD. The new Cavalier SRi won the Tow Car of the Year Award in the UK.

Not surprisingly, the manufacturing roll-out schedule led to shortages of the most wanted models. The decision had been taken to produce the low-end variants in volume first, particularly the L specification with the 1.4 and 1.6 litre engines. But, as it turned out, the greatest demand was for the 2.0 litre engines – partly because the pricing was right, partly because the performance was just that much better, partly because that is the trend of the market.

The CD model and SRi were also in demand. And the last minute tactical addition of sun-roofs as standard to all models except the base specification led to trouble, and to a supply that could not keep up with demand, exactly the situation Vauxhall had hoped to avoid. The automatic transmission proved to have vibration problems in the 1.6 litre model and had to be withdrawn. And customers noticed the absence of a 1.8 litre engine, and one of the existing engines had to be quickly added to the line-up.

These problems did not stop virtually every new Cavalier that could be produced from selling. In January 1989, the new Cavalier took third place on the new registration list, behind the Sierra and the Escort, with 6008 copies sold. By October 1989, the new Cavalier edged past the Escort and was in striking distance of the Sierra. In that month, 11,405 new Cavaliers were registered versus 11,503 for Sierra. Vauxhall was now firmly in second place, in terms of share of domestic sales, well ahead of Rover.

The story was the same in Germany. Opel was, in effect, sold out of Vectras. As many as they could make, at present capacities, they could sell. These were exciting days for the people in Zurich, in Rüsselsheim and at Luton.

But, no matter what the press may say, no matter how many cars the fleet operators choose to buy, it's still a cold, hard world out there for a fledgling product. On that launch day, 14 October 1988, the new Cavalier was pushed out into the world. Although it received more than its share of attendant hype, persuasion and explanation, the outcome still came down to that most intimate of new product confrontations: potential customer approaches car and forms a first impression. It was happening all over the country, at dealerships, airports, mainline railway stations and motorway service stations.

That Saturday I stopped at the Scratchwood service station on the way up the M1. It was a busy day, grey and threatening rain, and the service station was filled with people. They stood around outside the loos or milled around their cars, picking up litter from the floors or rearranging luggage in the boot. They wandered in and out of the various restaurants.

And there, rather forlornly displayed in the car park with a pyramidal banner nearby, stood a new Cavalier hatch. There was no attendant fanfare. It was just there. The 'personality girl' had taken temporary shelter elsewhere, so the new car was truly alone, almost abandoned.

Two men, one of them sucking at his teeth for lingering remnants of lunch, studied the new model. They scowled, not because they didn't like the car but because you must scowl when studying any new product that costs nearly £10,000. One of the gentlemen noticed something, reached forward and picked at a bit of rubber protruding from around the rear window, a section of door seal that was less than perfect.

'Look at that,' the man said to his mate, 'hasn't got a patch on my Mazda.' That was that. One pick at a bit of rubber. One negative pronouncement. That was all the new Cavalier got from those two: about forty seconds of study and a failing grade based on an errant piece of rubber, which had probably been dislodged by an earlier critic anyway.

And that is typical of the automotive market today. That is why Fritz Lohr, Wayne Cherry, the twenty-five designers, the aerodynamicists, the computer experts and 4,000 engineers fight such prolonged battles. It is why Peter Bonner and the manufacturing team so diligently mark defects with little blue and green and yellow dots all over the pilot cars.

As Peter Batchelor puts it, 'There are no bad cars any more. Just varying degrees of good ones.' And everybody knows it.

10 · FUTURE

'Ford is no longer fireproof.'

*Paul Tosch, Chairman and Managing
Director, Vauxhall Motors Ltd*

Press day for the 1989 Frankfurt Motor Show was Tuesday, 12 September. The show was held at the Frankfurt Airgrounds, and all the car manufacturers were exhibiting there, along with makers of commercial vehicles and many suppliers.

The Opel stand was in Hall 8, the central one, occupying a space across from Seat, adjacent to BMW, where the new 850 was displayed, and not far from Volkswagen. On its left flank was a small stand occupied by General Motors, touting American-made cars for export to Europe.

The Opel stand was a large two-tiered structure, focused around a kind of circular forecourt. The rear half of the circle was faced with a wall of fifty-four video projection panels. The forward half was defined by little nozzles that, on command, shot wavery jets of water upwards, but it was otherwise open to the passing public. The circular floor itself was white and flat, with a tell-tale groove that made you suspect it could guide and support a car when the time came.

An open space on the opposite side of the stand was devoted to a circular track. Here a small, transparent, operating scale model of the four-wheel-drive J'89 could be put through its paces – around corners, up a hill – by remote control. The upper level was a broad open area, enclosed only by a waist-high rail, from which you could overlook much of the rest of the hall. This space was entirely devoted to conversation and refreshment – an open bar and, at lunch time, a hot and cold buffet.

On the back of the stand a black Vectra had been bolted into a spectacular piece of display machinery that rotated the car through 360 degrees on its longitudinal axis, allowing the watcher to see the car from virtually every angle. Many a passing spectator was enraptured by it and stood before the huge, rotating metal structure for minutes at a time as if mesmerized.

Everyone from GME seemed to be there. Fritz Lohr, looking like a contented burgher presiding over a small, bustling city; Paul Tosch, seeming slightly uncomfortable with all the hoopla and flesh-pressing; Wayne Cherry, roving happily to and fro, sometimes holding court on the upper level, sometimes making lone forays to inspect the competitive merchandise; Erhard Schnell, intently inspecting an aqua/turquoise concept vehicle called Futura at the Volkswagen stand; and Chris Mattingley, from Opel public relations, trying to keep contact with the dozens of journalists present. Young women in crisp white outfits, the Opel information staff, resembled an efficient team of automotive industry nurses.

The big moment at the Opel stand was to be the unveiling of the new Calibra, a coupé based on the J'89 platform, at one o'clock in the afternoon. At the GM US stand, they were planning an unveiling of their own: three new models available for purchase in Europe. The new cars were properly concealed beneath grey cloths, emblazoned with their 'You'll be impressed' slogan.

A large screen overlooked them, flanked by skirted podiums. A video crew was completing last-minute preparations. Young ladies in short dresses were standing by. A number of GM people tending the show stand, recognizable by their blue suits and blue GM badges, shifted from one foot to the other. As the appointed moment approached, a crowd began to gather, perhaps drawn as much by the evidence of impending food and drink visible at the far end of the stand, as by the expectation of electrifying news.

A live video image of the podium now appeared on screen, and a large woman dressed in dramatic red took the stage. She spoke in German and proceeded to introduce a speaker from General Motors in the States. He was not an accomplished speaker, delivering his few remarks in stumbling English. 'GM has been selling North American produced cars and trucks for over sixty years. As we approach the '90s, we believe the time is right to expand our marketing efforts throughout the world to sell more American-made cars and trucks.' Unfortunately, there was a palpable lack of excitement for the idea from the crowd.

The actual descriptions of the new cars, and their unveiling, were overseen by a second American executive. The Corvette ZR1 came first. After describing all the 'features you would expect in a world class car', including six-speed manual transmission, ABS from Bosch, selective ride control and a sophisticated audio system, he completed his description with the comment: 'But nevertheless you can still drive it every day.' He didn't deliver it as if he knew it was meant to be a joke, nor did anyone take it that way.

Next he unveiled, or prompted the ladies to unveil, a Pontiac Transport, known as an APV or all purpose vehicle. 'It could easily be mistaken for a prototype or research and development car, but it's a real production model,' he assured the audience. 'You can use it to haul bicycles up north for the weekend, or picnic with kids or friends.' It was hard to tell which north he was thinking of – northern Germany or northern Michigan? He described the features in best brochure jargon. 'The driver faces a fully functional driver-oriented analogue instrument cluster,' he said. 'Let's have a further look inside the vehicle.'

We were able to have just such a look inside, thanks to an ambulatory video cameraman, whose images were being transmitted live to the large projection screen. As the spokesman began to describe the utility features, one of the girls bounded into the driver's seat and grabbed the key in the ignition, apparently expecting it to be functional.

The key, however, would not turn. In panic, the girl looked desperately to the video cameraman who was poking his camera in through the opposite door. She realized, just a second too late, that she was being broadcast, and her angry, frustrated grimace briefly melted into horror before the video director cut to another shot. Such are the trials of trade show production. Throughout the unveiling of the cars, the second American responded in English to questions posed in German by the woman in red. The effect was bizarre.

At the Opel stand it was different. As one o'clock drew near, a crowd of many hundreds of people clustered around the circular show space. Many hundreds more hung over the railing of the second storey, looking down on to the staging area. Rumour had it that Steffi Graf, the young German tennis star, would be attending.

In a stroke of luck and foresight, Opel had signed her to a multi-year contract for promotional appearances before she became a superstar. At one o'clock, a German television host appeared and introduced Louis Hughes, the new Opel president. He is an American who had come to Opel only a few months before, but he had already perfected his German sufficiently to make the presentation in it. He was soon joined by Fritz Lohr, still looking mightily pleased, but slightly sheepish as a stage performer.

After a dramatic multi-projector presentation, the rear walls parted and the Calibra emerged, slowly drawn forward by cables. Water shot out of the nozzles, creating a rather feeble-looking fountain. Calibra came to rest centre stage and, after the applause, it was Steffi's turn. Clad in a short black dress, she answered questions about herself and tennis put to her by the television interviewer. Fritz Lohr hovered in the background, the proud corporate father.

Then, in response to shouts from photographers, Steffi gamely draped herself over various parts of the new car. She was obviously not cut out for this role and, although willing, couldn't muster whatever it takes to slither yourself into truly provocative postures around a fender or boot. She seemed at once resigned, amused and embarrassed by all the attention, retaining a sweet half-smile throughout the proceedings but never looking relaxed. When it was done, she made a no-nonsense exit through the rear door of the stage, pausing not one moment to chat with the Opel executives or to banter with the crowd.

After the show, Fritz stood close by the Calibra. It is an attractive machine and was receiving extremely favourable reviews. Some writers, after the event, even called it the star of the show – high praise when it was competing with a long-awaited new model from BMW. The excitement of the Calibra, following on the success of J'89, combined with the profitability of both Opel and Vauxhall in Europe brought an aura of success and excitement to the Opel stand.

'We always wanted to do a coupé like this,' said Fritz Lohr, 'but we couldn't afford it. But we saved enough money on J'89 to make it possible.' The new coupé had been brought to market quickly – just eighteen months after the introduction of J'89. It looked like a winner. And it would fill a niche in the market – the European-made, reasonably priced coupé – a niche which the Opel Manta and Ford Capri had once occupied, but which Japanese models now dominated. Lohr beamed. Paul Tosch acted like a happy child at a motor show. Wayne Cherry stood proudly by.

GM Europe was on an up after years of struggling, and it could last a long time.

But, then again, it might not. That the motor industry is changing, and has already changed rapidly and dramatically, is obvious. The next several years promise even greater change – possibly the most tumultuous years the industry has ever experienced – so that it will look very different in the year 2000 from what it does in the year 1990.

When dallying with automotive predictions, motoring writers often concentrate on the 'car of the future', and we see illustrations of fabulous cars equipped with spacecraft-like systems and every possible convenience feature. But it's likely that the most important changes in the automotive world over the next several years will be in the structures and processes that surround the product: the development process; organization within the large manufacturing companies; the global structure of the industry; the role of cars in the societies where they operate; how cars are built, how they are marketed.

Such a restructuring of the industry could lead to a marketplace where:

- Not a single European auto manufacturer is still operating as we know it now. They have all merged with others, failed, been carved up or swallowed up by American or Japanese companies.

- Increase in European production capacity has come from the Japanese transplants and joint ventures in Eastern Europe, where GME, Fiat, Rover and others already have established partnerships.

- There is even more intense competition among the multinational manufacturers in Europe. After 1992, sales across Europe are facilitated because standards have been unified and transport regulations have been simplified. There are price and specification wars.

- Also in the wake of the completion of the single European market, the Japanese share of market climbs to 30% across Europe.

- Japanese and East Asian domestic markets are booming, bringing greater prosperity to those countries and making them even stronger competitors in the world market.

- The Russian and Eastern European car industry is also booming, taking the role that first Japan and then Korea played earlier, providing low-cost cars to markets throughout the world.

- In America, Chrysler is no longer. Ford and General Motors fight for smaller and smaller chunks of the market.

For General Motors Europe, many changes could be in store. With market share slipping away in the US, an increased emphasis on Europe by the parent company is likely. The European division's fortunes could continue to rise. GM's thwarted attempt to buy Jaguar in late 1989 showed that they were thinking seriously about how to capture the high end of the market.

Although the J'89 GSi 2000 and the Senator are supposed to help them in that effort, they're probably not enough. General Motors may still be looking to purchase a small, prestige maker in addition to Saab or to set up a separate marque as Nissan did with Infiniti.

But ask Wayne Cherry or Paul Tosch if they expect to be where they are in the next year, the next month – tomorrow – and all you get is a smile. 'It's like the army,' says Cherry. 'They don't necessarily tell you when they're going to ship you out, and when they do you don't necessarily know where you're headed.'

The gradual development of the single European market will affect the motor industry in dozens of definable, practical ways, and in some less clear-cut, emotional and psychological ways. Currently, any new car must receive Type Approval (certification that the car platform meets all legal requirements) by the government of the country in which the manufacturer intends it to be sold. To offer a car for sale across Europe means getting National Type Approval in each country.

Although there are some uniform standards (for crash test results, for example) there are also requirements unique to each country, both for special tests and for standard required equipment: for example, dim-dip lighting in the UK, yellow headlamp bulbs in France, headlamp cleaning in Finland. And, perhaps most important, exhaust emissions standards vary widely, as do the deadlines for each country to conform to new standards. According to Peter Batchelor, the thicket of standards is currently so dense that 'the paperwork required to sell a single model throughout Europe practically fills a room'.

The acceptance of a single set of Type Approval standards would make life much easier and, arguably, somewhat less expensive for the manufacturer. Not only would the process of approval be streamlined and shortened, but manufacturing would be simplified through a reduction of the number of variants needed. Moving the cars from one country to another throughout Europe should also be much easier after 1992, with the abolition of border checks and streamlining of customs documentation.

The effect of standardization and removal of barriers should be the desired one: freer movement of automobiles around Europe and a general opening of the market. It will matter less where production plants are located, and it will be easier to source production at several plants. The issue of local content will virtually disappear because local suppliers will be defined as EC-based suppliers, not just those from the country where the manufacturing plant is based. All of which leads to the second, and thorniest, question facing governments and car manufacturers for 1992: what should be done about the Japanese?

The Japanese car manufacturers are threatening to do just as they have done in the US passenger car market: keep gobbling up share. Through imports, and now primarily through production at US-based 'transplants', the Japanese car companies now own about 30% of the car market in the US. In Europe, many countries have protected themselves with import quotas. The UK quota is at 10.8%. Italy has been fierce, with a quota of about 2%. In some countries where there is no quota, the Japanese companies, in aggregate, have gained a market share as high as 40%.

The two obvious routes for Europe are to adopt a uniform quota or to adopt no quota at all. Even if a quota is adopted, it could not apply to Japanese plants based in Europe, because local content require-ments would be satisfied. The Japanese companies are building new plants in Europe and maintaining their cost advantages.

As Bob Eaton, President of GM Europe, put it, 'This phenomenon is perhaps the most advanced in the US automobile industry, where the Japanese have been able to maintain about 80% of their cost advantage, even while using American labour. There is reason to believe that the Japanese will be able to reproduce these productivity levels in Europe as well.'

Then there is the extremely complex set of issues concerning taxes, banking and financial services. Some of Vauxhall's worst years would not have been so bad but for the relationship of the pound to the deutschmark.

Underlying all these issues is another one: that of national identity and cultural pride. For the car industry, two traits are bound to find themselves in conflict as the market opens. First, British industry has a strong preference for buying British goods. With fleet sales account-ing for nearly half of all new car sales in the UK, the adherence to local goods made with a reasonably high content of locally produced parts has helped keep the British-based manufacturers, particularly Rover, afloat during hard times.

Although neither Ford nor Vauxhall is truly a British manufacturer, they have been operating in the UK long enough, and are good enough citizens, to be thought of as British. One of the reasons GM dropped the Opel marque in the UK was that, according to one insider, 'we couldn't get in the boardrooms with the Opel name.' Meaning, of course, a German name.

But with the broadening of the definition of 'local' to mean Europe and the increasing awareness of car makers as multi-national, it will be hard to tell who is a British maker and who isn't. This will feed in to another national trait: car obsession. Not only do the British love cars, but the British company car driver is obsessed with his motor as a symbol of his standing within the organization. There has already been a great increase in the number of corporate 'user-choosers', and if the approved list now includes more models from more European makers the big three British manufacturers are sure to lose some sales.

At the same time, although the European market may be opening, that doesn't mean national tastes are going to change immediately. It is likely that, as basic mechanical and safety specifications become standardized, there will be greater customization for national and even regional markets, and specific market segments.

It won't be a question of headlamps or mechanical systems – it will probably be a matter of colours and special editions. Peter Negus proved the point with photographs of a special edition of the Opel Corsa, intended for sale in the Spanish market. This had been conceived by Don Algodon, the Spanish fashion designer, and featured darting accents of baby blue – at the air intakes and on seat covers. It had been offered to the UK packagers as a possibility for a special Nova edition. 'It would never fly in the UK,' Negus chuckled. 'No way.'

As the marketplace changes, so does the role of the car, and as the role of the car changes, so does the marketplace change some more. The 'car of the future' will be more and more defined by forces larger than itself, particularly the move for greater safety and a cleaner, less cluttered environment. Manufacturers already wince at what they consider to be the onerous burdens placed on them in terms of standards and tests and certifications. But automobiles have a vast and often negative effect on the world around them and need to be controlled.

Currently, the car is a personal transport vehicle designed primarily for long-haul, high-speed motorway use. Although you can buy smaller, more efficient cars with lower top speeds, they tend to be less safe and less comfortable than the larger models.

Manufacturers are far more interested in the larger cars for at least two reasons. First, the profit margins are higher. Second, there is a deeply ingrained, long-standing and virtually unspoken attitude that speed, power and glamour are what cars are really all about. Look at the drawings and models of transportation students who will one day be the corporate designers. There are a few students who are trying to rethink the car as a method of transportation, but it seems that the majority are still operating under the same assumptions: the best cars are the fastest, meanest, hottest, most powerful.

Many people in the industry – including designers, fleet operators and car makers – agree that the evaluation of a car based on maximum top speed and acceleration from nought to sixty is not only useless but wrong. The controversy rages in government as well.

In an all-day debate in the House of Commons in 1988, Robert Atkins, the minister responsible for road safety, told MPs: 'All too often the central feature of the promotion of a new car is its acceleration or the extent to which it is capable of exceeding the legal speed limit. I do not think it is enough to say, "That is what people want". Advertising forms attitudes as well as responding to them.'

The obsession with top speed seems particularly ludicrous in the light of the actual top speeds motorists are able to reach most of the time. Some analysts predict that the average motorway speed in Los Angeles will be about 30 kph by the year 2000. You're lucky to travel that fast on the M4 or M40 during the rush hour in or out of London. The personal car, as opposed to the taxi, represents an inefficient and wasteful mode of transport for use in cities and large towns, especially old cities with narrow streets.

For years, the solution for traffic congestion has been to build more and bigger motorways. This has had the effect of attracting more traffic and it might be impossible to build a motorway so big that it could handle all the traffic it would eventually attract. Larger motorways don't solve congestion problems in the cities. A trip across London by car can take two hours, and the rush hour seems to extend from as early as 6.00 in the morning to as late as 10.00 or 10.30 A.M., and to start up again as early as 3.30 and last until 7.30 or 8.00 P.M.. Not only is this frustrating, it is a great drain on the productivity of a nation.

In the United States, the US Department of Transportation estimates that traffic delays cost the country $73 billion each year in lost productivity. It calculates that the 110 million US commuters spend as much as two billion hours a year in traffic jams, and that these will get five times worse by the turn of the century.

Although cars are safer than ever before, they still represent a major cause of death and injury. In the United Kingdom, 239,063 road accidents were reported to the police in 1987, and they involved 387,521 vehicles. 5,125 people were killed in these accidents, of whom 1,703 were neither drivers nor passengers but pedestrians. Motor vehicles are the leading cause of accidental death, just ahead of suicide. Nearly one thousand of the deaths in 1988 were the result of accidents in which the driver or motorcycle rider was drunk.

Another 306,348 people were seriously injured in motor accidents. The driver is the person most likely to be injured, with adult pedestrians a close second, passengers third, motorcycle riders fourth and child pedestrians the next. 5,472 children aged nought to fourteen were injured by motor vehicles in Great Britain in 1987.

Although these figures sound bad, the UK has a good safety record in comparison to other countries of the world. Measured in number of deaths per 100,000 population per year, the UK has the fewest with 9.9, nearly tied with Japan which has ten. This compares to the US with nineteen per 100,000 and Portugal, one of the worse, with 26.4 deaths. Even so, 5000 deaths and a quarter of a million injuries per year amount to a great deal of human suffering, pain, lives ruined, horror endured, money wasted and time lost.

The motor industry is also a great polluter. Exhaust emissions which account for a large percentage of air pollution in cities are not the only source: there is pollution from the manufacture of automotive raw materials, particularly steel, plastic and rubber; pollution from the manufacture and assembly of the cars themselves; and much pollution from the refining of petroleum products.

In addition, there is the pollution that comes from discarded materials – the plastics and metals and oils in scrap cars, not to mention the tons of rubber that are worn off the tyres of the twenty million cars in use in Great Britain and which seep slowly into the tarmac and surrounding countryside.

In the light of these issues, car makers and their designers cannot continue to think of the car as they always have, in virtual isolation from the problems that surround it. Opel, in particular, prides itself on being a 'green' company in many ways, and General Motors cars were among the first in Europe to run on unleaded fuel. But where American companies are showing concepts for bigger, sleeker, more technologically sophisticated future models, some Japanese companies appear to be rethinking the automobile in a more radical way with non-traditional designs for 'people movers'.

The solutions to these various ills will not be found solely in the designs of the cars themselves. There are a number of organizations with pilot programmes underway searching for solutions that involve a rethinking of how highways and traffic are controlled.

In Europe, the PROMETHEUS project (or Programme for European Traffic with Highest Efficiency and Unprecedented Safety) is a joint research programme of thirteen European automobile manufacturers (GME not among them) and a variety of universities, research institutes and government agencies. It was established in 1986 to find solutions to the various problems that plague us, and to examine ways of reducing the number of Europeans killed (about 55,000) and injured (about 1.5 million) each year, lessening the amount of money wasted each year (some £2,400 million) due to poor traffic routing, and reducing the stress on drivers. They are researching a variety of approaches including new in-car safety technologies, better communications between traffic authorities and drivers, and so-called 'smart' highways.

In Los Angeles, where the traffic is as bad as it is anywhere in the United States, an automated traffic surveillance system is being tested. It consists of a number of sensors placed in the road-bed which monitor traffic flow and vehicle speeds. The information gathered is used to adjust the timing of traffic lights and to direct traffic away from the clogged areas.

Another project in Los Angeles, called Project Pathfinder, which is partially funded by GM, is designed to evaluate how effective such systems can really be. Once you give drivers information about road conditions, will they use the information at all, and, if they do, will they use it effectively?

Most of the ideas proposed for overcoming traffic congestion concentrate on guidance and navigational technologies placed in the car, and sensing and control technologies sited in the highways and at central command stations. There are already a number of guidance and navigational systems available.

A guidance system generally consists of a computer display mounted in the fascia, with a compact disk reader mounted, for instance, under the seat. The compact disk itself is similar to musical CDs but is filled with data, and is known as CD-ROM, for 'compact disk, read only memory'. The ROM part means that the disk can only be played back, not programmed; no new information can be stored.

The disk contains maps of the area you are travelling through, showing all significant roads. After setting your car's location on the map, your position is constantly re-plotted based upon information coming from sensors on the non-drive wheels. The sensors determine your car's speed and the direction of turn of the wheels, and the computer software translates it into map position.

True navigational systems, which are also in development, require some sort of reference point outside the car, either a series of land-based beacons that create a grid of radio signals, which the car system analyses and uses to plot position, or a satellite system similar to the inertial navigation system used by aircraft. These systems would be more accurate.

The theory is that drivers equipped with either of these systems when confronted with traffic which they see ahead or hear reported on the radio, would be able to seek alternative routes, without getting lost. Both systems have the facility for planning routes, based upon a destination input by the driver.

The next step is a vastly more complicated one and involves a system of electronic sensors placed either in the road-bed or along the side of the road, not only to monitor traffic, but also to control it. At first, the information could simply be used to monitor traffic, supplying information in real time to radio stations or a dedicated communications source.

But the most ambitious and long-range plan calls for a two-way system, in which the motorways are equipped with electronic guide paths. The paths monitor flow of traffic and relay the information to a computerized control centre, where the information is analysed and translated into commands which are then sent back to the 'smart' motorways to regulate the speed of cars. In other words, once the car is on the motorway, the motorway drives the car.

To realize such a vision will require enormous expenditure and inter-agency co-operation throughout the world: to produce digitized maps of the entire world, plant sensors in every road-bed, create computer programming that sensibly controls traffic. Yet the central problem will probably remain: too many cars for too little motorway. Even if motorists could be warned of jams ahead, there are still too few alternative routes to be had.

For the automobile industry, the future is not as far away as it is for other industries. With product development cycles of approximately five years and a product life of another five, this means that designers and managers are routinely thinking a decade ahead. And so the car makers look for ways both to predict the future and to manage it, to make it unfold as they would like it to. One way they do this is through basic research, and General Motors spends more money on research and development than any other company in the world, $5 billion in 1989.

Another way is by creating self-fulfilling prophecies. The manufacturers have advance design groups which develop concepts for the 'car of the future'. These are based on designers' own tastes, their reading of the market and their sense of what they could conceivably build. The advance groups build models – concept cars – and show them at the motor exhibitions and promote them in the press. These are often exercises in styling and packaging, rather than engineering, and sometimes are made for internal evaluation only. Others are shown to the public to create comment, tease people into accepting the idea of regular change and provide a reading for the car maker on what people do and do not like.

At the motor shows you can amuse yourself by studying extreme body shapes (duck tails, high hats, bulbous noses, seamless glass canopies), alternative door and seat treatments (sliders, gull-wings, swivelers) and revised fascia and control configurations (centre consoles, electronic steering or 'drive by wire'). There are other cars that are more appropriately called experimental or developmental cars – working vehicles which are built to test new mechanical systems, engines, electronics, new materials.

For example, General Motors claims that its Firebird concept cars of the late 1950s incorporated technologies that later became standard in production cars, including cruise control and an anti-skid braking system. Another GM concept car had radar sensors in nose cones which graced the fender tips, to warn of approaching cars – something you do not find on production cars today. The 1982 Sierra was closely based on the series of Ford concept cars called Probe which were shown throughout the late 1970s at European auto shows.

Perhaps the most striking experimental car of recent years was built by General Motors and may hold the record for the most efficient and aerodynamically successful car ever designed. Called the Sunraycer, it was designed and built to compete in the World Solar Challenge in September 1987. This was an international race to encourage the development of solar power for automobiles – a race across Australia, some 3200 km along the Stuart Highway, beginning in Darwin and ending in Adelaide.

Sunraycer has been described as looking like a giant cockroach or a prehistoric tadpole. It has a tapered body six metres in length and only a metre high, which starts from a rounded head and tapers to flat back, ending in a squared off stern.

The car is powered by solar cells that look like bluish scales or tiles and encrust the entire body except for the very nose, which is a glass canopy covering the driver's compartment. There are virtually no surface protuberances with the exception of two small, vertical fins called strakes that pop up from the top surface and help improve stability in crosswinds, rather like the Sierra's.

The wheels are thin with bicycle-like tyres, the spokes covered with plastic discs, and because of the solar-powered engine there is no need for a front air intake. To keep the driver cool, the canopy is coated with gold, which reflects 90% of visible light and 98% of infra-red radiation.

To reduce weight, the body is constructed of aluminium and Kevlar composite honeycomb sandwich materials. General Motors developed a direct current four horsepower motor especially for the car, which can propel it from nought to forty in twenty seconds.

The aerodynamics were developed by GM, working with its subsidiary Hughes Aircraft. Dr Paul MacCready, the man who designed the first man-powered aircraft to cross the English Channel, and his company AeroVironment Inc of Monrovia, California, were involved with the design and production of the car. They used an advanced computer program called VSAERO, developed by the US National Aeronautics and Space Administration.

With all this extraordinary talent and technical firepower trained on the Cd number, you would expect good results. Tests made of a quarter-scale model in a small wind tunnel in California showed the lowest Cd ever measured for a road vehicle. Although GM does not publish these figures, the Cd of the final product is reported to be an astonishing .099, approaching the smoothness of an aircraft wing.

Sunraycer won the race hands down. It opened up a lead of over 100 km on the first day and crossed the finishing line some twenty hours before the second place finisher, from Ford of Australia. Sunraycer averaged nearly 67 kph and reached a top speed of 112 kph.

It is impossible, of course, to say which of Sunraycer's technologies will be applied to production cars – and when, if ever. In its current state it is an unworkable production design, in terms both of cost and function. The cost of production was over a million dollars. The car seats one person. Although it has a back-up battery, it cannot be driven at night because of the gold plating which reduces the visibility severely. There are no headlamps. The top must be put in place by someone other than the driver. There are no bumpers.

Although few concept or experimental cars are ever realized as production cars precisely as they were originally imagined, that's not the point. The 'car of the future' is an ever-receding, ever-evolving phenomenon. But by imagining the future and making it tangible, the car maker goes a long way towards creating it.

The development of a volume passenger car will continue to balance the demands for novelty, genuine improvement and increased reliability and performance at the lowest possible price. For the most part, however, the concept car offers clues about how a manufacturer is thinking, and what ideas are under development.

In fact, the design approach and many of the technologies pioneered in the Sunraycer have been incorporated in GM's electric-powered prototype car, called Impact, which was unveiled in early 1990. The car was created by a team of designers based at GM's Advanced Concepts Center in Thousand Oaks, California, and built by AeroVironment. The Impact is a front-wheel-drive car, powered by two AC (alternating current) induction-type motors, and has an extremely low Cd of .19.

The problem with most electric car prototypes has been sluggish performance, but GM claims that the Impact can accelerate from 0–60 mph in under eight seconds – faster than some petrol-powered sports cars of similar size. In addition, GM claims that Impact can travel 120 miles between battery charges. The drawbacks remain the high cost of producing the car (about twice that of a similar petrol-powered vehicle), the cost of battery replacement and the time it takes for a recharge (about six hours).

Even so, Dr MacCready of AeroVironment is optimistic about the car's future. He was quoted in *Business Week* magazine as saying, 'There's a 50-50 chance the internal combustion engine will go the way of the buggy whip by 2005.'

Most designers, with a knowing gleam in their eye, predict an end to the tyranny of aerodynamics, without losing the benefits of aerodynamic design. Designers and engineers have learned enough about which features contribute to an aerodynamically efficient car to take advantage of them without creating lookalike shapes.

The wedge or teardrop shape, with smooth surfaces, small gaps and no protuberances can be applied to lots of different body styles, which should lead to models of greater individuality and character. 'Look at the aerodynamic forms in nature,' says Ron Hill, 'birds and fish all have aero shapes, and they all look different.'

After a certain level of aerodynamic efficiency becomes standard, with an average Cd of about .25 or so, further increases will probably be seen as too expensive and too intrusive to accomplish. The advantages of enclosed underbodies, seamless glass greenhouses and extremely low-profile bodies may not win over the customer.

But 'good aero design is not necessarily good people design,' as Italian designer Giugiaro has put it. As the demands of aerodynamics grow too great, the demands of customers will no doubt reinforce themselves. The youthfulness of a car, or the appeal of the car to young people, has been an important consideration in car marketing for years. But as the average age of the population increases there will be less and less tolerance of low-slung, aero designs that require people to contort themselves to get in and out of the car.

As safety regulations grow stricter, visibility from inside will become an increasingly important consideration. Low driving positions and dark-tint canopies may not be legally acceptable. As manufacturers work harder and harder to provide cars the customers want, they will probably become more sensitive to the needs of women drivers, allowing for a greater range of adjustment for seats and steering wheel, and smaller cars that are as safe and feature-laden (and as expensive) as the larger ones.

The future car will incorporate many materials that are not now standard, some of which have been growing in acceptance for years. The most obvious one is plastic. Plastics are already being used for individual exterior components such as fenders and tailgates, and have been a major bumper system material since the early 1980s.

The trend, eventually, will be to view the exterior body as totally non-structural. Currently, the sheet metal that sheaths the car contributes to its strength, stiffness, structural integrity and crashworthiness. The increased use of plastic, particularly composites based on fibre-reinforced plastics, may lead to a new structural approach. This would be based on a metal cage, with large plastic panels glued or snap-fitted to it.

Because plastic is so flexible and easy to form, it allows designers to create complex curves and bends that would be too expensive or time-consuming to create in steel. Plastic tooling is relatively inexpensive in comparison to steel tools and easy to change from one mould to another.

This, combined with non-structural exteriors, could lead to the production of many more exterior configurations than exist now, in small runs designed to capture the attention of smaller and smaller niche markets. In addition to these marketing and packaging advantages, plastic also has the benefit of resisting dents. In many impacts it merely deforms and then pops back into shape. It also reduces weight, which improves fuel efficiency, and doesn't corrode.

Other developments will create new exterior looks. A new kind of headlamp, developed by Ford and General Electric, is called the arc discharge lamp. The major advantage is its size; the actual lamp and filament are about the size of a small match, which means that the entire headlamp can be about the size of a golf ball. If you think of the front end of a car as being its most characteristic and most defining aspect, the headlamps have always been a major part of that look.

Designers have constantly tried to minimize the impact of headlamps by making them smaller and, in sports cars and upmarket models, hiding them away completely. But with a reduction in the size of headlamps, the whole character of the front end could change. No longer will designers have to deal with those large expanses of relatively ugly glass, or worry about the aerodynamic losses caused by the gaps around them. The lights could also be made photo-sensitive, responding to the ambient light level and delivering only the amount of illumination required to see, but not enough to blind fellow-travellers.

There is little doubt that the quantity of electronics in every car will increase for some time to come, with computer control of virtually every system in the car. New suspension systems are being investigated that will sense the terrain and adjust the inflation of tyres and height of the wheels accordingly, even to the point where a car can essentially 'lift' a wheel up to 25 cm to step over a bump. ABS will certainly become standard on most cars.

GM has announced that new models as early as 1993 will have the brains of the Apple Mac II computer under the bonnet: a thirty-two-bit chip with 442,000 transistors which can monitor and regulate the engine, the transmission, brakes, suspension, cruise control and engine emissions.

A few electronic systems are less likely to catch on soon, primarily because they are too expensive. But car marketers like to talk about aircraft style 'head-up displays' which show all the conventional information normally found on fascia gauges – speed, rpm, fuel levels – projected into the windscreen. This is so the driver does not have to look down at the controls and gauges, which should ensure a safer ride.

GM and other manufacturers are considering several alternative types of engines, including the Stirling engine, a two-stroke 'orbital engine', ceramic diesel engines, the gas turbine. And, of course, the debate about alternative fuels – especially methanol – is heating up, especially in the States, where new legislation will probably lead to the creation of at least some models that burn alternative fuels by the early 1990s. Engineers do not believe that current engine designs can be made to burn clean enough on petrol. The most likely candidates for cleaner-burning engines are natural gas and alcohol-based fuels such as methanol and ethanol.

And then there are any number of gadgets and gizmos, from microwave ovens in the glove box to fascia fax machines, that will come and go according to fashion and taste.

J'89 was promoted in the splashiest new car launch ever in the UK as 'the car of the future'. Appealing as the concept may have been, well-executed and pervasive as the campaign was, one thing was fundamentally wrong with it. The new Cavalier incorporates features that may have been considered futuristic in the late 1950s – 'scientific streamlining, self-tuning engine, non-locking brakes, power-assisted steering' – but in 1989 they were the features you could find in any number of cars.

The real message seems to have been that these features were being offered in an automobile which you, the customer, might not have expected in a car as seemingly ordinary as the Cavalier. But, truly, the new Cavalier had nothing to do with the car of the future: it was the quintessential car of the present.

In Rüsselsheim, work has begun on the successor to J'89. Many of the faults of the J'89 have been identified. When you try to raise the partially concealed wipers off the windscreen to replace or clean them, the shaft bumps into the trailing edge of the bonnet. This is a minor annoyance, easily fixed. The wraparound doors continue to cause manufacturing problems; the tolerances are very close.

Although rear entrance has improved, the back seat accommodation still doesn't measure up to that found in some of the competitors. Some drivers in the UK complain that the new engines don't have the acceleration at the low end they used to have. They can't floor the new Cavalier the way they could the old. This is a more complicated issue and one that can be solved – but should it be?

These design and product issues will continue to be thrashed out by the squads of designers, marketing people, engineers, product people in Luton, Rüsselsheim, Detroit. But the process will change. General Motors say they are planning shortened product development cycles, as short as a year for a new model based on an existing platform.

This is made possible through the increased use of computers in virtually every stage of development, and through an approach to development called simultaneous engineering – an extension of the team approach, which calls for the development of engine and mechanical systems and exterior and interior design and styling to be undertaken in parallel. Through the use of a single computer database, this approach is now possible.

The shortening of product development cycles is considered critical to compete with the Japanese, particularly in Europe. 'It just takes discipline,' says Paul Tosch. 'At every stage you simply say, no changes. That's how you do it.'

So J'95 might be J'94 or it might not be a J car at all. The platform dimension might alter to move the Cavalier into a different position in the product line, or to accommodate some new technology, or to respond to some unforeseen development.

Much as the car makers control the process of developing a new car, much as any manufacturer wants to control the process of developing any new product – they are as much responding to demand as they are supplying it. The price of petrol, the behaviour of the wind, the state of the highways, the number of deaths, the health of the economy, the opinion of the press, the reaction of the customer, the health of the environment, the inclinations of the government, the emergence of new technologies or materials, the rise of a new competitor, gravity, inertia, history, futurism, money, chance – all these things influence the design of the car.

Which is why, although we might prefer to think that the Rolls-Royce Corniche or BMW 750 is the best reflection of who we are and what the nature of our society is today, J'89 is probably the more accurate one.

One day I sat in a meeting in an uninspiring conference room in T block, at Vauxhall headquarters in Luton. It was late in the afternoon of a hot summer's day. Our business was almost completed.

We got sidetracked on to the subject of old Vauxhall Motors models, a surprisingly rare occurrence for a company of car buffs. John Butterfield was shuffling through some photographs when he came across one that stopped his gaze. He held it up for us all to see.

It was a picture of a Cavalier coupé circa 1975. As Butterfield looked at it, I saw a gleam in his eye I hadn't witnessed before. To me, the car looked uninteresting and out-of-date, which of course it was by that time. But to him the car obviously represented an exciting achievement that I could not fully appreciate.

'It was an instant success,' said Butterfield. 'The coupé version really did attract the dealers. I mean, go back to '75, it was a very attractive motor car,' he said, with a touch of genuine feeling interlaced with something I took to be nostalgia or regret, or perhaps a sense of the passing of time. 'It really was a wow,' he concluded.

And some day the car that in 1989 was dubbed 'the car of the future' will be just like its predecessor, having passed through its product life cycle. From the freshness of a new release, it will have become a bread-and-butter model, then an aging warhorse, finally descending into obsolescence, before – possibly – finding renewed status as a fondly remembered classic.

The features that now seem so 'bang up to date', the styling that seems so strikingly aerodynamic, will slowly come to look not-so-new and then suddenly, one day, passé. Later, J'89 may become a new type of exemplar: a good representative of the period.

At some other conference table some other car enthusiast may fish out a photograph of the 1989 Vauxhall Cavalier and shake his head with a mixture of fondness and regret, amusement and remembrance, and say, 'That really was a wow'.

APPENDIX: Development Sequence

This is a general timing of events in the development process. Some cars take longer than others to develop; sometimes a programme will start and then be put on hold, then begin again some months later. Some phases overlap others. At General Motors Europe, all disciplines are involved in all phases to some degree. The early stages are design intensive, the later stages more engineering and manufacturing intensive.

MONTHS 1-10: CONCEPT

Design creates pencil and marker sketches, full-scale renderings, third-scale clay models and full-scale clay and fibreglass models.

Engineering develops initial specifications, cost and investment estimates, and makes fifth-scale clay models for aerodynamic testing.

During this period the Development Team holds weekly programme review meetings. These involve discussion of the package, aerodynamics, interior and exterior design, cost and investment issues and manufacturing implications.

MONTH 11: CONCEPT PRESENTATION

A presentation is made in the GME Development Centre in Russelsheim to a group of managers representing the key disciplines, as well as senior managers including the President of GM Europe. It includes concepts for exterior, interior and trim; the engineering package includes key dimensions and specifications.

The presentation of the models is supported with storyboards and verbal explanations.

MONTHS 12-17: CONCEPT REFINEMENT

Design continues to refine and develop interior and exterior surfaces and elements. Engineering runs road tests with component cars. These cars usually are based on an existing platform, with varying numbers of new elements and components added.

MONTH 14: FIRST PRODUCT CLINIC

Results from the product clinic are received, analysed and incorporated into the design.

MONTH 17: CONCEPT APPROVAL

This includes design 'freeze', when the exterior and interior surfaces have been finalized. The project team presents programme viability for management review.

MONTHS 18-20: DIGITIZATION

The surfaces are digitized, entered into a database and then sweetened through computer-aided design.

MONTH 20: DESIGN RELEASE

At this point, design hands over the surface data to engineering and manufacturing. Any changes that will affect the surfaces visually must be approved by management from here on.
Engineering begins identifying sources for long lead items, such as the instrument panel and bumper system.

MONTHS 20-28: ENGINEERING DEVELOPMENT

Engineering develops designs and drawings for all components and continues road and proving ground testing.

MONTH 28: PROTOTYPE COMPLETE

The first full, functioning prototype of the new car is completed. This is composed of mostly handmade components.

MONTH 32: FINAL APPROVAL

Management signs off on the new car programme. This is where 'real money' will now be committed to the project, particularly for tooling and purchase of equipment and supplies.

MONTHS 32-43: ENGINEERING TESTING AND MANUFACTURING TOOLING

Engineering develops several iterations of prototypes and conducts tests.
Manufacturing designs, develops and fabricates tooling. New tools often are installed in a separate test area of a manufacturing facility, so that the new car can gradually ramp up into production.

MONTH 44-53: PILOT PROGRAMME

The pilot programme is essentially a period of testing the manufacturing process. At the beginning of the programme, the new car is being produced with about 80% parts produced with final production tools. The other 20% are handmade or carry-over components.
By the end of the pilot period, the car should be composed entirely of production parts.
During the pilot programme, the product continues to be tested – including proving ground tests and quality and durability tests of individual systems or components (such as shock absorbers, brakes and seat springs).
During this period, national type approvals are sought.

MONTH 53: SOP OR START OF PRODUCTION

The car is manufactured. Manufacturing usually begins at a slower-than-optimal rate of production, measured as cars-per-hour, until workers are fully up to speed and the bugs have been worked out.
Engineering, manufacturing and design personnel continue to refine and tweak the car and the production processes.

BIBLIOGRAPHY

Books

Adeney, Martin. *The Motor Makers.* London. William Collins, 1988.

Automobile Quarterly Magazine, *General Motors: The First 75 Years of Transportation Products.* Princeton, New Jersey. Automobile Quarterly Magazine and General Motors.

Betjeman, John. *Collected Poems.* London. John Murray, 1958.

Boyne, Walter J. *Power Behind the Wheel.* London. Conran Octopus Ltd, 1988.

British Petroleum. *BP Statistical Review of World Energy.* 1989.

Bush, Donald J. *The Streamlined Decade.* New York. George Braziller, 1975.

Cecchini, Paolo with Michel Catinat and Alexis Jacquemin. *1992 The European Challenge.* Aldershot. Wildwood House Ltd, 1988.

Clayton, Ken. *Jaguar, Rebirth of a Legend.* London. Century Hutchinson, 1988.

Dennis, Geoff. (ed). *Annual Abstract of Statistics, 1989 Edition.* Norwich. Her Majesty's Stationery Office, 1989.

Economic Commission for Europe. *Statistics of Road Traffic Accidents in Europe.* New York. United Nations, 1986.

Energy Information Administration. *Petroleum Supply Annual 1988.* Washington, DC. US Department of Energy, 1988.

Fersen, Olaf von, Frére, Paul, Ludvigsen, Karl, Rogliatti, Gianni. *Opel Wheels to the World.* Automobile Quarterly Publications. Stuttgart, 1984.

Gustin, Lawrence R. *Billy Durant, Creator of General Motors.* Grand Rapids, Michigan. William B. Eerdmans Publishing Company, 1973.

Halberstam, David. *The Reckoning.* New York. William Morrow and Company, 1986.

Heraud, Daniel. *Road Report 1989.* Chicago, Illinois. Contemporary Books, 1988.

Howard, Geoffrey. *Automobile Aerodynamics.* London. Osprey Publishing Ltd, 1986.

Itten, Johannes. *Design and Form.* London. Thames and Hudson, 1963.

Keller, Maryann. *Rude Awakening.* New York. William Morrow and Company, 1989.

Lacey, Robert. *Ford, The Men and the Machine.* Boston, Toronto. Little, Brown and Company, 1986.

Lee, Albert. *Call Me Roger.* Chicago, New York. Contemporary Books, 1988.

Loewy, Raymond. *Industrial Design.* Woodstock, New York. The Overlook Press, 1979.

Lorenz, Christopher. *The Design Dimension.* Oxford. Basil Blackwell, 1986.

Lucie-Smith, Edward. *A History of Industrial Design*. Oxford. Phaidon Press, 1983.

McAlhone, Beryl (ed). *Directors on Design, The Car Industry*. London. The Design Council, 1985.

Morita, Akio. *Akio Morita and Sony, Made in Japan*. London. William Collins, 1987.

Moskowitz, Milton. *The Global Marketplace*. New York. Macmillan Publishing Company, 1987.

Motor Vehicle Manufacturers Association of United States. *World Motor Vehicle Data*. Detroit, Michigan. MVMA, 1989 and 1990 editions.

Nahum, Andrew. *Alec Issigonis*. London. The Design Council, 1988.

Nixon, St John C. *The Story of the SMMT*. London, printed privately by the SMMT, 1952.

Rajan, Amin and Thompson, Marc. *Economic Significance of the UK Motor Vehicle Manufacturing Industry*. London. Institute of Manpower Studies and the SMMT, 1989.

Robson, Graham. *The Rover Story*. Wellingborough. Patrick Stephens Ltd, 1988.

Scarlett, Michael. Managing Editor. *Automotive Technology International '87*. Sterling Publications Ltd. London, 1986.

Sloan, Alfred P. Jr *My Years with General Motors*. New York. Doubleday, 1963.

Smith, Hubert 'Skip'. *The Illustrated Guide to Aerodynamics*. Blue Ridge Summit, Pennsylvania. Tab Books, 1985.

Society of Motor Manufacturers and Traders. *Motor Industry of Great Britain 1988*. London. SMMT, 1988 (also 1989 edition).

Stewart, Richard. *Design and British Industry*. London. John Murray, 1987.

Taylor, John. *How It Is Made – Motor Cars*. London. Faber and Faber, 1987.

United Nations Centre on Transnational Corporations. *Transnational Corporations in the International Auto Industry*. New York. United Nations, 1983.

United Nations Industrial Development Organization. *Industry and Development Global Report 1988/9*. Vienna. United Nations, 1988.

Wise, Daniel Burgess, (ed). *The Illustrated Encyclopedia of Automobiles*. London. New Burlington Books, 1988.

Pamphlets, Unpublished Papers etc

Batchelor, P.R. 'EC 1992, The Manufacturer's Viewpoint'. September 1988.

Berneburg, Dr Ing. Helmut. 'Technical Workshop "Driving Resistance" German-Netherlands Wind Tunnel'. Emmeloord, Holland, July 1986.

Department of Trade and Industry. 'Selling in the single market'. London, November 1988.

Department of Trade and Industry. 'The single market – the facts'. November 1988.

Eaton, Robert J. 'A Single EC Market – A view from a European Company of American Parentage'. November 1988.

Eurostat. 'Europe in Figures'. Luxembourg: Office for Official Publications of the European Communities. 1988.

Folksam. 'The Sum of 700,000 Car Accidents'. 1987.

Motor Vehicle Manufacturers Association. 'MVMA Motor Vehicle Facts and Figures '89'. Detroit, 1989.

Public Relations Department of Vauxhall Motors Ltd. 'A History of Vauxhall'. 1980 and 1990 editions.

Servais, Dominique. 'The Single Financial Market'. Commission of the European Communities. Luxembourg, 1988.

Society of Motor Manufacturers and Traders. 'Part of Our Lives, The Commercial Vehicle and the Community'. London.

Tosch, Paul J. Speech to the Institute of the Motor Industry. May 1988.

Williams, M. and Preston, N.C.G.N. 'The Prometheus Project'.

Newspaper and *Magazine Articles*

Amos, Bill. 'Quality and Performance . . . At a Price!' *Scottish Field.* November 1988.

Baker, Sue. 'New Model Army'. *The Observer.* 28 August 1988.

Barker, John. 'Droop Snoot'. *Motor.* 14 May 1988.

Bell, Roger. 'Cavalier ready for a Fight'. *Country Life.* 27 October 1988.

Benson, David. 'Car Wars!' *Daily Express.* 30 March 1982.

Benson, David (Motoring Editor). 'Guide to World Cars '89'. *Daily Express* and *Sunday Express.* 1988.

Benson, David. 'Sierra, the winner that started with a defeat'. *Daily Express.* 24 September 1982.

Blick, Kevin. 'Impressions – Vauxhall Cavalier'. *Performance Car.* November 1988.

Borrus, Amy and Lee, Dinah and English, Victoria and Riemer, Blanca. 'Who's the Biggest of them All?' *Business Week.* 17 July 1989.

Bremner, Richard. 'Cavalier shows off its good manners'. *Independent.* 8 October 1988.

Brinton, Alan. 'John Bagshaw'. *Motor Trade Executive.* December 1981.

Campbell, Shaun. 'Fine new Cavalier fulfils its promise'. *Autocar and Motor.* 5 October 1988.

Chapman, Giles. 'Dinosaurs'. *High Performance.*

Cinti, Fulvio. 'Opel Vectra, from the Package to the Shape'. *Auto and Design Magazine.* Turin, February–March 1989.

Cinti, Fulvio. 'Those Tyrannical Aerodynamics'. *Auto and Design magazine.* Turin, July 1989.

Courtney, Geoff. 'The Opel Vauxhall, World Exclusive – The first picture'. *Luton Evening Post.* 9 October 1975.

Darlin, Damon. 'Korea's Car Companies Expand Like Crazy Despite Lagging Sales'. *Wall Street Journal.* 10 March 1990.

Dodsworth, Terry. 'Vauxhall Cavalier is further evidence of "Opelization"'. *Financial Times.* 10 October 1975.

Done, Kevin. 'Sharp Recovery from GM in Europe'. *Financial Times.* 16 February 1989.

Dryden, Colin. 'Ford Launches price war on car imports'. *Daily Telegraph.* 30 March 1982.

Dryden, Colin. 'Renewing the Cavalier versus roundeds battle'. *Daily Telegraph.* 18 October 1988.

Eason, Kevin. 'Shadow of the Rising Sun'. *The Times.* 10 May 1989.

Eason, Kevin. 'Who is proud to be British?' *The Times.* 3 November 1989.

Ensor, James. 'Get rid of the big, old bad GM image'. *Financial Times.* 18 November 1975.

Faliva, Guiliano. 'Pininfarina, The Design Dynasty'. *Autocar and Motor.* 12 October 1988.

Fisher, Lawrence M. 'Uniting Low Power and Efficiency'. *New York Times.* 25 February 1990.

Glancey, Jonathan. 'To be first among equals'. *Independent.* 29 October 1988.

Gooding, Kenneth. 'Ford pins its hopes on Sierra'. *Financial Times.* 21 September 1982.

Gooding, Kenneth. 'Vauxhall Sales hit 13-year high'. *Financial Times.* 10 May 1982.

Gooding, Kenneth. 'Vauxhall suffers record loss'. *Financial Times.*

Goodwin, Stephen. 'Car makers criticised for emphasis on speed when selling vehicles'. *The Times.*

Gray, Charles L. Jr and Alson, Jeffrey A. 'The Case for Methanol'. *Scientific American.* November 1989.

Green, Gavin. '30 Things You've Always Wanted to Ask Graham Day'. *Car.* August 1989.

Greenhouse, Steven. 'The Car Boom

Sweeping Europe'. *New York Times.* 9 March 1989.

Griffiths, John. 'Vauxhall to cut 2,000 more jobs'. *The Guardian.*

Hellen, Nicholas. 'Will the Cavalier have the last laugh?' *Marketing Week.* 30 September 1988.

Hubbard, Bryan. 'Vauxhall MD: We're on the Right Path'. *Chiltern Enterprise.* May 1983.

Hutton, Ray. 'A Car is Born'. *Daily Express.* 16 October 1988.

Jackson, Judith. 'Cavalier fashion'. *The Guardian.* 15 October 1988.

Jackson, Judith. 'Heir to the Cortina Millions'. *Sunday Times.* 26 September 1982.

Jackson, Judith. 'Survival of the Fittest'. *The Guardian.* 3 November 1988.

Kemp, Michael. 'Si! Si! Sierra!' *Daily Mail.* 21 September 1982.

Kemp, Michael. 'Stop this foreign British Car'. *Daily Mail.* 10 October 1975.

Kupfer, Andrew. 'The Methanol Car in Your Future'. *Fortune.* 25 September 1989.

Langley, John. 'The pick of the bunch in Paris'. *Daily Telegraph.* 29 September 1982.

Langley, John. 'Vauxhall's new models will be imported from Belgium'. *Daily Telegraph.* 10 October 1975.

Leinster, Colin interview with Roger Smith. 'The US Must Do As GM Has Done'. *Fortune.* 13 February 1989.

Levin, Doron P. 'Breaking Up Is Hard to Do'. *New York Times Magazine.* 26 March 1989.

MacMinn, Strother. 'In Memoriam: William L. Mitchell, 1912-1988'. *Road and Track.*

Mennem, Patrick. 'Ford launch a cut price car war'. *Daily Mirror.* 30 March 1982.

Mennem, Patrick. 'High hopes for the Sierra'. *Daily Mirror.* 21 September 1982.

Millar, Fiona. 'A car that puts you into space'. *Daily Express.* 7 October 1988.

Mouland, Bill. 'Nice Car, Shame about the Bimbo'. *Today.* 22 October 1988.

Nakajima, Yoshikazu. 'Following the World Solar Challenge'. *Car Styling.* March 1988.

Page, Frank. 'Motorists Drive an Easy Bargain'. *Daily Mail.*

Parisi, Anthony J. 'How R&D Spending Pays Off'. *Business Week.* Innovation Issue 1989.

Piatti, Roberto. 'Opel Calibra, the "importance of a coupé"'. *Auto and Design.* November 1989.

Prokesch, Steven. 'GM Europe: How to Get Something Right'. *New York Times.* 4 February 1990.

Rae, Charles. 'Car Price War'. *Daily Star.* 30 March 1982.

Revkin, Andrew C. '2001 Transportation, A Car with a Mind of its Own'. *Discover.* November 1988.

Robinson, Peter. 'A new car every year – GM's secret weapon'. *Autocar and Motor.* 14 June 1989.

Rowlands, David. 'The Route Master'. *Autocar and Motor.* 12 July 1989.

Stertz, Bradley A. and White, Joseph B. 'Driving into the Next Decade'. *Wall Street Journal.* 12 July 1989.

Taylor III, Alex. 'Why US Carmakers Are Losing Ground'. *Fortune.* 23 October 1989

Townsend, Edward. 'New models could put Vauxhall back on profits by 1983'. *The Times.* 20 August 1981.

Truell, Peter. 'All Exports Aren't Created Equal'. *Wall Street Journal.* 3 July 1989.

Tully, Shawn. 'Now Japan's Autos Push Into Europe'. *Fortune.* 29 January 1990.

Vivian, David. 'No laughing matter'. *Motor.* 27 August 1988.

Ward, Daniel. 'Advertising Costs Favour Best-Sellers'. *Car.* May 1989.

Webb, Clifford. 'After the Cortina, the Sierra'. *Financial Times.* September 1982.

West, Ted. 'The Battle of Paris'. *Road and Track*. January 1989.

Williams, Lyndon. 'First J-Car rolls out of Vauxhall'. *Dunstable Gazette*. 19 August 1981.

Witcher, Gregory. 'Smart Cars, Smart Highways'. *Wall Street Journal*.

Yoo, John. 'As Highways Decay, Their State Becomes Drag on Economy'. *Wall Street Journal*. 30 August 1989.

(The following articles appeared without an author's byline, were the work of several authors or the author could not be determined.)

'All the facts: the born-again Cavalier'. *Autocar*. August 1988.

'Arrivals: New Cavalier Driving the Range'. *Autocar and Motor*. 5 October 1988.

'Cars of the Year'. *What Car?* April 1989.

'Cavalier Fashion'. *What Car?* November 1988.

'Cavalier Leads the Pack'. *Financial Times*. 1 October 1988.

'Dawn of a new age'. *Autocar and Motor*. 5 October 1988.

Financial Times Survey. *World Car Industry*. 13 September 1989.

'The 500 Largest Foreign Companies'. *Forbes Magazine*. 24 July 1989.

'The Fortune 500 Largest Industrials'. *Fortune*. 24 April 1989.

'GM J-car: fruit of five continents'. *Sunday Times Magazine*. 18 October 1981.

'Group Test: Cavalier-v-Sierra-v-405'. *Autocar and Motor*. 5 October 1988.

'Laughing Cavalier'. *The London Evening Standard*. 7 October 1988.

'Luton Vanguard'. *Car*. November 1988.

'New Generation Cavalier Gets Vauxhall's Family Look'. *What Car?* October 1988.

'Paul Tosch interview'. *Car*. November 1988.

'Playing Safe with Styling'. *Sunday Times*. 28 August 1988.

'Road Test – Vauxhall Cavalier 1.6L'. *Autocar and Motor*. 26 October 1988.

'Rounded Cavalier'. *Car*. November 1988.

'Testing Time for Cavalier'. *The Times*. 7 October 1988.

'Top Brass'. *What Car?* October 1989.

'Vauxhall Rivals Get Cavalier Treatment'. *Sunday Times*. 9 May 1982.

'Vauxhall stand a show in itself'. *Guardian Motorshow Supplement*. October 1988.

'Well, Have You Seen a Sierra?' *Mail on Sunday*. 16 November 1982.

INDEX